Interest Representation in Soviet Policymaking

About the Book and Author

Dr. Chung examines a little-known facet of Soviet decisionmaking--pressure-group politics and policy formation. He focuses on the "pro-Siberian" forces involved with the development of energy resources in West Siberia, an area rich in oil and natural gas. Because West Siberia is a remote and relatively unexplored region, controversy arose over the location of the highest-yielding fields and the areas to which funds and materials should be allocated. Dr. Chung shows that the decision to accelerate the development of the West Siberian energy complex was influenced strongly by what he calls a "policy coalition" composed primarily of local officials, enterprise managers, specialists, and academics. Demonstrating that this coalition is a stable and highly active pressure group, he illustrates how it gradually established ascendancy and eventually outflanked opposing elements in the government and planning agencies. He identifies key elements of the coalition's strategy, tracing the steps by which it swung the leadership over to its views on resource allocation. The coalition not only survived the recent Soviet leadership changes but also has been able to assert itself more strongly under Gorbachev.

Han-ku Chung is a visiting scholar at the Kennan Institute for Advanced Russian Studies, Woodrow Wilson International Center for Scholars.

Interest Representation in Soviet Policymaking

A Case Study of a West Siberian Energy Coalition

Han-ku Chung

Foreword by Peter Reddaway

Routledge
Taylor & Francis Group
LONDON AND NEW YORK

First published 1987 by Westview Press, Inc.

Published 2018 by Routledge
52 Vanderbilt Avenue, New York, NY 10017
2 Park Square, Milton Park, Abingdon, Oxon OX14 4RN

Routledge is an imprint of the Taylor & Francis Group, an informa business

Library of Congress Cataloging-in-Publication Data
Chung, Han-ku.
Interest representation in Soviet policymaking.
(Westview special studies on the Soviet Union and Eastern Europe)
Bibliography: p.
Includes index.
1. Petroleum industry and trade--Government policy--Russian S.F.S.R.--Siberia, Western--Decision making. I. Title. II. Series.
HD9575.S653S5735 1987 338.2'7282'0947 86-19109

ISBN 13: 978-0-367-01371-4 (hbk)
ISBN 13: 978-0-367-16358-7 (pbk)

To Yong-hee and Ki-yon

Contents

List of Tables and Figures xi
Foreword, *Peter Reddaway* xiii
Acknowledgments xvii

1. INTRODUCTION 1

2. ORGANIZATIONAL SETTING FOR ENERGY POLICY-MAKING. . . 15
   In Moscow. 15
   In West Siberia. 18

3. SOVIET ENERGY STRATEGY 25
   Soviet Oil Development: Achievements and Problems . 25
   Changing Emphases in Soviet Energy Policy. 34
   Trends in Soviet Energy Investment 44

4. THE CONTROVERSY OVER WEST SIBERIAN OIL 63
   Reserves 64
   Costs. 71

5. ARTICULATION OF PRO-WEST SIBERIAN DEMANDS. 83
   Manoeuvre for Development Priorities, 1968 - 1970. . 84
   Demands for Further Development, 1976 - 1978 95
   Recurring Demands for Priority, 1979 - 1981. 108

6. THE SOVIET LEADERSHIP ON WEST SIBERIAN OIL 129

7. THE FORMATION OF A PRO-WEST SIBERIAN POLICY COALITION 145
   1968 - 1970 145
   1976 - 1978 149
   1979 - 1981 153

8. CONCLUSION .169

List of Abbreviations. 175
Bibliography 177
Index 189

Tables and Figures

Tables

3.1 Soviet Fuel Production, 1960-1984. 26
3.2 Soviet Oil Production, 1965-1985 26
3.3 West Siberian Oil Production, 1965-1985. 27
3.4 Location of Soviet Oil Production, 1965-1980 . . . 29
3.5 Plan Fulfillment of Soviet Oil Reserves Growth, 1966-1972. 30
3.6 Technical-Economic Indices of Soviet Oil Production and Transportation, 1960-1980 31
3.7 Oil Yields in New Wells and Development Drilling in West Siberia. 33
3.8 Planned Increments of Soviet Energy Production . . 44
3.9 Capital Investment in Soviet Fuel Industries, 1965-1984. 46
3.10 Sectoral Share of Soviet Industrial Investment, 1966-1984. 47
3.11 Annual Percentage Shares each Fuel Industry obtained of Industrial Investment, 1966-1984 . . . 48
3.12 Annual Percentage Shares each Oil-producing Region obtained of Total National Investment, 1965-1975. 50
3.13 Capital Investment in West Siberian Fuel Development, 1966-1985 52
3.14 Trends in West Siberian Oil Drilling Activities, 1961-1980 54
7.1 Major Proponents of West Siberian Oil and Gas Development, 1968-1970 146
7.2 Main Advocates of the Continued Development of West Siberian Oil and Gas, 1976-1978. 150
7.3 Major Advocates of West Siberian Oil and Gas Development, 1979-1981 154
7.4 Leading Figures of the Pro-West Siberian Policy Coalition 159

Figures

2.1 Soviet Decision-making Structure with reference to West Siberian Oil and Gas Development 16

Foreword

This book tackles an area of Soviet politics which is under-researched and very difficult to explore. Key sources on the Soviet policy-making process are either unavailable, because they are state secrets, or have to be excavated from amidst thousands of low-value materials in Soviet books and journals. Moreover, the political actors do not normally make themselves accessible for interviews, and reveal little when they do.

Despite these formidable difficulties, Dr. Chung has done an impressive job of piecing together a picture of at least some of the policy inputs which operated over the period 1965-81 with regard to energy issues, and especially to oil production. Where the gaps in sources are most serious, he cautiously infers possible answers on the basis of his other evidence and of his sound understanding of how the Soviet system works as a whole. His book thus joins a small group of painstaking case studies which successfully use a similar methodology, notably Thane Gustafson's on Soviet land and water policies, Leslie Holmes's on the rise and decline of the production associations in Soviet industry, and Jiri Valenta's on the decision to invade Czechoslovakia in 1968.

Dr. Chung is concerned to show that the decision to accelerate the development of the West Siberian energy complex in the 1970s was strongly influenced by what he calls a "policy coalition" composed of specialists, local Party officials, and government officials associated with the West Siberian region. He demonstrates that this coalition formed a stable, highly active, though informal, "pressure group," which proved capable of mounting a sustained campaign to win Politburo backing for its view of the correct priorities on energy development.

In a carefully researched series of chapters he shows how this informal "group" gradually established its ascendancy, and, possibly assisted by a CIA report of 1977 which pointed to the probability of a sensational decline in Soviet oil extraction in the near future, proceeded to win the ear of the Party's Secretary General, Brezhnev. In this way it outflanked those elements in the government and planning agencies, including Prime Minister Kosygin, which favored a traditional, incremental development of all the main types of energy, and gained acceptance for a more radical and in some ways risky crash program to extract huge quantities of oil from the vast but little exploited West Siberian deposits.

Dr. Chung identifies the key elements in the coalition's strategy, and traces the steps by which they both swung the political leadership to their views on resource allocation, and also won endorsement for an administrative reorganization which affirmed the primacy of the West Siberian region in energy development. This reorganization gave authority to two new, cross-ministerial bodies which could pursue more rigorous and integrated policies.

Dr. Chung's case study is a valuable addition to the scanty literature of high quality on "pressure group" politics in the Soviet Union. The author advances our knowledge of the mechanics of policy formation in the field of energy, and, aided by his familiarity with existing, comparative, theoretical literature on policy formation, sheds light on the workings of the Soviet decision-making process in general.

This said, I might raise some questions for consideration both by readers and by Dr. Chung as he pursues his research and embarks on new case studies. First, did so much conflict over policy spill over into the Soviet press only because the issues were viewed by the Kremlin leadership as being more technical than political? If so, does the book describe bureaucratic jostling of a type not so different from what Fainsod and others have shown occurred even under Stalin's dictatorship, rather than real political conflict related to an oligarchic form of rule? To put it another way, did the oligarchic, Brezhnevian style of government change the nature of bureaucratic politics regarding such issues, or not? Did the localities gain some real power from the center, or not?

A second line of questioning raises the issue of whether Dr. Chung has devoted insufficient attention to external factors. What was the impact on the Kremlin of the dramatic world oil price rise of 1973-74, and the prospect that it would--with a crash oil development program--be able to cover its mounting grain deficits by purchasing grain abroad with enormously increased oil revenues? And did the above-mentioned CIA study help bring home to it the danger that, without such a program, the USSR might miss out on this golden opportunity?

As for conflict between individual Soviet leaders, does Dr. Chung perhaps exaggerate this somewhat, especially in the period up to the decision of December 1977 to abandon the balanced approach and embark on a crash program? In 1976-77, he shows, policy reflected the "balanced, Kosyginist approach." While this is true, might it not be the case that at this time Brezhnev did not consider the matter very important, so that, in a sense, the policy was Brezhnevist too? Circumstantial evidence suggests that Brezhnev was rather powerful at this time, having ousted five senior opponents from power in the years 1973-77--Polyansky, Shelest, Voronov, Shelepin and Podgorny. In this situation it seems questionable whether a Kosygin policy would have *prevailed over* simply a Brezhnev one (rather than simply being accepted by Brezhnev, who was busy with other matters). Subsequently, in late 1977, may not the leadership have noted the disappointing prospects for oil and coal production and the incentive provided by the world oil price, and reconciled itself to the huge costs of a crash oil program--all in more or less united fashion?

To the extent, however, that the Brezhnev forces pushed this program and the Kosyginist ones fought a rearguard action, readers may like to consider whether this reflects a traditional difference between the Party approach and the Government approach to economic matters. Historically, the Party has tended to adopt a campaigning, "storming" approach, while the government ministries, which are saddled with the blame if things go wrong, are inclined to be more cautious. An example is the Virgin Lands scheme of the mid-1950s, which Khrushchev and the Party embraced with vigor, while their government colleagues sat on the fence as long as they could, regarding the whole enterprise as rash and ill-planned.

Meanwhile, we should be thankful to Dr. Chung for assiduously "clearing the site" and setting before us a working hypothesis. I am also grateful to Terence McNeill of Hull University, England, for allowing me to incorporate in this foreword some of his perceptive thoughts on Dr. Chung's book.

Peter Reddaway
Secretary,
Kennan Institute for Advanced Russian Studies

Acknowledgments

This study evolved under the balanced direction of Peter Reddaway and Peter Wiles. To Mr. Reddaway I owe a particular debt of gratitude. It was he who initially helped spawn my interest in Soviet policy-making and supervised my work on the subject with unending patience while I was reading for a higher degree at the London School of Economics and Political Science (LSE). Professor Wiles, always with great kindness and humor, contributed to my general understanding of the Soviet economic system. His encouragement was especially important in spurring my interest in Soviet development policy. Without their stimulating ideas and rigorous reading of draft dissertations it would not have been possible for me to produce this work.

I also wish to thank Dr. Terence McNeill of the University of Hull for his valuable comments on my study.

Many other persons also have helped in the writing of this book. Simon Cosgrove, as friend and critic, generously read previous drafts and offered many constructive criticisms. It was a stimulating experience to discuss with him about Soviet politics in connection with my research. I am also indebted to Jane Dawson who kindly read the manuscript and made some valuable suggestions.

My deep appreciation also goes to the Kennan Institute for Advanced Russian Studies not only for sponsoring my new project but also for providing me with an opportunity to publish the present work.

Han-ku Chung

Interest Representation in Soviet Policymaking

1

Introduction

The purpose of this study is to explore the role of territorial interests in Soviet policy-making. Under the term "territorial interests" are here broadly included not only local Party and government organs but also various other institutions such as industrial enterprises operating in the locality. It has been asserted that these territorially-oriented organizations are governed by the Leninist principle of "democratic centralism," according to which they are obliged faithfully to implement national policies under the supervision of central departments in Moscow. Such organizations would exercise little or no discretionary powers. As a matter of fact, they have long been considered by most Western scholars to be non-participants or participants with little influence in central policy-making.[1] In recent years, however, there are fair indications that these territorial interests have become more assertive, at least on questions of economic development and appropriations. During the Brezhnev era, according to Joel Moses, "the increasing tendency of provincial political leaders to act in concert in bargaining with the centre, in asserting some autonomy in local policy making, and in competing with other provinces for their own regional interests and influence in the Soviet centre all seemed more clearly prevalent."[2]

Nevertheless, the potentially important role which territorial interests play in central policy-making has been neglected in current research efforts. Recent studies of Soviet politics bear witness to the growing participation of elements outside the political leadership in policy-making. According to these studies, various subleadership entities--most of them bureaucratic organizations and public institutions such as the USSR Academy of

Sciences--have grown accustomed to having their interests and views duly considered in the post-Stalin period.[3] The growing advisory role of specialists has also been demonstrated in such policy areas as environmental protection and criminal justice.[4] Since the 1960s, argues Peter Solomon, this trend towards wider participation by occupation groups "became institutionalized; that is, that participation...became a regular feature" of the policy process in criminal justice and other policy areas.[5] Seweryn Bialer similarly emphasizes the "stable representation" by bureaucratic interests as a characteristic feature of the present Soviet system: "There evolved a complex and regularized domestic decision-making process based on bargaining and compromise among major elite and bureaucratic groups which cut across organizational and functional lines."[6] Yet most of these studies have focused their main attention on what are called "functional" or "vertical" interests such as the specialized industrial ministries and the military establishment rather than on "territorial" interests and their influence in the Soviet policy process.

From time to time, the territorial aspect of Soviet policy-making has been touched upon by some scholars. As early as 1969, for instance, Jerry Hough found in his study of the provincial Party committee's role in industrial policy-making that provincial Party first secretaries act not only as overseers of central policy in their own areas, but also as spokesmen for local interests.[7] During Brezhnev's rule, according to George Breslauer, these provincial leaders, and especially younger ones, became more demanding and less ready simply to continue implementing new policies in their bailiwicks.[8] Howard Biddulph tries to identify the phenomenon of local interest articulation by republican and provincial Party and government leaders at the last four Party Congresses (1966-1981). He argues that regional participation has exercised "a modest but not insignificant influence on the revision of the (plan) *Guidelines* that the Party prepares."[9] When Moses speaks about the growing tendency of provincial leaders to assert themselves, he bases his argument on the general patterns of all-Union cadre policy in which an increasing proportion of newly elected provincial first Party secretaries since 1964 were deliberately selected from "locals" inside the same regions. In his opinion, this cadre change which broke from traditional patterns under the Stalin and Khrushchev eras has "profound implications in redefining the relationship between the centre and provincial locales in the Soviet system."[10] Similarly, John Miller contends that Moscow has apparently lacked "a strategy of combating regionalism by the maximum dispersal of staff throughout the union."[11] In close connection with these, scholars like Daniel Nelson have emphasized the phenomenon of "local power accretion" in the Soviet Union and several other Communist countries.[12] In the cases of Poland and Romania, he notes the efforts by local elites to achieve "horizontal integration," i.e. the attempt on the part of subnational institutions and local elites to "influence decisions made at higher levels by mobilizing and organizing local resources."[13] With the possible exception of Biddulph's study, however, the role of territorial interests in the Soviet policy process has not been treated in a systematic manner.

To this aspect of institutional participation in Soviet policy-making the present study will address itself. In particular, it will try to answer two questions: (1) Have territorially-based organizations undergone an expansion of their role in central policy-making? (2) If this is the case, what is the nature of their participation? What follows is a case study in Soviet industrial policy-making, focusing on the formation of the so-called "pro-Siberian" forces associated with the development of energy resources in West Siberia since the mid-1960s.

Case Study

In the history of Soviet energy development, the 1970s were characterized by the eastward movement of the oil- and gas-extracting industry.[14] Before this, growth in Soviet hydrocarbon production had been brought about by the development of fields in the European part of the country close to its main industrial centre. By the beginning of the decade, however, development prospects pointed to the increasing importance of areas to the east of the Urals, in particular West Siberia. The Soviets have since that time accorded high priority to a West Siberian energy development programme, pouring a huge amount of funds into this energy-rich, but remote and environmentally harsh, region. By 1980 West Siberia accounted for more than half of the country's entire oil output and nearly 40 percent of its gas production.

The West Siberian energy undertaking, apart from its economic significance, provides an interesting case showing how bureaucratic organizations in the Soviet Union participate in the policy process. As will be seen later, there have been considerable policy differences with regard to the development of West Siberian energy resources. Controversy arose in the context of Soviet energy policy as to where the greatest yields were to be found, and as to which regions should be given more funds and resources. The "Siberians" (*Sibiryaki*)--local geologists, oil and gas industry officials, Party and government bureaucrats, and academics--have been especially active in promoting their cause.

No serious attention, however, has been directed towards their role in this controversy. Of the key industries of the Soviet Union, the oil and gas industry is perhaps the one which has been most studied in the West and it has been the oil and gas resources in West Siberia that have attracted undivided attention. A controversy similar to that in the USSR took place among Western specialists over the oil and gas potential of West Siberia and the Soviet energy future.[15] But those taking part have been economists, geographers, and oil and gas industry specialists, whose main interest has lain in the content of the policy and its results rather than in the process by which policy decisions have been made. Sometimes they have touched upon institutional and regional influences, but these have always been peripheral to their main interest. Thane Gustafson may be cited as an exception to this. He has attempted to explain changes in Soviet energy policy in terms of policy differences among Soviet leaders.[16] He has also tried to show the role of various bureaucratic influences in the formation of a gas development programme for West Siberia.[17] On the whole, however, his concern has been more with energy decision-making at the national level than with the territorial representation involved in this process.

Coalition-formation in Soviet Politics

How do we identify the role of the pro-West Siberian elements in Soviet energy policy-making? An examination of what role organized interests in the Soviet Union play--that is, how they participate--in the policy process is inevitably a study of their influences on policy formation. In order to determine the influence of the pro-Siberian elements, an attempt will be made here to relate alterations in energy policy to what can be termed the "public discussions" which were conducted. Influence is said to exist where an actor A, "without resorting to either a tacit or an overt threat of severe deprivation, causes B to change his course of action."[18] But it is often difficult to establish such a relationship of influence in the real world. This is all the more so in Soviet politics as Soviet leaders rarely reveal that they have yielded to certain individuals and groups. For the study of Soviet politics, Donald Kelley has thus devised a measure of influence as follows: "perceptible alteration of policy along lines suggested by interest groups as seen in a comparison of the original proposal and the final legislation."[19] In the Soviet Union, however, the original policy proposals made at the top are often not known. If, therefore, we replace the word "the original proposal" with an existing policy line and "the final legislation" with a new decision, his operationalization of the influence concept could be used in the study of Soviet policy-making in many areas.

Public discussions are one form of policy-relevant suggestions published in the Soviet press. They include promotional arguments, complaints and demands. They are intended to "persuade" the decision-making authorities. It is not difficult to imagine that every organized interest in the Soviet Union is eager to contribute promotional articles (*obsuzhdeniya*) to *Pravda* and other mass-circulation newspapers. A *Literaturnaya gazeta* correspondent once revealed that when a scientific conference was held in Novosibirsk in Siberia in 1969 representatives of two rival local energy enterprises approached him for a lobby interview ("*Mne rasskazyvali v kuluarakh.*").[20] As will be seen later, the Siberians engaged extensively in this kind of promotional activity specifically with the energy decision-makers in Moscow in mind.

In dealing with Soviet-style public discussions and debates, a cautionary note may be heeded. There is concern that in the Soviet Union published expressions are filtered through so many constraints that they may not reflect the "true" opinions of the contributors. Concerning the reliability of "debates" aired in the Soviet press, however, Lilita Dzirkals and others observe:

> That such discussions do take place, and that they mirror to some extent the evolution of actual policy, no Western analyst can seriously doubt, because so many cases have been observed. Indeed, it is remarkable that during the Brezhnev period, as freedom of expression in cultural matters has diminished, the frankness of many technical discussions in the Soviet press has increased.[21]

They give major press controversy involving Soviet energy strategy in the 1970s as a case in point.[22] In any case, it should be noted that the probable direction of any bias resulting from censorship and other constraints would be toward the understatement of differences of opinion, rather than toward their overstatement. To the extent to which differences of opinion are identified, we can thus assume that real differences of at least that magnitude do exist.[23] At the same time, the demands and grievances printed in the Soviet press may be compared with desired policy changes in order to distinguish whether they are initiated by the leadership with a view to mobilizing support or by subleadership elements. If such demands are not met within a reasonable period of time, let us say, one year, then it may be deduced that they were made by those below the leadership. Demands for mobilization from the top cannot be ignored for long.

The public discussions analyzed in this study are restricted to those which have appeared in all-Union and Russian republic (RSFSR) newspapers and mass-circulation journals. This limitation is not only a result of the author's lack of access to Soviet provincial newspapers such as *Tyumenskaya pravda* but also due to the fact that the national-level newspapers and journals are more likely to be the media used for purposes of representing organizational interests in the central policy process. Local papers and specialized journals are presumably less effective in communicating demands to the central decision-making authorities.

If the pro-West Siberian elements were influential in the formation of Soviet energy policy, what was the nature of their participation? Soviet media debate, in the opinion of Dzirkals and associates, "is likely to involve interest groupings cutting across institutions."[24] As will be seen, a number of individuals and groups were involved in public discussions concerning Soviet energy policy. In this study, the analysis of public discussions will be used to investigate the possible formation of such groupings or coalitions. The term "coalition" is taken to mean here joint action by two or more actors--individuals or groups--to represent their common interests in specific policy areas. By definition, it is a policy-oriented grouping. According to some scholars, account needs also to be taken of factional groupings based not on policy differences but on personal allegiance. If these are to be included, there are at least three models of policy grouping in the Soviet policy process. What kind of grouping the pro-West Siberian elements belonged to--if they ever formed themselves into one--will determine the nature of their participation in Soviet energy policy-making.

(1) **Grouping as a faction:** Scholars advocating the factional view of Soviet politics would not deny that groups and other intermediate elements below the political leadership initiate policy proposals and that conflict among them is widespread. But they argue that many of these are factions based on personal ties to important leaders and that the Soviet policy process is primarily characterized as conflict between them as an extension of leadership conflict.[25] The intermediate elements are considered to be politically dependent. According to Uri Ra'anan, "factions in the USSR tend to be personality-oriented, i.e., they reflect a 'feudal' relationship of mutual obligation and fealty between certain leaders and their appointees and clients, rather than representing mainly the vested interests of sundry civilian and military agencies."[26] The independent initiative of these factions is therefore decisively constrained by "feudal" obligations: i.e. as a clientele they must render loyalty and support to their patron in return for the protection of the latter. Such patron-client relationships between Soviet leaders and factions dependent upon them have in the past been mediated by a wide variety of policy lines, including such as biological theories (Lysenkoism with N. V. Podgorny), agricultural methods (no more cultivation after autumn plowing with G. I. Voronov, opposition to shallow tillage with L. M. Kaganovich) and certain crops (corn with Khrushchev).[27]

Can it be proven that the Soviet policy process has continued to be characterized by factional conflict in the Brezhnev and post-Brezhnev periods? Unfortunately, and particularly in Soviet conditions, it is not often easy to identify patron-client relationships since they are usually highly informal.[28] But Soviet factions, according to Ra'anan, "display little long-term commitment to issues as such. They are inclined to advocate certain policies only as long as they are competing with rival groups that propagate a different approach. Once such competitors are defeated finally and unmistakably, the victorious faction seems to feel minimal compunction about 'picking up the fallen banners of the adversary from the battlefield.'"[29] For the "interests" of a faction are "personal" interests, not the "corporate" interests of an institution or a profession. Ra'anan also argues that "the various factions try their best to obtain a foothold in as many bureaucratic institutions as possible, so that their concerns and allegiances frequently run athwart departmental frontiers."[30] If his assertion is right, the length of commitment by officials and specialists to certain policy positions and the pattern of personnel change in any given institution and policy area would provide means of determining whether factional struggle is a dominant mode of the policy process in any given area during a certain period of time.

(2) **Coalition as a tendency of articulation:** To replace the totalitarian and "leadership conflict" models of Soviet politics, Franklyn Griffiths proposes to focus on "tendencies of articulation."[31] A tendency, according to him, is "a pattern of articulation associated with a loose coalition of actors operating at different levels of the political structure, whose articulations tend in the same direction but who are unlikely to be fully aware of the common thrust and consequences of their activity."[32] Based on the findings drawn from cases in the 1950s and 1960s, he insists that it is not structures--groups and institutions--but tendencies or different issue orientations that are vital to the Soviet policy process. Others talk of opinion groupings or "non-institutionalized, ad hoc lobbies." Philip Stewart, for example, employs the word "grouping" when "similar opinions on the same issue are expressed by more than one individual."[33] For such groupings, John Lowenhardt employs the term "policy coalitions." "Policy coalitions," according to him, "emerge when and if the common interests of sections (opinion groupings) of different groups and institutions appear to be stronger than the interests which bind each section to its 'own' group or institution."[34] Such policy coalitions share common outlooks on specific issues which cut across formal groups and institutions and, therefore, tend to be ephemeral and ill-formed. Lowenhardt argues that policy coalitions "coalesce around one policy position in an issue, and they will fall apart once the issue has died in a binding decision."[35] In short, according to these scholars, coalitions in the Soviet Union are not quite explicit but very implicit. They are short term, deal with only one temporally-bound issue and then disband. Finally, they combine individuals who only tacitly--or even unknowingly--represent particular interests.

(3) **Coalition as a policy "complex":** But other scholars have criticized the "tendency" approach for failing to give proper consideration to the importance of the institutional basis of Soviet politics. Timothy Colton argues, for example:

> It is important that in accepting intraorganizational diversity and cleavage we not lose sight of structural factors altogether.... The members of major Soviet organizations do share and pursue some common interests, and these interests can be very important ones...And, even if political alignments do not usually parallel the boundaries of formal organizations, such alignments are normally *not* without structure. Moreover, this structure is not without relation to the structure of institutions--or, at least, of administrative institutions such as the army and the party.[36]

Jerry Hough proposes the concept of "whirlpools" or "complexes"--comparable to the military-industrial complexes he identifies in the United States--to describe interest representation by institutional actors in Soviet politics. He introduces models of American politics as such, and examines the possibility of applying them to Soviet politics:

> The assumption of these models is that the political conflicts in the United States tend to be compartmentalized, with the debate in such policy area (or "whirlpool") being largely limited to those whose careers are associated with it, those most directly affected by the decision, and a few who have developed a special interest in it. .... In interbranch conflict, those in the whirlpool or complex are seen as usually uniting against those in competing whirlpools or complexes.
>
> ....
>
> (In the Soviet system) one can speak of "complexes"...and of "whirlpools"...of specialized party, state, "public," and scientific personnel working within the respective policy areas. The definition of goals formally remains the responsibility of the party leadership, but except for ensuring that the Marxist goals in social policy are pursued, the leadership is not to act with "voluntarism"--that is, it generally should follow the advice of the specialized "complexes" or "whirlpools" in their respective policy areas, limiting itself to a mediation of the

> conflicts that arise among them. In practice, policy-making power informally comes to be delegated to these complexes.[37]

According to these scholars, coalitions in Soviet politics are more or less clearly structured. They involve long-term alliances directed at broad issues in any given policy areas.

In what follows it will be seen which of these three models is the more useful in bringing light to the nature of the role of the pro-West Siberians in the making of energy policy concerning the development of West Siberian oil and gas resources. In the present study, I propose to argue that during the 1970s and early 1980s West Siberian territorial interests played a significant part in the formation of Soviet energy strategy. The West Siberians successfully pressed their demands for the maximum development of the oil and gas industry in their region. Both the West Siberians and their supporters in Moscow found themselves formed into a broad policy coalition in their attempts to influence the leadership. There is no evidence that the coalition, though supported by the Party leadership, was a factional grouping of the first type. And while it appears to have been loosely structured in conformity with the second coalition model, it was both highly stable over time and strongly rooted in specific organizations and institutions as is typical of coalitions of type three.

The following chapter describes various institutions involved in Soviet energy policy and, more narrowly, in the development of West Siberian energy resources and the ways in which these institutions may be assumed to interact with each other in the formation of policy. Chapter 3 discusses a series of changes in recent Soviet energy strategy with emphasis on the role of West Siberian oil and gas. In order to determine the impacts of these changes, this chapter also analyzes variations in the volume of capital investment allocated to respective fuel industry sectors and regions. Chapter 4 contrasts two rival arguments concerning the prospects for West Siberian hydrocarbon production. Against this background, Chapters 5 and 6 are concerned with a description of various efforts made to support West Siberian energy development and the leadership responses to them. In Chapter 7, it is then explained how a West Siberian energy coalition was formed and who the members of that coalition were. The study concludes with a discussion of the significance of such policy alignments in the Soviet system.

NOTES

1. For example, see Allen Kassof, "The Administered Society: Totalitarianism without Terror," *World Politics*, XVI (July 1964), 558-575.

2. Joel C. Moses, "Regionalism in Soviet Politics: Continuity as A Source of Change, 1953-1982," *Soviet Studies*, XXXVII (April 1985), 185.

3. As representative of this large body of scholarship, see the following: Sidney Ploss, *Conflict and Decision-Making in Soviet Russia: A Case Study of Agricultural Policy, 1953-1963* (Princeton, Princeton University Press, 1965); Theodore H. Friedgut, "Interests and Groups in Soviet Policy-Making: The MTS Reforms," *Soviet Studies*, XXVIII (October 1976), 524-547; Joel J. Schwartz and William R. Keech, "Group Influence and the Policy Process in the Soviet Union," *American Political Science Review*, LXII (September 1968), 840-851; Philip D. Stewart, "Soviet Interest Groups and the Policy Process: The Repeal of Production Education," *World Politics*, XXII (October 1969), 29-50; Donald R. Kelley, "Interest Groups in the USSR: The Impact of Political Sensitivity on Group Influence," *The Journal of Politics*, Vol. 34 (August 1972), 860-888; Abraham Katz, *The Politics of Economic Reform in the Soviet Union* (New York, Praeger, 1972); Erik P. Hoffmann and Robbin F. Laird, *The Politics of Economic Modernization in the Soviet Union* (Ithaca, N.Y., Cornell University Press, 1982); and Timothy J. Colton, *Commissars, Commanders, and Civilian Authority: The Structure of Soviet Military Politics* (Cambridge, Mass., Harvard University Press, 1979).

4. For a discussion of the policy-making role of Soviet specialists, see Donald R. Kelley, "Environmental Policy-Making in the USSR: The Role of Industrial and Environmental Interest Groups," *Soviet Studies*, XXVIII (October 1976), 570-589; Richard B. Remnek, *Soviet Scholars and Foreign Policy: A Case Study in Soviet Policy toward India* (Durham, N.C., Duke University Press, 1975); and Peter H. Solomon, Jr., *Soviet Criminologists and Criminal Policy: Specialists in Policy-Making* (London, Macmillan, 1978).

5. Solomon, pp. 149-150 and 160-161.

6. Seweryn Bialer, *Stalin's Successors: Leadership, Stability and Change in the Soviet Union* (Cambridge, Cambridge University Press, 1980), p. 50.

7. Jerry F. Hough, *The Soviet Prefects: The Local Party Organs in Industrial Decisionmaking* (Cambridge, Mass., Harvard University Press, 1969), Ch. XII.

8. George W. Breslauer, "Is There A Generation Gap in the Soviet Political Establishment?: Demand Articulation by RSFSR Provincial Party First Secretaries," *Soviet Studies*, XXXVI (January 1984), 1-25.

9. Howard L. Biddulph, "Local Interest Articulation at CPSU Congresses," *World Politics*, XXXVI (October 1983), 49. ( ) added.

10. Moses, p. 186. See also Robert E. Blackwell, Jr., "Cadres Policy in the Brezhnev Era," *Problems of Communism*, XXVIII (March-April 1979), 36-37.

11. John Miller, "Nomenklatura: Check on Localism?," in T. H. Rigby and Bohdan Harasymiw (eds.), *Leadership Selection and Patron-Client Relations in the USSR and Yugoslavia* (London, George Allen & Unwin, 1983), p. 90. In the post-Brezhnev era and especially under Mikhail Gorbachev, there have been sweeping changes especially in the composition of the key Party and government organizations. In connection with this, Archie Brown argues that "the days of 'Ivanov's turn' in Soviet politics are over. No longer can the first deputy head of a ministry, state committee or Central Committee department wait in confident expectation of filling his master's shoes." Archie Brown, "Change in the Soviet Union," *Foreign Affairs*, Vol. 64 (Summer 1986), 1050. It is yet to be determined that a similar trend can be found in the appointment of local cadres and especially of provincial Party first secretaries.

12. Daniel Nelson, "Conclusion: Participatory and Policymaking Dilemmas in Local Communist Politics," in Daniel Nelson (ed.), *Local Politics in Communist Countries* (Lexington, Ky., The University Press of Kentucky, 1980), pp. 211-224.

13. Daniel Nelson, "Vertical Integration and Political Control in Eastern Europe: The Polish and Romanian Cases," *Slavic Review*, Vol. 40 (Summer 1981), 211.

14. Other energy industries in the Soviet Union underwent similar locational changes during the period. See Yu. I. Maksimov, "Dobycha toplivno-energeticheskikh resursov v Sibiri," *Izvestiya Sibirskogo otdeleniya Akademii Nauk SSSR*, seriya obshchestvennykh nauk, No. 6 (1982), 34-38.

15. For a discussion of Soviet energy economy and the oil and gas industry in particular, see Robert W. Campbell,

The Economics of Soviet Oil and Gas (Baltimore, Md., Johns Hopkins University Press, 1968); R. W. Campbell, *Trends in the Soviet Oil and Gas Industry* (Baltimore, Md., Johns Hopkins University Press, 1976); Leslie Dienes and Theodore Shabad, *The Soviet Energy System: Resource Use and Policies* (New York, Wiley, 1979); Edward A. Hewett, *Energy, Economics, and Policy in the Soviet Union* (Washington, D.C., Brookings Institution, 1984); Arthur A. Meyerhoff, "Soviet Petroleum: History, Technology, Geology, Reserves, Potential and Policy," in Robert G. Jensen, Theodore Shabad and A. W. Wright (eds.), *Soviet Natural Resources in the World Economy* (Chicago, University of Chicago Press, 1983), pp. 306-362; D. Park, *Oil and Gas in Comecon Countries* (London, Kogan Page, 1978); Jonathan P. Stern, *Soviet Natural Gas Development to 1990* (Lexington, Mass., Lexington Books, 1980); and David Wilson, *Soviet Oil and Gas to 1990* (London, The Economist Intelligence Unit, 1980).

For a controversy about the prospects for Soviet oil production, see Central Intelligence Agency, *Prospects for Soviet Oil Production*, ER-77-10270 (April 1977); Central Intelligence Agency, Directorate of Intelligence, *Prospects for Soviet Oil Production: A Supplemental Analysis*, ER 77-10425 (July 1977); M. M. Jermol and L. A. Magnusson, *Soviet Preparations for Major Boost of Oil Exports* (Malmo, Sweden, PetroStudies Rept. GOP-782, 1978); and Marshall Goldman, *The Enigma of Soviet Petroleum: Half-empty or Half-full?* (London, George Allen & Unwin, 1980).

For an attempt to calculate the cost of Soviet oil production, see Peter Wiles, "A Note on the Cost of Soviet Oil," in NATO, Economic and Information Directorates (eds.), *CMEA: Energy, 1980-1990* (Newtonville, Mass., Oriental Research Partners, 1981), pp. 129-141.

For a discussion of changes in Soviet energy policy, see Thane Gustafson, "Soviet Energy Policy: From Big Coal to Big Gas," in Seweryn Bialer and Thane Gustafson (eds.), *The Soviet Union at the Crossroads: The 26th Congress of the CPSU* (London, George Allen & Unwin, 1982), pp. 121-139; and Thane Gustafson, *The Soviet Gas Campaign: Politics and Policy in Soviet Decision-making* (Santa Monica, Ca., Rand Corporation, 1983).

16. Gustafson, "Soviet Energy Policy."

17. Gustafson, *The Soviet Gas Campaign*.

18. Steven Lukes, *Power: A Radical View* (London, Macmillan, 1974), pp. 17-18.

19. Kelley, "Interest Groups in the USSR," p. 864.

20. *Literaturnaya gazeta*, June 4, 1969, p. 10.

21. Lilita Dzirkals, Thane Gustafson, and A. Ross

Johnson, *The Media and Intra-Elite Communication in the USSR* (Santa Monica, Ca., Rand Corporation, 1982), p. 72.

22. *Ibid.*, pp.73-74.

23. William A. Welsh, *Understanding Stability in East European Political Systems*, A monograph (Cologne, Bundes-institut fur Ostwissenschaftliche und Internationale Studien, 1980), p. 18.

24. Dzirkals and others, p. xii.

25. Carl A. Linden, *Khrushchev and the Soviet Leadership, 1957-1964* (Baltimore, The Johns Hopkins University Press, 1966), Especially pp. 1-9; and Michel Tatu, *Power in the Kremlin, From Khrushchev to Kosygin* (New York, Viking, 1968).

26. Uri Ra'anan, "Soviet Decision-Making and International Relations," *Problems of Communism*, XXIX (November-December 1980), 43. See also T. H. Rigby, "The Soviet Leadership: Towards A Self-Stabilizing Oligarchy?," *Soviet Studies*, XXII (October 1970), 177.

27. N. S. Khrushchev, *Khrushchev Remembers*, Trans. by S. Talbott (London, Andre Deutsch, 1971), pp. 241-242; N. S. Khrushchev, *Khrushchev Remembers: The Last Testament*, Trans. by Talbott (Boston, Little, Brown & Co., 1974), pp. 132-133; and Roy A. Medvedev and Zhores A. Medvedev, *Khrushchev: The Years in Power* (London, Oxford University Press, 1977), pp. 94-95 and 131.

28. For example, see T. H. Rigby and Bohdan Harasymiw (eds.), *Leadership Selection and Patron-Client Relations in the USSR and Yugoslavia* (London, George Allen & Unwin, 1983), Part Two.

29. Ra'anan, p. 43. See also William E. Odom, "A Dissenting View on the Group Approach to Soviet Politics," *World Politics*, XXVIII (1976), 552.

30. Ra'anan, p. 43.

31. Franklyn Griffiths, "A Tendency Analysis of Soviet Policy-Making," in H. Gordon Skilling and Franklyn Griffiths (eds.), *Interest Groups in Soviet Politics* (Princeton, Princeton University Press, 1971), pp. 335-377.

32. *Ibid.*, p. 358.

33. Stewart, p. 42.

34. John Lowenhardt, *Decisionmaking in Soviet Politics* (London, Macmillan, 1981), p. 87.

35. *Ibid.*

36. Colton, pp. 205-206. Emphasis in the original.

37. Jerry F. Hough and Merle Fainsod, *How the Soviet Union Is Governed* (Cambridge, Mass., Harvard University Press, 1979), pp. 525-526. ( ) added.

2

Organizational Setting for Energy Policy-making

Many organizations are engaged in the management of the Soviet energy economy.[1] Below the leadership, there are industrial bureaucracies in charge of fuel and power sectors and other related industries. But there is no formal organization which deals with the energy branch as a whole. Until 1980, there was also no unified authority in charge of the oil and gas complex in West Siberia.

A. In Moscow

Industrial Ministries: There are central ministries in Moscow which are in charge of the fuel and power industries. Of them, four are directly responsible for the oil and gas industry: the Ministry of the Oil Industry (*Minnefteprom*), the Ministry of the Gas Industry (*Mingazprom*), the Ministry of Geology (*Mingeo*), and the Ministry of Construction of Oil and Gas Industry Enterprises (*Minneftegazstroi*). The first two are all-Union ministries.[2] There is some inevitable overlap between these ministries in the production of oil and gas. In 1975, for instance, the Oil Ministry produced nearly one fifth of all natural gas while the Gas Ministry provided 1.5 percent of liquid hydrocarbons, mainly gas condensate.[3] The Geology Ministry has its counterparts in several republics including the Russian Republic (RSFSR). In oil and gas development, they are conducting most geological-exploratory work.[4] Finally, the Ministry of Construction of Oil and Gas Industry Enterprises which was created as an all-Union ministry in 1972, is charged with the work of laying pipelines and building other infrastructure needed by the oil and gas industry.[5]

Figure 2.1: Soviet Decision-making Structure with reference to West Siberian Oil and Gas Development

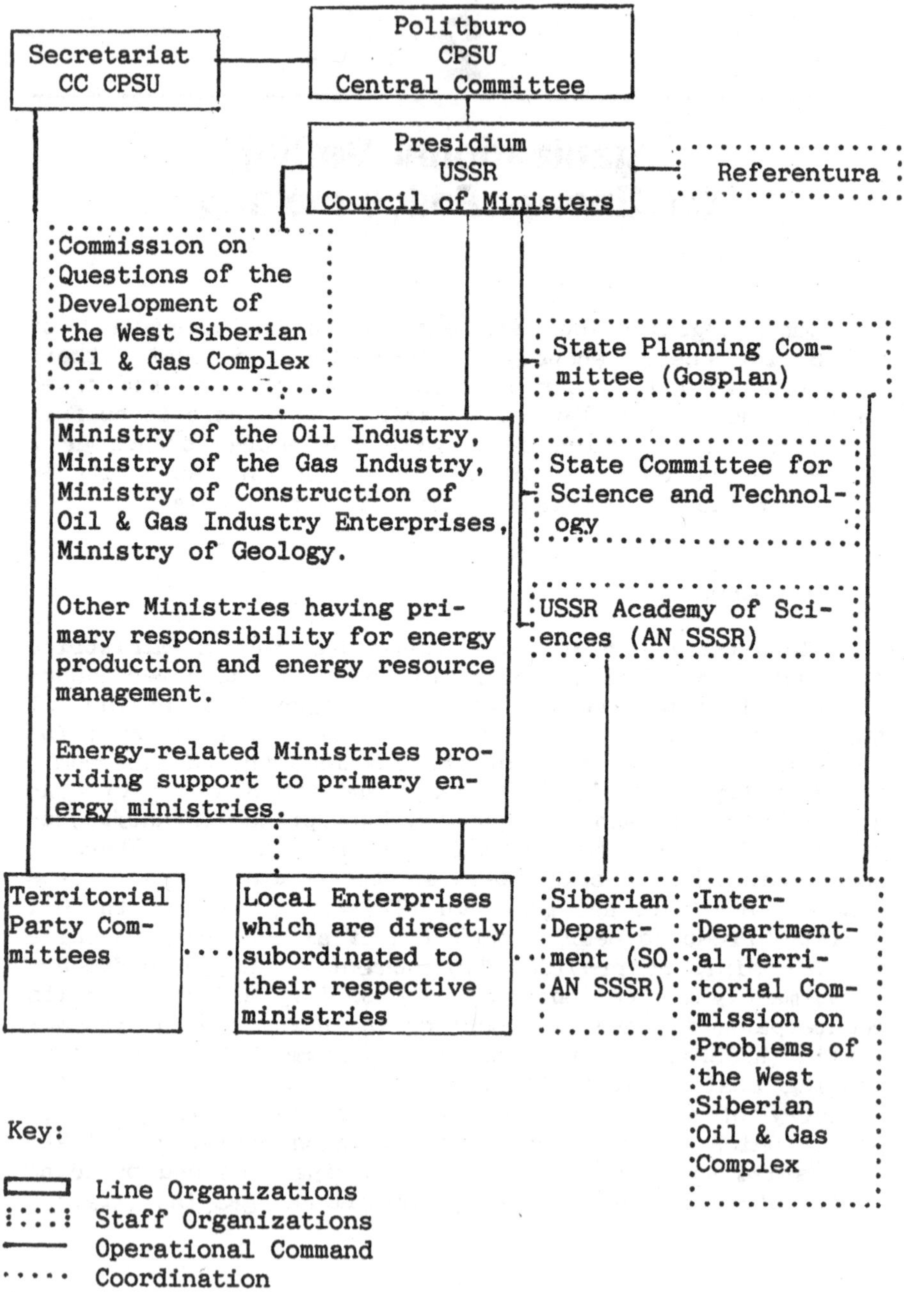

All of these ministries have their own institutes which conduct research and development and do a large part of the modelling for energy planning and strategy.[6] They also have their own planning departments, which carry out much of the planning involved in their respective areas. These ministries provide information, when requested, to the State Planning Committee (*Gosplan*), the State Committee for Science and Technology (*GKNT*), and a consultant body, called the *referentura*, for the Presidium of the USSR Council of Ministers.[7] This procedure is the same for other energy and energy-related ministries such as the Ministry of Power and Electrification (*Minenergo*) and the Ministry of the Medium Machine Building.

About 30 industrial ministries and departments are currently engaged in capital construction in the West Siberian energy complex.[8] By 1983 the Ministry of Construction of Oil and Gas Industry Enterprises alone had carried out about 60 percent of all the contract construction and installation works for the oil industry in West Siberia.[9]

Gosplan and Other Advisory Agencies: In addition to these ministries, there is Gosplan, the central planning body. One of its main tasks in the energy area is the selection and coordination of policy proposals by interested ministries and departments and their incorporation into five-year plans. It works out major programmes such as the development of territorial-production complexes (*TPK*) which involve numerous organizations. A Western observer reports that the authority by which the country's fuel and power balance is determined lies in a collegium of Gosplan.[10] It seems that senior officials recruited from appropriate ministries participate in the collegium.[11] Within the planning organ are to be found the Oil and Gas Industry Department and three advisory agencies; the Council for Study of Productive Forces (*SOPS*), the Institute of Complex Fuel and Power Problems, and the State Experts Commission. In addition to these bodies, Gosplan set up in 1980 the Interdepartmental Territorial Commission on Problems of the West Siberian Oil and Gas Complex (*ZapSibMVTK*) with its headquarters in West Siberia.[12]

There are two advisory organizations independent of the central planning agency, which provide technical advice to industrial ministries and departments. They are the State Committee for Science and Technology (*GKNT*) and the USSR Academy of Sciences (*AN SSSR*).[13] Of the research institutes and departments of the Academy of Sciences, the three which appear to be actively involved in the West

Siberian energy programme are: the Commission for Study of Productive Forces and Natural Resources, the Scientific Council for Complex Problems of Power, and the Siberian Department (*SO AN SSSR*) in Novosibirsk.

The USSR Council of Ministers and the Secretariat of the CPSU Central Committee: Higher up, the Presidium of the USSR Council of Ministers maintains the *referentura*, a consultative-advisory body which provides research on requested topics including the energy problem.[14] The Presidium also set up in 1980 a special organ, the Commission on Questions of the Development of the West Siberian Oil and Gas Complex.[15] Finally, the Party Secretariat which is responsible to the Politburo, the country's highest decision-making body, has oil and gas industry and geology sectors in its Heavy Industry Department. This Department "may provide policy proposals directly to the Council of Ministers' Presidium."[16] The high Party apparatus "does not have the manpower for detailed staff work in most economic sectors, however. For that it must rely on the government apparatus."[17]

B. In West Siberia

The Soviet fuel industries are organized along the branch-industry line as are other industries. In West Siberia, there are production and construction organizations which are directly subject to their respective ministries in Moscow.[18] The Chief Tyumen' Oil and Gas Administration (*Glavtyumenneftegaz*), the Oil Ministry's largest production organization, is responsible for oil production in Tyumen' and neighboring Tomsk provinces.[19] Being subordinated to the Gas Ministry, the Tyumen' Gas Industry Association (*Tyumengazprom*) is engaged in the development and production of natural gas mainly in the northern part of Tyumen' province.[20] Of the production funds brought into operation in the industrial sector of the province during the period of 1971-1980, the oil and gas industry accounted for 90 percent.[21] The Chief Tyumen' Geology Administration (*Glavtyumengeologiya*) conducts the bulk of geological-exploratory work in the area.[22] These organizations are the major customers (*zakazchiki*) of the many construction organizations working in West Siberia. One of their major contractors is the Chief Tyumen' Administration for the Construction of Oil and Gas Industry Enterprises (*Glavtyumenneftegazstroi*).[23]

In addition to these production and construction organizations, there are more than 50 research institutes (*NII*) and design-making offices (*KB*) working on the problems of the oil and gas industry in West Siberia.[24] In 1981, there were about 30 such organizations operating in Tyumen' alone.[25] The most prominent of these organizations are the Tyumen' State Oil and Gas Research-Design Institute (*Giprotyumenneftegaz*) and the West Siberian Geological-Prospecting and Oil Research Institute (*ZapsibNIGNI*). Many of these organizations are affiliates of the Siberian Department of the USSR Academy of Sciences.[26] Its two institutions--the Institute of Economics and Organization of Industrial Production and the Institute of Geology and Geophysics--are perhaps most actively involved in West Siberian oil and gas development.

We have seen that there are many organizations which are involved in the Soviet energy sector. Yet there exists no unified formal authority for energy policy amongst either the government or the Party organs. A Western observer puts it as follows:

> A striking aspect of the administrative structure for the energy economy is that there is no energy czar--no energy commissar. There is no administrative node above the ministries...with responsibility for energy as a whole. Executive control of these subdivisions of the energy sector is exercised only by the Council of Ministers as one aspect of its larger task of overseeing the whole economy. Many of the information threads come together in the Gosplan ..., but Gosplan has no executive power to make energy policy or decisions on its own.[27]

As late as 1980, S. Yatrov, Director of Gosplan's Institute of Complex Fuel and Power Problems, called for the creation of a "single economic organism" which would deal with the country's fuel and power complexes.[28] But such appeals seem to have gone unheeded. Perhaps the problem of achieving a global focus in energy policy is too complicated to be feasible. Similarly, there were no formal organization in exclusive charge of the development of the West Siberian energy complex at least until the end of the 1970s. As mentioned earlier, the Soviet government belatedly set up a high-level commission in 1980 to look after West Siberian oil and gas. Still, its task is limited to coordinating the activities of the ministries and departments engaged in the development of the complex "in main (policy) directions" (*po vazhneishim napravleniyam*).[29] Another commission has been created in Tyumen' as a special department of Gosplan. Though special, however, it is no more than a planning body and has no operational authority.[30] As late as 1982, according to its head, the commission was still in the stage of trying to "find its place in the 'enterprise-branch-Gosplan' system."[31]

This organizational structure for the management of the Soviet energy economy and, above all, for the development of the West Siberian complex seems to have important effects on the policy process. It is widely observed that in any bureaucracy a plurality of separate actors tend to pursue their separate and often conflicting interests in spite of the existence of formal institutions for authoritative conflict resolution. In the absence of such a unified formal authority, this tendency may have become more pronounced in Soviet energy policy-making. At the same time, at least something like unified control and coordination will be needed for the management of a given policy area or programme. In the Soviet energy area, this appears to have been provided by Party leaders at both central and local levels. It is indeed the Party that has frequently played the role of coordinator or "expediter" (*tolkach*) in the Soviet Union.[32] In the ensuing chapters, we will examine how organized interests as detailed above interact with one another in the considerations of Soviet energy policy and, especially, energy development programmes. We will first review recent changes in Soviet energy strategy in the next chapter.

NOTES

1. The term *energy* is used in this study to refer both to energy itself--such as electric power--and to fuels used to produce that energy.

2. The Oil Ministry was transformed from a Union-republican ministry into an all-Union ministry in May 1970.

3. Leslie Dienes and Theodore Shabad, *The Soviet Energy System: Resource Use and Policies* (New York, Wiley, 1979), p. 264.

4. The Oil and Gas Ministries also maintain their own exploration teams, though small in size.

5. On its activities, see *Pravda*, September 2, 1979.

6. Dienes and Shabad, p. 267; and Robert W. Campbell, *Soviet Energy Technologies: Planning, Policy, Research and Development* (Bloomington, Indiana University Press, 1980), Chapter 2.

7. Central Intelligence Agency, National Foreign Assessment Center, *Energy Decision Making in the Soviet Union: A Reference Aid*, An organizational chart, CR 80-10623 (August 1980).

8. V. P. Kuramin, S. S. Pesotskii, V. T. Permyakov, N. A. Sesin, and S. N. Starovoitov, "Problemy planirovaniya i upravleniya razvitiem Zapadno-Sibirskogo neftegazovogo kompleksa," in S. N. Starovoitov (ed.), *Problemy razvitiya Zapadno-Sibirskogo neftegazovogo kompleksa* (Novosibirsk, Nauka, 1983), p. 33.

9. Ye. P. Yefremov, M. K. Mikhalev, L. I. Churikov and G. L. Chudnovskii, "Sostoyanie i napravleniya dal'neishei realizatsii programmy kompleksnogo razvitiya neftedobyvayushchei promyshlennosti Zapadnoi Sibiri," in *Ibid.*, p. 74.

10. Murray Feshbach, "Report of A Visit by U.S. Systems Analysts to Moscow," Mimeo (1974), pp. 5-6 as quoted in D. Park, *Oil and Gas in Comecon Countries* (London, Kogan Page, 1978), p. 58.

11. Dienes and Shabad, p. 267. According to Jerry Hough, branch industry officials in Gosplan are mainly recruited from the respective industrial ministries and they "tend to serve as the representative, the negotiating agent of their respective ministries in the bargaining process by which a balanced plan is hammered out. In this process, they usually push for the maximum development of their own branch and the maximum allocations of supplies to it." Jerry F. Hough and Merle Fainsod, *How the Soviet Union Is Governed* (Cambridge, Mass., Harvard University Press, 1979), pp. 390-391. For the working of Soviet collegial bodies, see Ellen Jones, "Committee Decision Making in the Soviet Union," *World Politics*, XXXVI (January 1984), 165-188.

12. *Pravda*, February 24, 1981; and Starovoitov, p. 7.

13. On the energy role of the State Committee for Science and Technology, see *Ekonomicheskaya gazeta*, No. 42 (1972), p. 5; and *Pravda*, December 17, 1976.

14. Central Intelligence Agency, *Energy Decision Making*.

15. See footnote 12.

16. Central Intelligence Agency, *Energy Decision Making*.

17. Thane Gustafson, *The Soviet Gas Campaign: Politics and Policy in Soviet Decisionmaking* (Santa Monica, Ca., Rand Corporation, 1983), p. 17. In the early 1970s, it was estimated that there were just over 900 responsible staff workers and about 2,400 other personnel--responsible non-staff workers and technical staff--in the Party Central Committee. A. Pravdin and M. Matthews, "Inside the CPSU Central Committee: Interview by M. Matthews," *Survey*, Vol. 20 (Autumn 1974), 95.

18. By oil-producing regions in West Siberia, the Soviets usually mean two adjoining provinces. Tyumen' province (*oblast'*) is the major oil- and gas-producing region. Tomsk province is also producing oil but its contribution is small. Administrative associations and other main organizations are mostly located in Tyumen'. On the organizations working in Tomsk province, see *Izvestiya*, April 19, 1978.

19. In West Siberia, there are 17 oil-extracting associations (*NGDU*), most of which belong to *Glavtyumenneftegaz*. Starovoitov, p. 3. On *Glavtyumenneftegaz* and its relation with the Oil Ministry, see *Ekonomicheskaya gazeta*, No. 27 (1974), p. 2; and No. 45 (1974), p. 8.

20. *Tyumengazprom* has 4 gas-producing associations which are also in charge of transporting their products. Starovoitov, p. 3.

21. S. D. Ageeva and B. P. Orlov, "Nekotorye cherty investitsionnogo protsessa v Zapadno-Sibirskom neftegazovom komplekse," *Izvestiya Sibirskogo otdeleniya Akademii Nauk SSSR*, seriya obshchestvennykh nauk, No. 11 (1982), 85.

22. The Geology Ministry maintains a total of 19 geological-exploratory organizations in West Siberia, 12 of which belongs to *Glavtyumengeologiya* and 5 to the Tomsk Geology Administration. Starovoitov, p. 3. Organizationally, *Glavtyumengeologiya* is placed under the jurisdiction of the RSFSR Ministry of Geology. *Ekonomicheskaya gazeta*, No. 35 (1978), p. 7.

23. There are also such contractors as the Chief Siberian Pipeline Construction Administration and the Chief Tyumen' Industry Construction Administration. V. I. Muravlenko and V. I. Kremnev (eds.), *Sibirskaya neft'* (Moskva, Nedra, 1977), p. 98.

24. *Ibid.*, p. 230.

25. *Izvestiya*, October 25, 1981.

26. The Siberian Department was set up in 1957 at the same time as the creation of the Regional Economic Councils (*Sovnarkhozy*) to provide on-the-spot scientific and technical support for Khrushchev's Siberian development plans.

27. Campbell, p. 19.

28. S. Yatrov, "Toplivno-energeticheskii kompleks," *Ekonomicheskaya gazeta*, No. 10 (1980), p. 10.

29. Kuramin and others, p. 40.

30. *Ibid.* and *Sotsialisticheskaya industriya*, June 19, 1981.

31. *Pravda*, March 3, 1982.

32. Jerry F. Hough, *The Soviet Prefects: The Local Party Organs in Industrial Decisionmaking* (Cambridge, Harvard University Press, 1969); and Paul Cocks, "Administrative Rationality, Political Change, and the Role of the Party," in Karl W. Ryavec (ed.), *Soviet Society and the Communist Party* (Amherst, The University of Massachusetts Press, 1978), p. 54.

3

Soviet Energy Strategy

The Soviet Union has made several shifts of emphasis in its energy strategy since the late 1960s. They were initiated mainly in response to the growing difficulties confronting the oil industry. On the whole, however, policies advocating the priority development of oil have continued to prevail over others. In this chapter, we will examine the policy changes and their outcomes as reflected in capital investments. Before determining the role of various participants in policy-making, we should know what policy changes have been made and what effects they have actually brought about. This is the starting point from which we will work our way back into the policy process.

A. Soviet Oil Development: Achievements and Problems

As in other industrial countries, oil is the key industry of the energy sector in the Soviet Union. The mainstay of the Soviet oil industry has been the newly opened oilfields in West Siberia. Any serious difficulty in producing oil especially in this region would produce an important effect on overall Soviet energy strategy.

(1) Achievements

By the early 1970s, Soviet energy strategy was firmly based on the priority development of the oil industry. Since former Soviet leader Nikita Khrushchev announced in 1959 the policy of "giving priority to developing the extraction and refining of oil and gas," development preference has been given to these high-quality fuels, especially

Table 3.1: Soviet Fuel Production, 1960-1984
(%, standard fuel)*

Year	Total	Oil**	Gas	Coal	Others
1960	100	30.5	7.9	53.9	7.7
1970	100	41.1	19.1	35.4	4.4
1980	100	45.5	27.1	25.2	2.2
1984	100	42.0	33.3	22.8	1.9

* Excluding stocks.
** Including gas condensate.
Source: *Narodnoe khozyaistvo SSSR v 1984 g.* (Moskva, Statistika, 1985), p. 166. Henceforth, respective volumes of this statistical yearbook will be referred to simply as *Narkhoz* with the appropriate year.

oil, over other energy sources.[1] As is clear from Table 3.1, the country's fuel structure has shown a considerable improvement in terms of the share of oil and gas. The proportion of hydrocarbons in terms of the total Soviet fuel balance rose from about 60 percent in 1970 to over 72 percent in 1980. The share of oil alone already reached more

Table 3.2: Soviet Oil Production, 1965-1985
(million tons)*

Year	Original FYP Goals	Revised Annual Goals	Actual Output	Annual Growth Rate (%)
1965		(243)	242.9	+9
1970	(345-355)		353.0 (349)	+7
1971		(371)	377.1 (371.8)	+7
1972		(395)	400.4 (393.8)	+6
1973		(429)	429.0 (421.4)	+7
1974		(461)	458.9 (450.6)	+7
1975	(480-500)	505 (496)	490.8 (481.8)	+7
1976		520.6 (510.6)	519.7	+6
1977		550	545.8	+5
1978		575	571.5	+5
1979		593	585.6	+3
1980	620-640	606	603.2	+3
1981		610	608.8	+1
1982		614	612.6	+1
1983		619	616.3	+1
1984		624	612.7	-1
1985	620-645		595	-3

(Continued)

Table 3.2 (Cont.)

* Figures in the brackets are oil only. Those without brackets include both oil and gas condensate. Since the mid-1970s, Soviet statistics have started to lump condensate production together with oil output under the heading of oil production.

Sources: *Narkhoz*, various years; *Ekonomicheskaya gazeta*, No. 8 (1977), p. 1; and annual plan reports published in *Pravda*, various years.

than 41 percent in 1970, replacing coal as the country's major fuel. It achieved an all-time high of 45.5 percent in 1980 as the table shows.

The absolute increase in Soviet oil output amounted to over 137 million tons in 1971-1975, the largest rise on record in the USSR. The production rose by further 112 million tons in 1976-1980 (See Table 3.2.).

Table 3.3: West Siberian Oil Production, 1965-1985 (million tons)*

Year	Planned**		Actual Output	Annual Increment	Annual Growth Rate (%)
1965			0.95		
1970	20-25	30	31.41	10.1	+47
1971		44.2	44.8	13.4	+43
1972		60.5	62.7	17.9	+40
1973		82.4	87.7	25	+40
1974		103.5	116.4	28.7	+32
1975	120-125	147	148.04	31.6	+27
1976		180	181.7	33.7	+23
1977		214.5	218.3	36.6	+20
1978		254	254	35.7	+16
1979		284.7	283	29	+11
1980	300-310	315	312.61	29.6	+10
1981		334.3	335	22.4	+7
1982			352.9	17.9	+5
1983			369	16.1	+4.6
1984			378	9	+2.4
1985	385-395	399			

* Including gas condensate.

** Hyphenated figures are original five-year plan goals. Other figures are recently revised annual production goals.

(Continued)

Table 3.3 (Cont.)
Sources: *Narodnoe khozyaistvo Tyumenskoi oblasti za gody vos'moi pyatiletki (1966-1970 gody)* (Omsk, Statistika, 1971), p. 50; *Razvitie narodnogo khozyaistva Sibiri* (Novosibirsk, Nauka, 1978), p. 180; V. I. Muravlenko and V. I. Kremnev (eds.), *Sibirskaya neft'* (Moskva, Nedra, 1977), p. 175; S. N. Starovoitov (ed.), *Problemy razvitiya Zapadno-Sibirskogo neftegazovogo kompleksa* (Novosibirsk, Nauka, 1983), p. 64; *Ekonomicheskaya gazeta*, No. 19 (1975), p. 6; No. 8 (1977), p. 2; No. 16 (1977), p. 12; No. 17 (1978), p. 2; No. 4 (1979), p. 1; No. 14 (1981), p. 2; and No. 5 (1982), p. 1; *Izvestiya*, April 19, 1978; *Trud*, March 10, 1981 and May 17, 1981; and *Soviet Geography: Review and Translation*, Vol. XXVI (April 1985), 289.

The development of the Soviet oil industry has been accompanied by a locational shift of production. Before the 1970s, the growth in oil output had been mainly brought about by the development of reserves in the European part of the country; i.e. the Ukraine, the Transcaucasus, the North Caucasus and the Urals-Volga area. It was especially the Urals-Volga region that had produced the major portion of Soviet oil. But the importance of reserves in the regions farther to the east of the Urals was soon appreciated. In West Siberia, production of oil began in 1964 and had already reached 31 million tons by 1970. West Siberia took the first place in Soviet oil output in 1974. The share of oil from this region was more than 30 percent of the total of Soviet oil production in 1975, and over 50 percent in 1980 (See Tables 3.3 and 3.4.). More importantly, West Siberia accounted for 84 percent of the increment in oil output for the period of 1971-1975. It was true in the post-1977 period that growth in Soviet oil production was entirely dependent upon the development of oil resources there.[2] Table 3.4 details changes in the regional balance of oil production in the Soviet Union during the +period of 1965-1980. The eastern region sent 15 million tons of oil to the European USSR in 1970, 113 million tons in 1975, and 242 million tons in 1980.[3]

(2) Problems

For all its achievements, however, the prospects for the Soviet oil industry have remained uncertain.[4] There were in fact many indications that the Soviet oil industry was entering a critical period in the 1970s. Despite the increasing production in West Siberia, the Soviet oil in-

Table 3.4: Location of Soviet Oil Production, 1965-1980 (%)*

Zone	Production				Production Growth		
	1965	1970	1975	1980	1966-70	1971-75	1976-80
USSR	100	100	100	100	100	100	100
European regions	92.9	81.9	61.0	45.0	57.4	7.9	n.a.
Urals-Volga	71.5	59.1	46.6	n.a.	31.7	12.1	n.a.
Eastern regions	7.1	18.1	39.0	55.0	42.6	92.1	n.a.
West Siberia	0.4	8.9	30.3	51.8	27.7	84.0	146.5

* Including gas condensate.

Sources: Ya. A. Mazover, "Osnovnye napravleniya razvitiya i razmeshcheniya toplivnoi promyshlennosti," in Ya. A. Mazover (ed.), *Problemy razvitiya i razmeshcheniya toplivnykh baz SSSR* (Moskva, Nauka, 1982), pp. 10-11; T. B. Baranova, "Osnovnye pokazateli razvitiya promyshlennosti Sibiri v desyatoi pyatiletke," *Izvestiya Sibirskogo otdeleniya Akademii Nauk SSSR*, seriya obshchestvennykh nauk, No. 11 (1982), 74; and I. D. Kozlov, *Energeticheskoe khozyaistvo stran SEV* (Moskva, Nauka, 1980), p. 30.

dustry as a whole experienced a decrease in the incremental change after 1975. The growth rate fell from an annual increase of 7 percent or so in the early 1970s to 5 percent in 1977. It further decelerated to 3 percent in 1980 and to an alarming level of less than 1 percent in 1982 (See Table 3.2.). The oil industry's production goals have consistently not been met since the mid-1970s in spite of the continued downward revision of plan targets. Production shortfalls in the older oil regions have been largely blamed for this: Oilfields in Tatar ASSR (autonomous republic), Bashkir ASSR, Kuibyshev and other major oil regions of the European USSR were yielding less than they once did.[5] In the Eighth Five-Year Plan period, the Soviet Union required 50 percent of new production capacity to offset natural depletion. By 1971-1975, however, 63.5 percent of new capacity was required for depletion offset.[6] The West Siberian oilfields have been drawn on more heavily than planned in order to meet the overall production target in the absence of other back-up fields with as much potential. But output growth in West Siberia itself began to slow down (See Table 3.3.). The Samotlor oilfield, which contributed more than 50 percent of the oil extracted in West Siberia, "practically reached its maximum level" by 1976-1980.[7]

Despite the absence of official reserves data, it is evident that the Soviet Union was not adding to its new reserves as fast as it needed to. In 1971-1975, according to two Soviet academics, "oil extraction is scheduled to increase by 1.42 times, but its commercial reserves (*promyshlennye zapasy*) only by 30 percent."[8] The plan for the growth of reserves itself was consistently underfulfilled in many areas with the exception of West Siberia during the early 1970s, as Table 3.5 shows. In the European USSR, the Soviets failed to add to their dwindling reserves. Even the oilfields newly opened in the existing regions turned out to be small and less productive than previously developed fields. Of a total of 239 oilfields explored in the Urals-Volga region in 1966-1972, 225 fields or 94 percent proved to be small.[9] The reserves situation in the existing oil regions in the European USSR seems to have been far from satisfactory for the rest of the 1970s as well. The director of *Bashneft'* (Bashkir Oil Production Association) revealed as late as 1977 that exploratory work in his area had produced no significant results.[10] In West Siberia, oil reserves grew by 2.3 times in 1966-1970, 3.2 times in 1971-1975, and 3.3 times in 1976-1980, compared with those achieved during the previous period of 1948-1965.[11] This reveals that reserves growth rate has been markedly decelerated in West Siberia as well. In any case, new reserves there were apparently not enough to sustain the continued growth in Soviet oil production. Additions to the reserves in West Siberia were said to have been smaller than those

Table 3.5: Plan Fulfillment of Soviet Oil Reserves Growth, 1966-1972 (%)*

Area	1966-1970 (8th FYP)	1971-1972
USSR Total	98.8	80.4
European regions	67.9	51.7
Urals-Volga	77.5	49.8
Eastern regions	128.0	97.6
West Siberia	158.8	105.9

* 1966-1970 figures seem to be based on original five-year plan goals while figures for 1971-1972 are apparently calculated on the basis of annual growth targets.

Source: Yu. I. Maksimov and Z. R. Tsimtsina (eds.), *Optimizatsiya razvitiya i razmeshcheniya neftegazovoi promyshlennosti* (Novosibirsk, Nauka, 1977), p. 77.

that sustained the Soviet oil boom over the previous quarter century.[12]

Worse still, the Soviets have been confronted by the ever rising costs of oil production. According to a Soviet economist, the cost (*sebestoimost'*) of oil production increased by 41 percent in the Soviet Union during the eight years following the wholesale price revision of 1967.[13] He attributed the cost increase to the inevitable utilization of poorer deposits in remote and inaccessible parts of the country. Table 3.6 shows that this negative tendency became apparent especially after the mid-1970s. The average depth of the oil wells drilled--both exploratory and development wells--remained practically unchanged during the first half of the 1970s after having fallen by a factor of 1.6-1.7 times at the end of the previous decade. But this average increased sharply by more than 20 percent in the second half of the 1970s. More importantly, the average distance of the transportation of oil rapidly increased throughout the whole period. As a result, capital expenditures for the extraction, processing and transportation of oil in terms of the unit productive capacity commissioned during each five-year plan period increased by more than 1.4 times in the 1970s (See Table 3.6.).

Further expenditures were necessary for the enhanced recovery of oil in older oilfields. But a more important reason for the rising costs of oil production was that constituted by the difficulties which confronted the oil industry in West Siberia, to say nothing of the growing transport requirements. As the best part of the oil deposits in West Siberia had been exploited by the mid-1970s, any further increase in output there could be achieved only by tapping those less easily worked deposits which were

Table 3.6: Technical-Economic Indices of Soviet Oil Production and Transportation, 1960-1980

	1960	1965	1970	1975	1980
Average depth of wells drilled for 1 million tons of oil extraction (1,000m)	43	34	26	26	30
Average distance of pipeline transportation (km)	350	630	826	1395	2005
Capital investment required to increase capacity by one ton during each FYP (rubles)		57	67	73	97

Source: L. A. Melent'ev and A. A. Makarov, *Energeticheskii kompleks SSSR* (Moskva, Ekonomika, 1983), p. 53.

thinly spread in the more remote areas. In 1979, F. G. Arzhanov, head of Glavtyumenneftegaz, explained in an interview the difficulties of oil extraction in West Siberia:

> Oil extraction during the Tenth Five-Year Plan period is planned to increase 1.4 times in comparison with the increase during the Ninth Five-Year Plan period. To achieve this, the volume of drilling and capital construction is to grow...three times!
>
> .... During the Ninth Five-Year Plan period, 17 very large deposits were developed. These deposits in turn comprised the central and most productive oil-bearing areas. During the Tenth Five-Year Plan period, nine out of 17 deposits enter the stage of production decline, the other eight reach the maximum production level, and drilling is directed to the outlying and less productive areas. Whereas Samotlor accounted for 73 percent of the total increase in the extraction of Siberian oil during the past five-year plan period, it is slated for 33 percent for the current plan period.
>
> As the result, the structure of the output growth during the Tenth Five-Year Plan period is as follows: During the first three years, the 17 large deposits provided the bulk of the increase in oil extraction. Now the main increase is to be provided by new deposits we are developing during the current plan period. There are 29 such deposits! In terms of technical and economic indices, they are inferior to those developed earlier but superior to those which will come up to take their place. As we move on from the best oil-bearing areas to those that are average, well outputs are lowered. Therefore, a considerable portion of the new extraction capacities have to be used to compensate for the fall in more than half of now exploited deposits.[14]

Table 3.7 clearly shows that yields in new oil wells in West Siberia rapidly decreased since the mid-1970s while the volume of development drilling increased proportionately.

Production costs could not but rise sharply in this situation, to say nothing of the rising expenditures for prospecting for new deposits. If the *privedennye zatraty* for one ton of oil production on average over the period of 1971-1975 were taken as 100 percent, according to a Siberian oil economist, then for the oilfields in West Siberia

Table 3.7: Oil Yields in New Wells and Development Drilling in West Siberia, 1970-1980

	1970	1975	1980
Average yield of new wells (ton/day)			
USSR Total	n.a.	58.5	45.0 (plan)
West Siberia	111.8	148.7	66.2
Volume of development drilling (1,000m)			
USSR Total	n.a.	8768	17160 (plan)
West Siberia	919.6	2730.7	8306.4

Sources: Adapted from S. N. Starovoitov (ed.), *Problemy razvitiya Zapadno-Sibirskogo neftegazovogo kompleksa* (Novosibirsk, Nauka, 1983), p. 64; and V. Filanovskii, "Zapadno-Sibirskii neftegazovyi kompleks: rezul'taty i perspektivy," *Planovoe khozyaistvo*, No. 3 (1980), 23.

during 1976-1980 these could be calculated as follows: in Samotlor--161 percent, Pravdinsk--159 percent, and Sovetsk--192 percent.[15] The cost of developing infrastructure for the oil industry in the Middle Ob' region (West Siberia) was calculated on average as being twice as high as in the European regions of the country in the mid-1970s.[16] Compared with the cost of infrastructure development in this central oil region, those in the northern parts of West Siberia were estimated to reach as much as 1.5 to three times higher.[17]

To sum up, the Soviet Union managed to cope with its oil supply problem by the opening up of oil deposits in West Siberia in the 1970s. At the same time, however, there was uncertain prospect of the eastern region becoming the country's reliable oil producer. First, there were uncertainties with regard to the proven reserves in the region. The Soviets failed to discover any new reserves in West Siberia and elsewhere, which are comparable to Romashkino in the Urals-Volga region and Samotlor in West Siberia. Second, the production and transportation of West Siberian oil cost much more than it did before the mid-1970s. Many of the existing fields had been yielding less than they once did. In search of oil, the Soviets had to move farther north and east. But it required colossal capital investments as well as necessitating high operating costs to open up and exploit the energy resources of these remote and environmentally harsh areas, which lacked necessary infrastructure.

B. Changing Emphases in Soviet Energy Policy

Apparently in response to the uncertain prospects for the oil industry, the Soviets made several shifts of emphasis in their energy development policy during the 1970s and the early 1980s. Richly endowed with all sources of energy, they still had a number of viable energy options available from domestic sources. In fact, a constant theme in Soviet energy policy-making during the period was that a substitute should be found to help ease the burden on oil. Broadly, the changes represented either of two policy orientations--one for the continued attribution of priority to the development of Siberian oil and the other for a more balanced approach with relatively more important roles assigned to other oil regions and, at a later stage, to other types of energy sources.

(1) Siberian Oil: A Development Programme, 1969

On December 11, 1969, the Party Central Committee and the USSR Council of Ministers adopted a joint decree, "On Measures for the Accelerated Development of the Oil-extracting Industry in West Siberia."[18] Stressing the "realistic possibilities for a further increase in oil extraction in this region," it called for "the creation in the nearest future of a large new oil-extracting base of the country in West Siberia as *a highly important task* of the national economy."[19] It set the 1970 oil production target for the region at 30 million tons, as against the 20-25 million tons envisaged by the Directives of the Twenty-third Party Congress. Production was to reach 100-120 million tons by 1975 and 230-260 million tons by 1980.

The joint decree, which presumably carries more weight than an ordinary Party or government resolution, took a coordinated task-oriented approach (*programmno-tselevoi podkhod*).[20] Stressing that all the necessary up-to-date equipment and materials should be supplied for the development of the Siberian oilfields and related infrastructure, it assigned various tasks to a number of industrial ministries and other organizations. For instance, the oil and gas ministries along with five other industrial ministries and the RSFSR Council of Ministers were charged with "working out within a period of six months and, with the agreement of the USSR Gosplan and the USSR *Gossnab* (the State Committee for Material and Technical Supply), confirming concrete measures for accelerating the development of the oil-extracting industry in West Siberia in 1970-1975, and to this end intensifying the construction of oil and gas fields, oil pipelines, railway lines, power transmission lines, facilities of the construction industry and the building materials industries, housing, and cultural-service and other facilities." In all, four energy ministries, 13 energy-related industrial ministries and state committees, two central planning agencies, the RSFSR Council of Ministers, and other social, local Party and economic organizations were entrusted with assignments for the task. Even the Ministry of Defense Industry, which is one of the producers of weapons, was instructed to contribute to the project. Finally, Party organizations at various levels were instructed to take under their special supervision the fulfillment of the assignments for oil and gas production and related construction in the area.

The decree was the latest in a series of measures to develop the newly-discovered Siberian oil deposits. As early 1962, the USSR Council of Ministers envisaged in a decree that annual oil production in West Siberia would be increased to five million tons in 1970.[21] In 1964 following the extensive opening up of oil deposits in Tyumen' province, the Party Central Committee instructed Gosplan to study the feasibility of creating a base for the oil-extracting industry there.[22] Finally, the Twenty-third Party Congress, held in 1966, announced that "it is the most important task to create new oil- and gas-extracting centers in West Siberia and West Kazakhstan."[23] The Siberian programme was reaffirmed at the Twenty-fourth Party Congress in 1971 when it stressed that "the country's *largest* oil-industry base will be created in West Siberia."[24] At the Congress, the 1975 output target for the region was set at 120-125 million tons. West Siberia was planned to contribute about 6.4 percent of Soviet oil production by 1970, but 25 percent by 1975.

(2) "European" Oil: A Policy of Intensive Oil Recovery, 1974

In the later years of the Ninth Five-Year Plan (1971-1975), however, Soviet planners and oil industry officials supported a higher level of capital commitment in order to maintain or at least slow the decline in the existing oilfields of the European USSR, especially the Urals-Volga region, and thus to opt in favor of slower development of oil resources in West Siberia. They decided to maintain relatively high rates of drilling activity in those increasingly depleted oilfields along with the intensive application of recovery methods.

In 1974, Gosplan Chairman N. K. Baibakov proposed the policy of "giving new life to old deposits" (*Dat' novuyu zhizn' starym mestorozhdeniyam.*).[25] In his contribution to a Party weekly, *Ekonomicheskaya gazeta*, he claimed that "despite the substantial achievement in the development of the oil and gas industry, the utilization of geological reserves of oil is at a lower level" compared with that of other mineral resources. Emphasizing the importance of more effective methods of extracting oil, he said:

> It should be noted that the rapid increase in the extraction of oil and gas was the result not only of the opening up and assimilation of new large deposits, of the carrying out on a very extensive scale of drilling and construction works, but was also the result of the introduction of highly efficient up-to-date technology in the exploitation of these deposits.[26]

He then went on to stress the economic advantage of the stabilization of oil production in the old oilfields of the European part of the country.

> ...the volume of oil left in the deposit strata which are closed or in the late stage of exploitation is very considerable.
>
> The national-economic significance of raising oil output from the strata is confirmed with the large saving of capital investment, material and labor resources. If, for example, we put before ourselves the task of extracting one thousand million tons of oil, or approximately 70 million tons a year, additionally in the operating deposits during the perspective period (1976-1990) through the enhancement of oil extraction, then the economy resulting from the implementation of this measure may be valued at several hundred million rubles of capital investment. ....
>
> ....
>
> It is especially important to speed up works for the increase of oil output from the strata in the deposits of the European part of the Soviet Union.[27]

The planning chief hoped to see the rate of recovery raised to an average of 41-44 percent in the existing fields in the European USSR.[28]

Noting that the rate of oil recovery was far from satisfactory, Baibakov said that it was the reason why "the CC CPSU demanded that the oil industry workers intensify the work to enhance the effectiveness in working out oil deposits and to increase extraction of oil from the strata to a considerable degree."[29] No sooner had the chief planner advocated stepped-up recovery activity than an oil ministry official revealed that "in the Ministry of the Oil Industry work has been finished on determining the optimal limits of applying various (recovery) methods.... A plan for research and design work has been formulated."[30] The ensuing five-year plan, adopted in 1976, assigned the task of "increasing the yield of oil-bearing formations" to the oil industry, although it did not make any specific mention of the need to carry out an intensive recovery work in the European part of the country.[31] In that same year the Oil Ministry set up a programme to promote further recovery in the existing fields and by 1978 a special administration in charge of the task was formed within the ministry.[32]

The fresh emphasis on intensive recovery at that time coincided with the growing concern over the country's dwindling oil reserves. Pointing out that many old oil regions had failed to increase explored reserves, Baibakov and others underscored that the recovery problem lay at the heart of the reserves issue. In 1974, Oil Minister V. D. Shashin revealed that the plan for the growth in oil reserves was not fulfilled in 1971-1973.[33] He pointed out that the growth in Soviet oil production had in the past been largely based on the discovery of new large oil deposits. Commenting that such a trend would not be likely to continue in the future, he emphasized the necessity of maintaining the level of oil extraction from existing fields in compensation for the lack of new oil discoveries.[34] At that time, many argued that intensive recovery would not only effectively compensate for the natural depletion of existing deposits but also lessen the spiralling burden of the further development of oil resources in remote areas. As traditional fields had produced less oil, according to Baibakov, "an increasingly considerable quantity of oil and gas from the eastern regions of the country already at the present time has to be transported to the west (of the country), which demands huge capital investment, great quantities of pipes and equipment for the construction of main oil and gas pipelines, pumping and compressor stations and also huge labor expenses."[35] Intensive recovery in the old oil regions was apparently an attractive option because the existing wells, pipelines, refineries, and markets were already linked up and no new major capital investment was necessary. The 1974 policy was certainly motivated in part by such considerations.

(3) Coal: A Substitution Policy, 1976

In the history of Soviet energy strategy, one of the most important changes was introduced in 1976. In his report to the Twenty-fifth Party Congress, the then Chairman of the USSR Council of Ministers A. N. Kosygin urged that coal should be developed rapidly during the coming plan period as a substitute for oil and gas. Stressing the necessity to secure the rational and economical utilization of the country's fuel and power resources, he said:

> In this five-year plan, the foundation will be laid for further growth of our power-generating potential primarily through the use of water power, atomic fuel and cheap coal. As regards oil and gas, increments in their extraction will be increasingly channeled into technological needs.... Coal will begin to play a growing role in supplying the country with fuel and electric power, particularly in its eastern regions.
>
> The use of Ekibastuz and Kansk-Achinsk coal for the production of electric power will expand considerably during the Tenth Five-Year Plan period, and a number of large thermal power stations in the Urals and Volga regions will switch to the use of coal instead of *mazut* (residual fuel oil). To this end, the further development of the coal industry is planned, especially increases in the extraction of coal by the open-cast method in the Ekibastuz, Kansk-Achinsk, Kuznetsk and South Yakutiya basins.[36]

In accordance with Kosygin's proposal, the Congress instructed the energy industry to "improve the structure of the fuel and power balance" during the Tenth Five-Year Plan period.[37] The objectives of the energy industry set forth in its Directives were:

> To combine various types of fuel rationally; along with oil and gas, to make wider use of coal, shale, hydropower and atomic energy.
>
> ....
>
> To provide for the accelerated development of atomic power engineering in the European part of the USSR.

> ....
> To improve equipment and technology on a wide scale, and on this basis to ensure an accelerated growth rate for the extraction of coal.
> ....
> With a view to achieving a substantial increase in fuel and power resources in the long term, to accelerate the development of the South Yakutiya coal region, along with the development of existing coal basins.... To start work on the accelerated creation of the Kansk-Achinsk fuel and power complex and the fuller development of the Ekibastuz basin.[38]

As is evident from the above, the Soviets at that time wanted to substitute other types of energy sources, especially coal, for oil and gas as fuel. Kosygin mentioned hydropower and atomic energy, but their contribution to the Soviet production of electricity had been modest.[39] The pro-coal policy was apparently prompted by the uncertain prospects of the country's oil industry. Despite efforts at enhancing oil recovery, the Soviets were unable to prevent many existing oilfields from yielding less oil than they once did. Oil Minister Shashin predicted in 1975 that two-thirds (66 percent) of new productive capacity would be needed to compensate for oil depletion in 1976-1980.[40] By contrast, the coal industry had done a good job during the Ninth Five-Year Plan period.[41] In 1975, it produced a total of 701 million tons of coal against the plan target of 685-695 million tons. Seemingly encouraged by the performance of the coal industry, the Tenth Plan Directives called for an increase in coal output of 13 to 16 percent by 1980 as against the 10-11 percent increase envisaged in the previous plan period. The 1980 production target was set at 790-810 million tons. If coal were produced by the methods of modernized open-cast mining, its cost would be low enough to make it competitive with oil and gas. The 1976 Directives envisaged that oil production was to be increased by 26-30 percent in the Tenth Plan period, but it was far lower than the 38-43 percent increase planned for the previous five years. In early 1977, the Party Central Committee and the USSR Council of Ministers adopted a decree, "On the Creation of the Ekibastuz Fuel and Power Complex and Construction of a 1,500-kilovolt DC Transmission Line from Ekibastuz to the Center."[42] The construction of the Kansk-Achinsk Complex was also to begin in that year, with a target completion date of 1999.[43]

(4) Siberian Oil: A Crash Development Policy, 1977

The balanced approach advocated by Kosygin, however, turned out to be rather short-lived as the urgency of oil development was once again accentuated in late 1977. This time it was Party leader L. I. Brezhnev who came out in favor of the accelerated development of West Siberian oil resources. In his speech to the December plenum of the Party Central Committee, he declared:

> We have developed and will develop the extraction of coal and atomic energy, and will construct hydroelectric power stations. But looking at the things realistically, we certainly have to admit that the decisive role in supplying fuel and power for the country in the next 10 years will remain with oil and gas, first of all from Tyumen'.
>
> Therefore, the all-round opening up of the underground resources and the development of productive forces in West Siberia is a programme of especial importance for our national economy. ....
>
> It is important to concentrate resources and the possibilities for capital construction on this truly great construction site of our time and secure the settlement of a number of technical and transportation problems.[44]

He reiterated his policy position at the Eighteenth *Komsomol* (the Communist League of Youth) Congress in May the following year:

> In a matter of 10 years, we have turned this taiga land into the country's main oil base. ....
>
> We will live on the Tyumen' reserves for many years to come. In the next 10 years, we expect Tyumen' to account for the main increase in oil and gas extraction and in valuable chemical feedstocks produced from these resources. In this connection, we are beginning, or more precisely, have already entered, a new and more complicated stage in the development of West Siberia. The volume of all work there will be doubled or trebled. This will require new material and technical outlays and an influx of people.[45]

In short, Brezhnev spoke for the priority development of oil and gas, and especially for the part to be played in this by West Siberian oil. To this end, he advocated a big increase in capital investment in West Siberia. The national daily *Sovetskaya Rossiya* summarized the tasks to be accomplished during the Tenth Plan period in connection with the West Siberian energy development as follows:

- The volume of all the (capital construction) work to be increased by from two to three times;
- In 1980, 315 million tons of oil to be produced in West Siberia (as against the 310 million tons envisaged by the 1976 Plan Directives); and
- A total of 15-20 million square meters of housing to be built there.[46]

The renewed emphasis on Siberian oil appears to have been less a reversal of the balanced energy strategy as formulated in 1976 than a response to the increasing difficulties that confronted the oil industry. As to coal, its production had been growing steadily at least until 1978 although its annual increment was declining. The annual growth rate of coal production was 2.5 percent in 1974 and 1975, and 1.5 percent in the following two years.[47] Oil production also continued to expand even though its growth rate had slowed down and the gap between the plan targets and actual production figures had widened (See Tables 3.2 and 3.3.). For the first time in the previous 15 years, however, the Soviets failed to fulfil their planned growth in oil reserves in West Siberia for 1976 and 1977.[48] In these two years, as also in 1979, Siberian geologists failed to fulfil even their drilling assignments.[49] By the time of the adoption of the crash development programme of Siberian oil, there was growing uncertainty concerning the future of the Soviet oil industry.

(5) Siberian Gas: A Substitution Policy, 1981

In 1981, Brezhnev initiated another policy change in the energy area, which accorded high priority this time to the development of natural gas in West Siberia. In his report to the Twenty-sixth Party Congress, the General Secretary said:

> A necessary precondition for the accomplishment of all national-economic tasks--both production and social tasks--is the development of heavy industry. This applies especially to its basic branches, first

> of all to the *fuel and power* branches. I shall not cite the figures--you know them. I would like merely to emphasize that the task of improving the structure of the fuel and power balance is becoming more and more urgent. We must reduce the share of oil used as fuel and replace it with gas and coal, and we must develop atomic power engineering more swiftly, including fast breeder reactors. ....
>
> I consider it necessary to single out a rapid increase in the extraction of Siberian gas as a task of paramount economic and political importance. The West Siberian region's deposits are unique. The largest of them--at Urengoi--has reserves so gigantic that for many years they can provide for both the country's domestic requirements and its export needs, including exports to capitalist countries. The extraction of gas and oil in West Siberia and their transportation to the European part of the country must be made major elements of the energy programme for the Eleventh Five-Year Plan, and the Twelfth as well.[50]

Brezhnev's proposal was fully endorsed at the Congress. The Eleventh Plan Directives "consider the implementation of the programme for the accelerated development of gas extraction as a highly important (*vazhneishii*) task."[51] It was planned at that time that the gas industry would produce 600-640 billion cubic meters of natural gas by 1985, 330-370 billion cubic meters of which were to be extracted in West Siberia. The industry produced a total of 435 billion cubic meters of gas in 1980, 156 billion cubic meters of this being extracted in West Siberia.

What caused the Soviet leader to retreat from his previous all-out campaign for Siberian oil? There had been a steady fall in the rate of growth of Soviet oil production, but 1979 was the first year that the growth rate plummeted sharply. As shown in Table 3.2, it stood at five percent each in 1977 and 1978, but at three percent in 1979. In West Siberia, the annual increment of oil production began to fall off after 1977 (See Table 3.3.). The efforts to intensify oil recovery in existing fields apparently did not produce satisfactory results either, as evidenced by the dismissal of Deputy Oil Minister E. M. Khalimov who had been in charge of the task.[52] Even more striking, meanwhile, the coal industry actually experienced a reduction in production in 1979 for the first time since the beginning of the 1970s.[53] In November of that year, *Pravda* pointed out in an editorial that "the oil and the coal ministries have made serious mistakes in planning and management of production, utilization of capital investments. The planned tasks of Kuzbass and Karaganda miners and Tyumen' oil workers have not been fulfilled."[54] Against this background, the Party leader made a retreat to what appeared to be a more balanced energy strategy. Thus at the November 1979 plenum of the Party Central Committee, Brezhnev said:

> Looking to the 1980s, the task is to substantially improve the country's fuel and power balance and, first of all, to reduce oil's share in power-station fuel. Is this a realistic undertaking? Estimates show that it is quite realistic.
>
> To this end, it is necessary, first of all, to make an even more resolute effort to increase the extraction rates for gas, especially in West Siberia, and to ensure the wide-scale replacement of *mazut* by gas. Second, we need to develop atomic engineering faster. .... Third, we must accelerate the development of the Ekibastuz, Kansk-Achinsk and Kuznetsk fuel and power complexes and, of course, the construction of the necessary power transmission lines, above all the 1,500-kilovolt direct-current Ekibastuz-Center line.[55]

But the Soviet energy situation further deteriorated in the later 1970s. The coal industry performed especially poorly. The industry produced 716 million tons of coal in 1980, as against the 790-810 million tons envisaged in the Tenth Plan Directives. Much of the coal extracted was also of low quality. In such circumstances, oil as well as gas had to provide still larger shares of the fuel supply to thermal power stations.[56] As we have seen, however, the oil industry suffered a further decline in production in the late 1970s and the early 1980s. By contrast the gas industry was doing well, with the 1977, 1978, 1979 and 1980 output targets being overfulfilled by six to eight percent.[57] Clearly encouraged by the performance of the gas industry, Brezhnev finally accorded at the October 1980 Party plenum the highest development priority to gas, particularly gas in West Siberia, as the following passage shows.

> A rapid increase in natural gas extraction is assuming a special role. Gas reserves are enormous, especially in West Siberia. These resources make it

> possible to solve fuel and power problems more easily and to accelerate the development of the chemical industry and a number of other branches. The expansion of gas deliveries could help us satisfy more fully the needs of the countries of the socialist commonwealth. On the basis of these considerations, it has been proposed that a large-scale programme be worked out for the stepped-up development of the oil and gas industry in West Siberia. .... Making this programme a highly important element of the Eleventh Five-Year Plan, and even of the Twelfth, is a task for Gosplan.[58]

According to the Eleventh Plan Directives, planned increments in the output of respective energy sources were as follows:

Table 3.8: Planned Increments of Soviet Energy Production

	1971-1975	1976-1980	1981-1985(plan)
Oil (including condensate) million tons:	138*	112 (26-30%)**	17-42 (3-7%)
Natural gas billion cubic meters:	91	146 (38-50%)	165-205(38-47%)
Coal million tons:		15 (13-16%)	54-84 (7-12%)

* Absolute increases over previous plan period.
** Figures in parentheses are percentage increases over previous plan period.
Sources: Five-Year Plan Directives, 1971, 1976 and 1981.

It appears from the above figures that the Soviets had decided to stabilize oil production in the near future. Stabilization of gas extraction would come in the more distant future, while coal would play an important role in the Soviet energy structure only in the longer run. In 1981-1985, the main emphasis was clearly placed on the priority development of natural gas. No significant changes have been made in Soviet energy policy since the death of Brezhnev except the increasing attention given to energy conservation by his successors.

C. Trends in Soviet Energy Investment

Thus far, a series of changes in Soviet energy strategy have been examined. These changes differed in their emphases and recommendations, but had one thing in common: All of them demanded more funds and materials for their respective projects. It is widely observed that capital investment plans in the Soviet Union are the direct reflection of policy priorities.[59] By focusing on these, it may therefore be possible to determine the impact of the announced policy changes upon Soviet energy development priorities.

(1) Between Fuel Industries

Capital outlays for fuel supply in the Soviet Union have been estimated to have reached 16 billion rubles in 1980.[60] This figure includes expenditures on geological prospecting, extraction, treatment and pipeline transportation. If investment in power generation is added, it rose to 22.5-23 billion rubles. In all, capital investment in the Soviet energy economy is calculated to have amounted to 33.5-37 billion rubles or about 30 percent of the total national investment in that single year. Capital expenditures on fuel supply alone--not counting investments in the power industry--took about 12 percent of the total.[61]

During the 1970s, capital investments in both oil and gas industries appear to have risen sharply. Table 3.9 includes figures for Soviet fuel investments derived from Soviet official statistics and other sources. Not counting expenditures on supporting industries, capital investment in the oil industry (mainly production and pipeline construction) grew from a level of 18-19 billion rubles in 1971-1975 to some 30 billion rubles in 1976-1980. That of the gas industry probably grew from 11-14 billion rubles to 21.5-28.5 billion rubles. These figures are greater than those tabulated in the official statistical handbook which apparently do not include transport construction and many other development costs. This is especially the case with the gas industry, in which 50 to 80 percent of capital expenditures are said to be spent in the construction of pipelines.[62] In 1980, B. Shcherbina, Minister of the Construction of Oil and Gas Industry Enterprises, revealed that the annual volume of pipeline construction work carried out by his ministry for both oil and gas industries, amounted to nearly four billion rubles.[63]

The Soviet Union has so far failed to publish any official statistics which include detailed figures of capital outlays for energy transport and other related infrastructure construction. Nevertheless, the general trends of

Table 3.9: Capital Investment in Soviet Fuel Industries, 1965-1984 (billion rubles)

		1966-70	1971-75	1976-80	1981-84
Oil Industry					
Production	*Narkhoz*	11.1	16.0	26.4	38.4
Production &	*Lalayants*	12.0	19.4		
Pipeline	*Shashin*		18		
	Hewett		19	30.4	
Gas Industry					
Production	*Narkhoz*	4.5	7.3	10.2	11.8
Production &	*Margulov*		10.9		
Pipeline	*Orudzhev*			21.5	
	Hewett		13.8	28.5	
Coal Industry					
Production	*Narkhoz*	7.2	8.3	9.7	10.6

Sources: *Narkhoz, 1977*, p. 354; *1980*, p. 338; *1922-1982*, p. 371; *1982*, p. 341; and *1984*, p. 381.

Lalayants: A. Lalayants, Vice Chairman of USSR Gosplan, gave unit capital investment figures in the oil and gas industries for the Eighth and Ninth Five-Year Plan periods. The figures in the table are calculated from them. A. Lalayants, "Dva obshchestva--dve linii v razvitii toplivno-energeticheskogo kompleksa," *Planovoe khozyaistvo*, No. 4 (1975), p. 28.

Shashin: Oil Minister V. Shashin, *Ekonomicheskaya gazeta*, No. 22 (1976), p. 4.

Hewett: E. A. Hewett calculates "extraction plus transportation costs" for both fuels during the Ninth and Tenth Plan periods on the basis of some Soviet data on pipeline investments. The numbers in the table are adapted from his. Edward A. Hewett, *Energy, Economics, and Foreign Policy in the Soviet Union* (Washington, D.C., The Brookings Institution, 1984), pp. 41 and 176. According to I. Ya. Furman, 4.05 billion rubles and 13.86 billion rubles were invested in the gas industry (extraction and transportation) in 1966-1970 and 1971-1975, respectively. I. Ya. Furman, *Ekonomika magistral'nogo transporta gaza* (Moskva, Nedra, 1978), p. 5.

Margulov: R. D. Margulov, *Razvitie gazovoi promyshlennosti i analiz tekhniko-ekonomicheskikh pokazatelei* (Moskva, VNIIE Gazprom, 1976), p. 17.

Orudzhev: Gas Minister S. A. Orudzhev, "Zadachi rabotnikov gazovoi promyshlennosti na 1980 god," *Gazovaya promyshlennost*, No. 2 (1980), 5-6.

Soviet energy investment may still be observed by analyzing the official statistics. It is assumed here that the overall capital expenditures spent in the development of each fuel industry will on the whole be proportional to the respective figures given in the official statistics.[64] As shown in Table 3.10, the 1970s and the first half of the 1980s were characterized by a rapid increase in investment in the oil and gas industry.[65] The oil industry in particular increased its share of total industrial investment in the Tenth and Eleventh Five-Year Plan periods. This shift in priorities occurred at the expense of several other industries such as the coal industry in the energy sector, and ferrous metallurgy. The share of the oil industry as a percentage of industrial investment increased by 5.3 percentage points in 10 years--from 8.9 percent in 1970 to 14.2 percent in 1980--while that of Machine-Building and Metal-Working gained only 3.7 percentage points during the same period.

The Soviet oil industry consistently lost its share of industrial investment during the period of 1966-1969 (See Table 3.11.). Nevertheless, plan targets were fulfilled or overfulfilled until the early 1970s. But in the second half of the 1970s its share began to grow, steadily at first, and then at an accelerating pace. The period was indeed characterized by an explosion of investment in the industry both in terms of absolute expenditures and in terms of the share of overall investment. In this process, the year 1970 proved to be a turning-point after which the

Table 3.10: Sectoral Share of Soviet Industrial Investment, 1966-1984 (%)

	1966-70	1971-75	1976-80	1981-84
Electricity	11.4	10.2(-1.2)	9.1(-1.1)	9.3(+0.2)
Coal	6.1	5.1(-1.0)	4.5(-0.6)	4.5(0)
Oil	9.2	9.1(-0.1)	11.7(+2.6)	16.4(+4.7)
Gas	3.7	4.2(+0.5)	4.5(+0.3)	5.0(+0.5)
Ferrous Metallurgy	8.3	7.6(-0.7)	6.8(-0.8)	6.1(-0.7)
Chemicals & Petrochemicals	9.2	9.0(-0.2)	9.9(+0.9)	7.7(-2.2)
Machine-Building & Metal-Working	18.8	22.0(+3.2)	24.2(+2.2)	24.2(0)
Others	22.3	21.3(-1.0)	18.9(-2.4)	17.3(-1.6)

Source: *Narkhoz, 1980*, p. 338; and *1984*, p. 381. ( ) is five-year change (four-year change in the last column) in investment share. About 10 percent of the industrial investment are not reported in the statistical yearbook.

industry began to add to its capital share. During the period of 1966-1984, the average annual variations in the share each fuel industry enjoyed of the total industrial investment were 0.26 and 0.22 percent, respectively, for the gas and the coal industries, and 0.63 percent of the oil industry. The increment in the capital share of the oil industry has consistently far exceeded that average figure since 1978. In the case of the gas industry, its share also grew sharply in 1973-1974 and again in 1977. After three to four years of relative decline, the percentage increase in its share of capital investment again rose above the average in 1982-1984. But the huge capital requirements for pipeline construction in the industry must be taken into account. It may be possible that the Soviets concentrated their efforts more on pipeline construction than on gas production during the period of relative decline in the increase of capital share of the gas industry itself. Meanwhile, the share of capital investment in the coal industry diminished throughout the 1960s and early 1970s, then rose slightly from 4.3 percent in 1976 and 1977 to 4.6 percent in 1980. But the industry experienced a

Table 3.11: Annual Percentage Shares each Fuel Industry obtained of Industrial Investment, 1966-1984

	1966	1967	1968	1969	1970	1971	1972	1973	1974
Oil	10.1	9.4	8.9	8.7	8.9	9.1	9.3	9.0	9.5
		-0.7	-0.5	-0.2	+0.2	+0.2	+0.2	-0.3	+0.5
Gas	3.5	3.7	3.7	3.6	3.7	3.7	3.8	4.3	4.7
		+0.2	0	-0.1	+0.1	0	+0.1	+0.5	+0.4
Coal	6.9	6.6	6.0	5.6	5.4	5.4	5.3	5.1	4.7
		-0.3	-0.6	-0.4	-0.2	0	-0.1	-0.2	-0.4

	1975	1976	1977	1978	1979	1980	1981	1982	1983	1984
Oil	9.4	10.0	10.6	11.6	12.9	14.2	16.3	17.0	17.0	16.1
	-0.1	+0.6	+0.6	+1.0	+1.3	+1.3	+2.1	+0.7	0	-0.9
Gas	4.5	4.5	4.8	4.9	4.5	4.3	4.1	4.6	5.0	5.9
	-0.2	0	+0.3	+0.1	-0.4	-0.2	-0.2	+0.5	+0.4	+0.9
Coal	4.5	4.3	4.3	4.5	4.5	4.6	4.1	4.3	4.3	4.6
	-0.2	-0.2	0	+0.2	0	+0.1	-0.5	+0.2	0	+0.3

* Numerators are percentage shares; denominators are annual changes in the share.

** Industrial investment figures used here do not include investments by collective farms and private individuals for any years except 1980-1984.

Sources: *Narkhoz*, various years.

setback in its relative share in 1981 when it lost 0.5 percentage points.

So far as can be judged from the incomplete data available, continued emphasis was laid upon both the oil industry and, to a lesser extent, the gas industry during the 1970s. It is interesting to note that the upturn in the oil industry's share of industrial investment in 1970 was preceded by a decision in 1969 to accelerate the development of West Siberian oil resources. Another decision in 1977 for the crash development of Siberian oil was clearly related to the great upsurge of oil investment in the ensuing years. Meanwhile, the balanced energy policy of 1976 apparently helped the coal industry to boost its investment share during the period 1978-1980. Finally, the share of the gas industry in overall industrial investment continued to fall by 0.2 percentage points in 1981 despite the big gas policy announced early in that year. But gas achieved a substantial gain of 0.5, 0.4 and 0.9 percentage points, respectively, in its share in 1982, 1983 and 1984.

(2) Between Regions

The Soviet energy policies which have been examined thus far have strong locational biases of their own. The 1969 programme was, for instance, intended for the oil industry in West Siberia, not for the oil industry as a whole. The same is true for the 1977 oil strategy. The policy of enhanced oil recovery in the mid-1970s was concerned primarily with the European oil regions of the country. Finally, the pro-coal policy of 1976 was based on the development of "eastern coal reserves."[66] The problem of just where to produce has been one of the major issues bedeviling Soviet energy strategy and in particular that part of the strategy concerned with oil. Should oil industry development continue to be concentrated in the established fields which are close to the country's industrial center, but have dwindling reserves? Or would it be better to develop the industry in the remote and harsh, but relatively oil-rich eastern areas?

Until 1975, the eastern regions of the Soviet Union--West Siberia, East Siberia and the Soviet Far East--had never received more than 17 percent of total national investment (except for a brief period during World War II). Their share was 15.2 percent in 1966-1970 and 16.8 percent in the following five-year period.[67] Minas Chentemirov,

First Vice Chairman of the USSR State Committee on Construction, however, disclosed that their share had jumped to 20 percent in 1978.[68] According to Boris Rumer, such a "disturbance" in the territorial structure of capital investment was "associated with the equally dramatic shift in the branch structure of industrial investment toward the fuel and energy complex."[69] In his opinion, all efforts had been directed to one "supertask" in the Soviet Union: "to maximize production of oil and gas, no matter what the cost."[70] Soviet economists have revealed that the regions which took the lion's share of investment in Siberia in the 1970s were Tyumen' province and Krasnoyarsk territory (*krat*).[71] Tyumen's share of the West Siberian investment rose from 23 percent in the Eighth Five-Year Plan period to 33 percent in the Ninth and finally to over 50 percent in the ensuing plan period.[72] In fact, capital investment in Tyumen' province grew by six times in 1970-1978. Also compared with the capital outlays expended in the province in 1965, they rose by 2.6 times by 1970, 7.0 times by 1975, 7.8 times by 1977 and finally a record 15.9 times by 1978.[73] Investment trends in the province of Tyumen' and

Table 3.12: Annual Percentage Shares each Oil-producing Region obtained of Total National Investment, 1965-1975

	1965	1966	1967	1968	1969
Tyumen' province	0.97	1.19 +0.22	1.44 +0.25	1.41 -0.03	1.46 +0.05
Bashkir ASSR	1.67	1.78 +0.11	1.84 +0.06	1.71 -0.13	1.62 -0.09
Tatar ASSR	1.22	1.35 +0.13	1.24 -0.11	1.26 +0.02	1.29 +0.03

	1970	1971	1972	1973	1974	1975
Tyumen' province	1.58 +0.12	1.75 +0.17	2.08 +0.33	2.38 +0.30	2.56 +0.18	2.84 +0.28
Bashkir ASSR	1.67 +0.05	1.55 -0.12	1.53 -0.02	1.49 -0.04	1.46 -0.03	1.49 +0.03
Tatar ASSR	1.44 +0.15	1.72 +0.28	1.88 +0.16	1.94 +0.06	2.04 +0.10	2.54 +0.50

* Numerators are percentage shares and denominators annual changes in the share.

Sources: *Narkhoz RSFSR, 1975*, pp. 328-329; and *Narkhoz, 1975*, p. 502.

in two older oil-producing autonomous republics (*ASSR*) up to 1975 are shown in Table 3.12.[74] The share of Tyumen' increased by 1.26 percentage points in five years from 1.58 percent in 1970 to 2.84 percent in 1975, while Bashkir ASSR lost 0.18 points. Tatar ASSR was the only oil province in the European USSR which was able to increase its share during the period, but it also fell behind the West Siberian province. During the whole period 1965-1975, the average annual changes in the share of these regions in the total Soviet investment were 0.19 percent for Tyumen' province, 0.07 percent for Bashkir ASSR, and 0.15 percent for Tatar ASSR. Tyumen's share exceeded that average in 1972-1973 and in 1975, but it had already begun to rise after 1969 following a year of decline.

How much have the Soviets actually spent on the West Siberian fuel development programme? As our data given in Table 3.13 are highly fragmentary, the inferences drawn must be tentative. Assuming that our data is reasonably correct, however, the share West Siberia obtained of the overall investment in the oil industry increased from nearly 20 percent in 1971-1975 to about 40 percent in 1976-1980. According to a Siberian economist, West Siberia actually received 38.3 percent of the total investment in the oil industry as a whole in 1976-1980.[75] Capital expenditures on the gas industry in West Siberia also grew rapidly and were equivalent to 80 percent of the volume of oil investment in the region in the Tenth Plan period.[76] During the period, both oil and gas industries received more than 60 percent of the total investment in the West Siberian energy complex (Table 3.13). The Eleventh Five-Year Plan earmarked for the complex almost all of the increase in overall investment in West Siberia as a whole.[77]

A trend such as this can also be discerned in the allocation of drilling activity, which is said to be absorbing 40 to 50 percent of capital investments in oil and gas production throughout the first half of the 1970s.[78] As shown in Table 3.14, the volume of development drilling has rapidly increased in West Siberia. West Siberia's share of total national drilling rose from 31 percent in 1975 to nearly 44 percent in 1978. Exploratory drilling to establish the presence of hydrocarbons in West Siberia also substantially increased in the late 1970s. As is evident from the table, West Siberia had earlier experienced a downturn in the volume of exploratory drilling. In 1972, Siberian drillers carried out as little as 385 thousand meters of exploratory drilling. According to a Soviet source, capital investment in exploratory drilling for oil in West

Table 3.13: Capital Investment in West Siberian Fuel Development, 1966-1985 (billion rubles)

	1966-70	1971-75	1976-80	1981-85(plan)
In Tyumen' & Tomsk oblasti(1)	6.7	14.6		
In the West Siberian TPK(2)			35	
In the Oil & Gas Industries(3)			22	40-55
In the Oil Industry alone(4)		3.5	(13)	26

Sources: (1) Both figures are overall investments in two oil-producing provinces in West Siberia. *Narkhoz RSFSR, 1975* p. 329.

(2) *Pravda*, February 11, 1980. A Soviet specialist revealed that capital outlays for the development of the West Siberian Territorial-Production Complex (*TPK*) amounted to about 50 billion rubles in 1965-1980. N. Feitel'man, "Mineral'no-syr'evaya baza SSSR i perspektivy ee razvitiya," *Voprosy ekonomiki*, No. 12 (1982), 66. According to another Soviet source, more than 55 billion rubles were invested in the complex during the period of 1964-1980. V. I. Lipanovich, "Osobennosti dinamiki i struktury kapital'nykh vlozhenii v shirotnykh mezhregionakh Zapadnoi Sibiri," in A. G. Granberg (ed.), *Ekonomika Sibiri v razreze shirotnykh zon* (Novosibirsk, Nauka, 1985), pp. 64-65.

(3) 1976-80 figure: V. Filanovskii, "Zapadno-Sibirskii neftegazovyi kompleks: rezul'taty i perspektivy," *Planovoe khozyaistvo*, No. 3 (1980), 20.

1981-1985 plan figures: V. Kuramin, Chairman of Gosplan's West Siberian Commission, revealed in 1982 that capital investment in the oil and gas complex would be 40 billion rubles in the Eleventh Plan period, almost twice the level of the previous five years. But Tyumen' Party Secretary B. Trofimov set the figure at 55 billion rubles for the fuel-extracting complex, which he also claimed to be twice the level of the previous plan period. See V. Kuramin, *Pravda*, March 3, 1982; and B. Trofimov, "Formirovanie Tyumenskogo neftegazovogo kompleksa," *Planovoe khozyaistvo*, No. 9 (1981), 85.

(4) 1971-75: According to V. Muravlenko, former head of *Glavtyumenneftegaz*, and others, a total of 3,485 million rubles were invested in the oil industry in West

(Continued)

Table 3.13 (Cont.)
Siberia during the period of 1971-1975. V. I. Muravlenko and V. I. Kremnev (eds.), *Sibirskaya neft'* (Moskva, Nedra, 1977), p. 95; and *Trud*, April 11, 1978.

1976-85: R. Bulgakov, head of Glavtyumenneftegaz, revealed that capital investments in oil in West Siberia would be 26 billion rubles in the Eleventh Plan period. The figure seems to include capital expenditures for development of supporting sectors in the area as well. *Trud*, May 17, 1981. Two Soviet academics stated that the volume of capital investment in the oil industry of West Siberia in 1981-1985 would grow by two times in comparison with the Tenth Plan period. Thus, the figure of 13 billion rubles are obtained by dividing Bulgakov's figure in half. S. D. Ageeva and B. P. Orlov, "Nekotorye cherty investitsionnogo protsessa v Zapadno-Sibirskom neftegazovom komplekse," *Izvestiya Sibirskogo otdeleniya AN SSSR*, seriya obshchestvennykh nauk, No. 11 (1982), 86. B. S. Trofimov, a Tyumen' obkom section head, was quoted as saying in 1982 that over 17 billion rubles were allocated to Tyumengazprom in the Eleventh Plan period. *Sotsialisticheskaya industriya*, November 2, 1982.

Siberia began to dwindle after 1969 and this trend continued until 1973.[79] The downturn took place at a time when the total number of meters drilled in exploratory wells around the country rose from 3,239 thousand meters in 1970 to 3,788 thousand meters in 1975. Nevertheless, West Siberia eventually gained two percentage points in its share of exploratory drilling over five years from 12.9 percent in the Eighth Plan period to 14.9 percent in the Ninth Plan period. This increase was primarily achieved in the latter part of the 1971-1975 plan period. This is because the Soviets had apparently decided to conduct prospecting and exploratory drilling for oil in more conveniently located areas in the late 1960s and the early 1970s. In fact, about 65 percent of the exploratory drilling in the Soviet Union had been allocated to the European part of the country during the Ninth Plan period.[80] But having failed to add more reserves to the old oil regions, the Soviets seem to have switched the exploratory work to the eastern part of the country. At the same time, they certainly turned their attention to increasing output of the existing fields by extensive use of the techniques of enhancing recovery.

In sum, the 1969 decision for the full-scale development of West Siberian oil seems to have added momentum to the eastward movement of the Soviet oil industry. But confronted by large increases in costs in the industry, the Soviets proceeded to commit relatively greater funds to the older oilfields close to the place of consumption in an

Table 3.14: Trends in West Siberian Oil Drilling Activities, 1961-1980 (thousand meters)

Year	Development Drilling		Exploratory Drilling	
	USSR Total[1]	West Siberia[2]	USSR Total[3]	West Siberia[4]
1961-65			16500	1070
1967				500
1970		919.6	3239	
1966-70		2863.9	16190	2090
1972				385
1975	8768	2730.7	3788	728
1971-75		9188.9	17760	2650
1976		3400		
1977		3800		
1978	11576	5045		
1980		8306.4		over 1000
1976-80		26770.7		

Sources: 1. V. Filanovskii, "Zapadno-Sibirskii neftegazovyi kompleks: rezul'taty i perspektivy," *Planovoe khozyaistvo*, No. 3 (1980), 23.

2. The 1976-1977 figures are from *Neftyanoe khozyaistvo*, No.5 (1977), 7 and No. 5 (1978), 4 as quoted in J. Richard Lee and James R. Lecky, "Soviet Oil Developments," in U.S. Congress, Joint Economic Committee, *Soviet Economy in A Time of Change*, Vol. 1 (Washington, D.C., 1979), p. 592. The 1978 figure is in Filanovskii, p. 23. The remaining numbers are from S. N. Starovoitov (ed.), *Problemy razvitiya Zapadno-Sibirskogo neftegazovogo kompleksa* (Moskva, Nauka, 1983), p. 64.

3. Five-year figures are from Ya. A. Mazover (ed.), *Problemy razvitiya i razmeshcheniya toplivnykh baz SSSR* (Moskva, Nauka, 1982), p. 98. The 1970 and 1975 figures are from "Razvedochnoe burenie na neft' v SSSR," *Ekonomika i organizatsiya promyshlennogo proizvodstva*, No. 6 (1977), 37.

4. Five-year figures are from Mazover, p. 98. The numbers of 1967 and 1972 are from *Sovetskaya Rossiya*, December 8, 1978. The 1975 figure is given by V. I. Muravlenko and V. I. Kremnev (eds.), *Sibirskaya neft'* (Moskva, Nedra, 1977), p. 16. The figure for 1980 is obtained from B. Trofimov, "Formirovanie Tyumenskogo neftegazovogo kompleksa," *Planovoe khozyaistvo*, No. 9 (1981), 84.

attempt to discover oil reserves there and, especially later, to maintain the output from the existing wells. With the unabated decline in oil production in these traditional fields, together with the uncertainty of the reserves situation in the eastern part of the country, they then turned their attention to the country's more abundant coal resources as a possible substitute for oil. But this coal policy was soon abandoned. In 1977, the decision was taken to accelerate the development of Siberian oil resources, and this was done with tremendous impact upon resource allocation throughout the whole economy. The pro-oil policy was reaffirmed in 1981, although this time with relatively more emphasis being attached to natural gas resources in West Siberia as another substitute for oil. We have seen that all of these shifts in Soviet energy strategy had their impact upon Soviet investment activities. For all such changes, however, it was West Siberian oil that continued to have received preference in the allocation of resources.

NOTES

1. Nikita S. Khrushchev, "O kontrol'nykh tsifrakh razvitiya narodnogo khozyaistva SSSR na 1959-1965 gody," *Vneocherednoi XXI s'ezd KPSS*, stenograficheskii otchet, I (Moskva, Gospolitizdat, 1959), p. 27.

2. Ye. P. Yefremov, M. K. Mikhalev, L. I. Churikov and G. L. Chudnovskii, "Sostoyanie i napravleniya dal'neishei realizatsii programmy kompleksnogo razvitiya neftedobyvayushchei promyshlennosti Zapadnoi Sibiri," in S. N. Starovoitov (ed.), *Problemy razvitiya Zapadno-Sibirskogo neftegazovogo kompleksa* (Novosibirsk, Nauka, 1983), pp. 62-63.

3. I. D. Kozlov, *Energeticheskoe khozyaistvo stran SEV* (Moskva, Nauka, 1980), p. 30.

4. The problems besetting the Soviet oil industry have been widely discussed in the West. See Chapter I, footnote 15.

5. *Ekonomicheskaya gazeta*, No. 42 (1972), p. 5.

6. S. N. Starovoitov, "Voprosy nadezhnosti v perspektivnom planirovanii razvitiya neftyanoi promyshlennosti," in Yu. I. Maksimov and Z. R. Tsimtsina (eds.), *Optimizatsiya razvitiya i razmeshcheniya neftegazovoi promyshlennosti* (Novosibirsk, Nauka, 1977), pp. 88-89.

7. V. Filanovskii, "Zapadno-Sibirskii neftegazovyi kompleks: rezul'taty i perspektivy," *Planovoe khozyaistvo*, No. 3 (1980), 22.

8. N. Mel'nikov and V. Shelest, "Toplivno-energeticheskii kompleks SSSR," *Planovoe khozyaistvo*, No. 2 (1975), 11. "Commercial reserves" include three categories of reserves, A+B+C_1 in Soviet terminology, which roughly correspond to the Western categories of "proved," "probable," and some "possible" reserves. By commercial reserves the Soviets seem to mean the reserves which are commercially exploitable with available technology and equipment.
It is interesting to note that data on Soviet oil reserves are secret and there are a variety of Western estimates of the Soviet reserves, not all of which specify whether the reserves cover A+B+C_1 or more. On Soviet reserves classification system, see Arthur A. Meyerhoff, "Soviet Petroleum: History, Technology, Geology, Reserves, Potential and Policy," in R. G. Jensen, T. Shabad, A. W. Wright (eds.), *Soviet Natural Resources in the World Economy* (Chicago, University of Chicago Press, 1983), pp. 327-330. For a discussion of Western estimates of the Soviet reserves, for instance, see Marshall I. Goldman, *The Enigma of Soviet Petroleum: Half-empty or Half-full?* (London, George Allen & Unwin, 1980), pp. 115f.

9. *Razvitie narodnogo khozyaistva Sibiri* (Novosibirsk, Nauka, 1978), p. 183.

10. *Pravda*, May 8, 1977.

11. Yefremov and others, pp. 58-59.

12. *Pravda*, June 11, 1975.

13. Yu. Yakovets, "Ekonomicheskie rychagi i povyshenie effektivnosti mineral'no-syr'evogo kompleksa," *Planovoe khozyaistvo*, No. 1 (1978), 69.

14. F. G. Arzhanov, "Vokrug burovoi," *Ekonomika i organizatsiya promyshlennogo proizvodstva*, No. 2 (1979), 23-24.

15. L. P. Guzhnovskii, "Neftyanaya i gazovaya promyshlennost'," in V. E. Popov (ed.), *Toplivno-energeticheskii kompleks Sibiri* (Novosibirsk, Nauka, 1978), p. 49.
Privedennye zatraty is a cost measure including an allowance for the opportunity cost of capital along with current operating costs. The Soviets use the following formula in calculating the *privedennye zatraty*: *Privedennye zatraty* = Prime cost (*sebestoimost'*) + 0.12xCapital investments. The figure 0.12 is a coefficient of effectiveness of the capital inputs or an annual interest rate which is used in the Soviet energy economy. See K. Maksimov, "Sistema

pokazatelei effektivnosti kapital'nykh vlozhenii v toplivnykh otraslyakh," *Planovoe khozyaistvo*, No. 6 (1984), 28.

16. Ya. A. Mazover (ed.), *Problemy razvitiya i razmeshcheniya toplivnykh baz SSSR* (Moskva, Nauka, 1982), p. 43.

17. *Ibid.*, pp. 43, 103-104.

18. "O merakh po uskorennomu razvitiyu neftedobyvayushchei promyshlennosti v Zapadnoi Sibiri," *KPSS v rezolyutsiyakh i resheniyakh s'ezdov, konferentsii i plenumov TsK*, Vol. 10, 1969-1971 (Moskva, Politizdat, 1972), pp. 130-139; and *Pravda*, January 15, 1970.

19. *Ibid.* Emphasis added.

20. B. P. Orlov and R. I. Shniper, "Obzor opyta programmnogo resheniya narodnokhozyaistvennykh problem v Sibiri," *Izvestiya Sibirskogo otdeleniya Akademii Nauk SSSR*, seriya obshchestvennykh nauk, No. 6 (1980), 15.

21. "O merakh po usileniyu geologorazvedochnykh rabot na neft' i gaz v raionoi Sibiri," *Resheniya partii i pravitel'stva po khozyaistvennym voprosam*, Vol. 5, 1962-1965 (Moskva, Politizdat, 1968), pp. 87-90.

22. B. Ye. Shcherbina, "Novye rubezhi tyumenskikh neftyanikov," *Ekonomicheskaya gazeta*, No. 6 (1970), p. 5.

23. "Direktivy XXIII s'ezda KPSS po pyatiletnemu planu razvitiya narodnogo khozyaistva SSSR na 1966-1970 gody," *XXIII s'ezd KPSS*, stenograficheskii otchet, II (Moskva, Politizdat, 1966), p. 334.

24. "Direktivy XXIV s'ezda KPSS po pyatiletnemu planu razvitiya narodnogo khozyaistva SSSR na 1971-1975 gody," *XXIV s'ezd KPSS*, stenograficheskii otchet, II (Moskva, Politizdat, 1971), p. 258. Emphasis added.

25. N. K. Baibakov, "Zadacha narodnokhozyaistvennoi vazhnosti," *Ekonomicheskaya gazeta*, No. 11 (1974), pp. 7-8. He showed interest in enhanced oil recovery as early as 1965 when he was the Chairman of the State Committee for the Oil Industry. N. Baibakov, "Progressivnye metody dobychi nefti," *Ekonomicheskaya gazeta*, No. 38 (1965), pp. 4-5.

26. *Ibid.*, p. 7.

27. *Ibid.*

28. According to Baibakov, there were various recovery estimates for the operating fields of the European USSR: i.e. 50 percent of oil in place with the maintenance of artificial well pressure and 20-30 percent without it. *Ibid.* In the West, the expected ultimate recovery by primary methods (oil gusher) amounts to 22 percent of oil in place, and those by secondary (water injection) and tertiary (mainly chemical treatment) recovery methods 10 and 5-10

percent, respectively. *Enhanced Oil Recovery*, Shell Briefing Service (March 1979), p. 4.

29. Baibakov, p. 7.

30. G. Grigorashchenko, "Progressivnym metodam dobychi nefti--shirokuyu dorogu," *Ekonomicheskaya gazeta*, No. 23 (1974), p. 10. ( ) added.

31. "Osnovnye napravleniya razvitiya narodnogo khozyaistva SSSR na 1976-1980 gody," *Materialy XXV s'ezda KPSS* (Moskva, Politizdat, 1976)p. 177. In fact, two previous five-year plans had also called for "stabilization" of production in the old oilfields along with the bringing into operation of new deposits. The 1971 Plan Directives, for instance, envisioned that no less than 75 percent of total oil output would be obtained with the use of the method of artificial pressure on the strata. *Pravda*, April 11, 1971.

32. *Sotsialisticheskaya industriya*, April 2, 1981 and October 4, 1981.

33. *Sotsialisticheskaya industriya*, June 6, 1974.

34. At that time, Academician A. Krylov and others also advocated intensive oil recovery. See, for example, *Ekonomicheskaya gazeta*, No. 14 (1974), p. 10; and No. 17 (1974), p. 8.

35. Baibakov, p. 7. ( ) added.

36. A. N. Kosygin, "Osnovnye napravleniya razvitiya narodnogo khozyaistva SSSR na 1976-1980 gody," (March 1, 1976), *Materialy XXV s'ezda KPSS*, p. 140. ( ) added.

37. "Osnovnye napravleniya razvitiya narodnogo khozyaistva SSSR na 1976-1980 gody," p. 176.

38. *Ibid.*, pp. 176-179.

39. Both hydro-electric and atomic power stations generated 14.1 percent of total Soviet electricity output in 1975.

40. Starovoitov, "Voprosy nadezhnosti v perspektivnom planirovanii razvitiya neftyanoi promyshlennosti," p. 89.

41. For example, see *Sovetskaya Rossiya*, May 14, 1976.

42. *Izvestiya*, April 29, 1977.

43. "Start KATEKa," *Ekonomika i organizatsiya promyshlennogo proizvodstva*, No. 1 (1977), 19.

44. L. I. Brezhnev, "Iz vystupleniya na plenume TsK KPSS," (December 13, 1977), in L. I. Brezhnev, *Ob osnovnykh voprosakh ekonomicheskoi politiki KPSS na sovremennom etape, rechi i doklady*, Vol. 2 (Moskva, Politizdat, 1979), pp. 452-453.

45. *Pravda*, April 26, 1978.

46. *Sovetskaya Rossiya*, May 16, 1978. ( ) added.

47. Based on *Narkhoz, 1922-1982*, p. 182.

48. *Pravda*, August 10, 1977.

49. *Sovetskaya Rossiya*, March 24, 1977; *Trud*, February 21, 1978; *Pravda*, July 12, 1980; and Filanovskii, p. 21.

50. L. I. Brezhnev, "Otchet Tsentral'nogo Komiteta KPSS XXVI s'ezda KPSS i ocherednye zadachi partii v oblasti vnutrennei i vneshnei politiki," (February 23, 1981), *Pravda*, February 24, 1981. Emphasis original.

51. "Osnovnye napravleniya ekonomicheskogo i sotsial'nogo razvitiya SSSR na 1981-1985 gody i na period do 1990 goda," *Pravda*, March 5, 1981.

52. *Sotsialisticheskaya industriya*, October 4, 1981. Khalimov was criticized for making false reports on the progress of oil recovery work and was dismissed from the post in 1981.

53. Based on *Narkhoz, 1922-1982*, p. 182. Coal production recorded minus growth in 1980 and 1981 as well.

54. *Pravda*, November 12, 1979.

55. *Ibid.*, November 28, 1979.

56. In the case of thermal power stations operating under the jurisdiction of the USSR Ministry of Power and Electrification, oil (*mazut*) consumption increased in the second half of the 1970s contrary to the expectation of Kosygin and Brezhnev. Oil accounted for 29.5 percent of the total amount of fuel consumed by them in 1975, but 35.7 percent in 1980. See A. M. Nekrasov and A. A. Troitskii (eds.), *Energetika SSSR v 1981-1985 godakh* (Moskva, Energoizdat, 1981), p. 230.

57. Based on *Narkhoz, 1922-1982*, p. 182; and annual plan reports published in *Pravda*, various years.

58. *Pravda*, October 22, 1980.

59. Though investment outlays are only part of all government spending in the Soviet Union, according to Donna Bahry, "they do offer a virtually exhaustive measure of one conceptually distinct set of policy choices." Donna Bahry, "Measuring Communist Priorities: Budgets, Investments and the Problem of Equivalence," *Comparative Political Studies*, XIII (October 1980), 274.

60. L. A. Melent'ev and A. A. Makarov (eds.), *Energeticheskii kompleks SSSR* (Moskva, Ekonomika, 1983), p. 199; and Yu. D. Kononov, "Toplivno-energeticheskii kompleks v sisteme narodnokhozyaistvennykh svyazei," *Ekonomika i organizatsiya promyshlennogo proizvodstva*, No. 4 (1983), 21.

61. In 1980, the total capital investment in the Soviet Union amounted to 133.7 billion rubles, 120.2 billion rubles of which were investments by the "state and

cooperative enterprises and organizations." *Narkhoz, 1922-1982*, p. 365.

62. L. M. Umanskii and M. M. Umanskii, *Ekonomika neftyanoi i gazovoi promyshlennosti* (Moskva, Nedra, 1965), p. 173; V. A. Dinkov, "Gazovaya promyshlennost' na marshe pyatiletki," *Ekonomicheskaya gazeta*, No. 2 (1982), p. 2; and A. G. Aganbegyan, *Zapadnaya Sibiri na rubezhe vekov* (Sverdlovsk, Sredne-Ural'skoe izdatel'stvo, 1984), p. 37.

63. B. Shcherbina, "Industrial'nye metody sooruzheniya ob'ektov toplivnoi energetiki," *Planovoe khozyaistvo*, No. 3 (1980), p. 3. In the article (p. 5), he said that the construction of 1420-mm pipelines cost more than one billion rubles per 1,000 km.

64. At this point, it may be in order to consider the way the Soviet statistics work in the area of fuel industry investment. Broadly, capital outlays for fuel development consist of "direct" (*pryamoi*) expenditures and expenditures in related areas such as the building of infrastructure. In design-making, however, only direct outlays are taken into account (Mazover, p. 76). Direct expenditures include, in the main, investments in the facilities of basic production purposes and certain auxiliary facilities of general use such as power and water supply and transportation (*Ibid.*, pp. 72-74; and Umanskii and Umanskii, pp. 172-173). By function, direct expenditures can be classified in four categories: geological prospecting, extraction, treatment (refining and enrichment), and transportation.

By definition, *Narkhoz* excludes all the related (*sopryazhennyi*) expenditures from the category of fuel and power investment. In the case of the power industry, they are included in the investment activities of the USSR Ministry of Power and Electrification but not under the investment category of "power industry" (Nekrasov and Troitskii, p. 266).

In connection with oil refining, there is a separate investment category of "chemical and petrochemical industry" in *Narkhoz*.

In the case of oil and gas prospecting, their respective investment categories in *Narkhoz* include only part of their expenditures. Expenditures on geological prospecting and drilling work which is connected with the search for oil and gas in unproved (*nerazvedannye*) areas are considered as so-called operating costs (*operatsionnye raskhody*) of geology, not capital investments. *Narkhoz* makes it clear that its investment figures do not include expenditures on geological prospecting unconnected with construction (See *Narkhoz, 1977*, p. 348, for example.). But the cost of exploratory wells, which are under construction to outline already opened fields and to open up new deposits at depth or adjacent areas of these fields, is included in capital outlays (Umanskii and Umanskii, pp. 170-171).

As for investments in fuel transport construction, some Western scholars believe that the Soviet official statistics include all or at least a part of them in the investment categories of the fuel industries (For example, see R. W. Campbell, "Energy," in A. Bergson and H. S. Levine (eds.), *The Soviet Economy: Toward the Year 2000* (London, George Allen & Unwin, 1983), p. 213; and Gustafson, *The Soviet Gas Campaign*, p. 41n.). But *Narkhoz, 1963* (p. 453n) stated that "capital investments in pipeline transport (from now on) will be included in (the category of) 'transport and communications,' and not in the oil and gas industry."

65. In the main, there are two ways of measuring changes in patterns of capital investment expenditures. One is to analyze the pattern of gross expenditure changes over time and the other is to examine shifts in the shares of investment expenditures. The latter seems to be more important measure. This is especially true because Soviet investment data are often inconsistent and evidently not comparable. Prices, for example, have changed continuously and without explanation. After revising their accounting prices in 1969, the Soviets have since adjusted them three times. As a result, there are not infrequently two or more different investment figures for the same branch or sector in the same year. They do not seem to be easily reconcilable with one another. Thus, gross investment data are too fragmentary. But the Soviet statistics carry the annual percentage share each industrial sector enjoys of industrial investment expenditures. There are not many readjustments of the annual percentage change in the share of investment expenditures. In this regard, the share data appear to be more suitable for our purpose.

66. The Tenth Plan Directives envisaged that "more than 90 percent of the increment in coal extraction...be provided by the country's eastern regions." *Pravda*, March 7, 1976.

67. *Narkhoz RSFSR, 1975*, pp. 328-329; and *Narkhoz, 1975*, p. 502.

68. Quoted in Boris Rumer, "Soviet Investment Policy: Unresolved Problems," *Problems of Communism*, XXXI (September-October 1982), 62.

69. *Ibid.*

70. *Ibid.*

71. B. P. Orlov, "Razvitie ekonomiki Sibiri na otdel'nykh etapakh sotsialisticheskogo stroitel'stva," *Izvestiya Sibirskogo otdeleniya AN SSSR*, seriya obshchestvennykh nauk, No. 11 (1982), 68; S. D. Ageeva and B. P. Orlov, "Nekotorye cherty investitsionnogo protsessa v Zapadno-Sibirskom neftegazovom komplekse," *Ibid.*, 85; and *Sovetskaya Rossiya*, June 7, 1978.

72. Orlov, p. 68; and Ageeva and Orlov, p. 85.

73. *Ekonomika i organizatsiya promyshlennogo proizvodstva*, No. 2 (1979), 19.

74. There are no official Soviet statistics on the regional breakdown of industrial investment. There are only global statistics for the volume of investment in the individual regions, which of course do not reveal how the respective funds are allocated among the various sectors of the regional economics. Worse still, even these data disappeared from the Soviet statistical yearbook after 1975.

75. V. V. Alekseev, *Ocherki ekonomiki Sibiri* (Novosibirsk, Nauka, 1980), p. 108.

76. M. K. Bandman, V. A. Kalmyk, B. P. Orlov, and Z. R. Tsimdina (eds.), *Sibir' v edinom narodnokhozyaistvennom komplekse* (Novosibirsk, Nauka, 1980), p. 255.

77. Orlov, p. 69.

78. For example, see Umanskii and Umanskii, p. 173; *Pravda*, March 16, 1971 and June 26, 1973; and M. Brenner, "Effektivnost' ispol'zovaniya toplivno-energeticheskikh resursov," *Voprosy ekonomiki*, No. 6 (1977), 43.

79. I. Ognev, "Yevropa-Sibir'," *Ekonomika i organizatsiya promyshlennogo proizvodstva*, No. 4 (1976), 174-175.

80. V. A. Smirnov, Yu. I. Maksimov, V. I. Konstantinov, I. F. Maksimova, "Spetsializirovannye modeli perspektivnogo planirovaniya gazovoi promyshlennosti," in Yu. I. Maksimov and Z. R. Tsimtsina (eds.), *Optimizatsiya razvitiya i razmeshcheniya neftegazovoi promyshlennosti*, (Novosibirsk, Nauka, 1977), p. 59.

4

The Controversy over West Siberian Oil

In the previous chapter, we have discussed Soviet energy strategy on the assumption that public policy of any significance could be made by the rational choice of a single decision-maker for the whole society. But such an assumption is unlikely, if not impossible, in the real world. A decision-maker with undisputed authority and omniscient rationality is unlikely to be found. In the world of a plurality of actors with separate identities and separate goals, policy formulation and policy implementation will be inevitably the result of interactions among them. This will be especially true in the case of the Soviet energy economy, which is vast and complicated. As for the Soviet oil industry, we have examined the situation with which it was confronted in the 1970s and early 1980s. There seems to have been general agreement among Soviet energy officials and specialists that the situation had become serious. But how serious? Here ended their agreement. The West Siberian oil industry, the centerpiece of Soviet energy strategy, became the focus of much controversy throughout the last decade. In this chapter, we will examine such controversy in which a number of participants had taken up a variety of positions on the issue of the West Siberian energy development.

As far as West Siberian oil is concerned, there were two conflicting prognoses from the very beginning of its development. In 1970, for instance, Tyumen' Party leader B. Shcherbina claimed that there had been many "skeptics and opponents" of oil and gas exploration in West Siberia.[1] Those who rallied to his side in support of West Siberian oil and gas had asserted that opposition to their development had been based on two grounds: the paucity of oil and gas resources in West Siberia and their low economic efficacy. According to a central Party official, the opponents argued, first of all, that "there is theoretically no possibility that oil and gas deposits have been formed" in the eastern region of the country and "there is little prospect that such deposits, if found, are of any size."[2] Another rationale put forward by them was: "Although such deposits may be discovered, their development would not be economically advisable (*tselesoobraznyi*)."[3] Naturally, the pro-West Siberians had tended to emphasize the richness of West Siberian seams and the low cost of extracting oil and gas there. Such controversy continued throughout the 1970s.

A. Reserves

As early as 1965, Tyumen' Party Secretary A. Protozanov stressed that oil and natural gas deposits in West Siberia are "unique" (*unikal'nye*) among the country's hydrocarbon-producing regions in terms of both quantity and quality.[4] He was soon echoed by four local academics and specialists when they claimed that their region occupied the first place among the country's oil regions with regard to the volume of prospective oil and gas reserves. According to them, there are hydrocarbon resources equivalent to 10 billion tons of standard fuel in West Siberia.[5] Similar claims continued to appear in the press in the ensuing years. In 1968, for instance, Academician A. A. Trofimuk and Siberian geologist G. P. Bogomyakov emphasized that "today specialists have no doubt that the West Siberian lowland has reserves which can provide for the extraction of 400-500 million tons of oil and no less than 500-600 billion cubic meters of gas a year."[6] At a conference held in Tyumen' the following year, it was concluded that there were at least five trillion cubic meters of explored gas reserves in the province. The amount of the newly-found oil reserves in West Siberia was not yet determined at that time. But the conference expected that oil production in West Siberia could reach 500 million tons and gas production 600-700 billion cubic meters a year in the near future.[7] At that time, Academician N. N. Nekrasov, Chairman of the USSR Gosplan's Council for Study of Productive Forces (*SOPS*), also said that "according to geological data, projected oil and natural gas reserves are so great that in Tyumen' province alone the prospective annual production of oil could reach 500 million tons."[8] In 1970, Tyumen' leader Shcherbina revealed that there were about two billion tons of oil in the Samotlor oilfield alone.[9] There were a number of similar claims made by the pro-West Siberian figures. For instance, two Siberian economists, M. Simzen and V. Udovenko, noting that more than half of the fuel and power resources of the Soviet Union lie in Siberia, predicted that 260 million tons of oil and 300-350 billion cubic meters of gas would be extracted there annually.[10] In the early 1970s, the pro-West Siberians were especially eager to demonstrate the huge amount of gas reserves in the eastern region. Academician Trofimuk and his Siberian colleagues--Yu. G. Erv'e, I. I. Nesterov, and Ye. N. Altunin--claimed in 1971 that "the reserves of gas explored in the north of Tyumen' province can be brought to as much as 40 trillion cubic meters."[11]

In retrospect, the pro-West Siberian claims in the early 1970s seem to have been much exaggerated. Their forecasts for oil production in West Siberia ranged from 260 to 500 million tons a year. In actuality, it took more than 10 years to attain the annual output level of 300 million tons there. The inflated forecast figures may in part have been due to the inherent difficulties of sizing up underground resources. But they were also certainly due to the desire on the part of the West Siberians and their supporters to make the best of the opportunities presented by the newly discovered resources in the face of both real and potential competition for development funds, mainly by the so-called "pro-Europeans."

The advocates of the continued development of fuel resources in the European part of the country long maintained that there were still sufficient resources in those regions. Former USSR Geology Minister A. V. Sidorenko seemed to endorse this view when he declared in 1970 that oil and gas resources in the European area "are far from being exhausted."[12] In a contribution to Party organ *Kommunist*, he emphasized that "mineral resources of the European part of the country are potentially no less rich than those of Siberia."[13] Pointing out that the western regions, "not counting the Urals, give 67 percent of all the oil extracted and 71 percent of natural gas," he claimed that "about 45 percent of the territory of the European part of the country is believed to contain oil-bearing sediments."[14] He then expressed concern that "intensive oil extraction is not sufficiently made up for by the growth of explored reserves in the oil- and gas-extracting regions of the European part" and advocated more geological prospecting there.[15] About a month before the opening of the Twenty-fourth Party Congress, he repeated his claim that "it is a major problem to supply explored oil and gas reserves in the principal producing areas of the country..., the solution of which has begun to lag behind."[16] While the geology minister may have had in mind primarily the Urals-Volga area, the largest oil region in the European USSR, the pro-Europeans emphasized the oil and gas potentials of their respective regions. Two Ukrainian geologists argued in 1971 that the slow pace of oil industry development in their republic did not mean that the earth was barren but that the scale of exploratory work was inadequate.[17] Similar claims were made by N. A. Mal'tsev. head of the Perm' Oil Association (*Permneft'*), and by many oil administrators and specialists in Azerbaidzhan and other old oil-producing regions.[18]

Such claims concerning the potential reserves of oil and gas in the European USSR had largely disappeared from the Soviet press by the mid-1970s. There was apparently little prospect for expansion of production there as the stepped-up exploratory work had produced disappointing results. By that time, however, cautionary voices began to be heard concerning oil reserves in West Siberia itself. As early as 1973, a Soviet oil specialist argued that the Middle Ob' fields, the main oil area in West Siberia, could not provide an adequate base for further expansion of Soviet oil production after 1980.[19] As mentioned earlier, Oil Minister V. D. Shashin had expressed concern over the failure to find the big new fields needed to expand reserves. He was critical of the Geology Ministry for such a failure, particularly in West Siberia.[20] Academician A. P. Krylov, Chairman of the USSR Academy of Sciences' Research Council on Oilfield Development, and many others began to favor a sharp reduction in oil consumption and a greater use of other fuels.[21]

But those who were attached to the West Siberian energy development programme refused to give up their view that there were still vast potential oil reserves in West Siberia. In general, local geologists proved to be more sanguine concerning the prospects for oil in the region than their colleagues who were responsible for actual production. The "critical" reserves situation, in their opinion, was caused by past "mistakes" in planning. F. K. Salmanov, *Glavtyumengeologiya*'s chief geologist, argued in 1976 that there were two views which misrepresented the future of West Siberian oil.[22] "Optimists," according to him, mistakenly believed that Siberia's oil riches were boundless and would discover themselves, while "pessimists" claimed that Tyumen' geologists had already discovered everything there was to discover in Siberia. Implicating USSR Gosplan and the USSR Ministry of Geology in the first category, he criticized them for not having devoted adequate attention to the needs and concerns of Tyumen' geologists. "Strange as it may seem," he added, "discoveries in this area have created the illusion that prospecting for new deposits in Tyumen' province is an easy task."[23] As early as 1975, a *Pravda* article contrasted the concerns of the Siberians over the "uncertain" prospects for oil production in West Siberia with the optimism of Gosplan officials: N. Strizhov, Deputy Chief of Gosplan's Oil and Gas Industry Department, was quoted as saying that "Now, we are in peace. Good for the Siberians! Some other oil regions did badly, but the plan will still be fulfilled--Tyumen' has overfulfilled...."[24] He then went on to express disapproval of the wary attitudes of the Siberian oil workers and geologists. In 1977, another article by two *Pravda* correspondents, S. Vtorushin and A. Murzin, still criticized such "illusions" which they said were cherished by central planning and geology ministry officials:

> Discoveries of oil and gas deposits in West Siberia grew at such a pace that this created, among senior officials of the RSFSR and USSR Ministries of Geology and also of all-Union Gosplan, the illusion that it is exceptionally easy to search for underground resources here. .... That is why, beginning in 1968, the two ministries and USSR Gosplan have each year reduced allocations of material-technical resources to Glavtyumengeologiya. .... In 1973, the RSFSR Ministry of Geology...even issued a special decree, which banned the prospecting for gas in Tyumen' province, considering that the explored reserves would be sufficient for many years.[25]

Academician Trofimuk pointed out that this illusion should be blamed not only for the failure to increase, but even for the curtailment of, the volume of prospecting work and exploratory drilling in the area throughout the 1970s.[26] Describing such failure as a "mistake," V. Filanovskii, Chief of Gosplan's Oil and Gas Industry Department who was formerly a chief oil industry engineer in West Siberia, also remarked that "complacency has prevailed in both the RSFSR and USSR Ministries of Geology, and also in planning organs."[27]

In addition, the pro-West Siberians also criticized what they termed the "pessimist" view as totally inaccurate. At a conference held in Tyumen' in 1978 following the announcement of a crash development policy of Siberian oil, I. I. Nesterov, Director of the West Siberian Geological-Prospecting and Oil Research Institute (*ZapsibNIGNI*), said:

> In Tyumen' province, the estimate of (oil) resources grew many times in the last 15-18 years. The present advances...were thought unrealistic at the close of the 1950s. Regrettably, many specialists still consider that the reserves (in West Siberia)... are not well substantiated. ....
>
> As much as five years ago, it was considered that the earth of Tyumen' was so well-known that unexpected discoveries may no longer be likely. However, it became apparent in the past few years that there has not yet been sufficient study of the underground resources in Tyumen'.[28]

Arguing a similar view, G. Shmal', a Tyumen' *obkom* secretary, said in 1976 that "voices are still heard, asserting that in the northern regions of the province commercial deposits of oil may not be discovered."[29] Gosplan's oil chief Filanovskii also revealed that many scholars and specialists had considered that there could be no oil reserves above latitude 64 degrees north.[30] He said that they were proved wrong as a result of exploratory works carried out in the Tenth Plan period. However, skepticism apparently persisted as to the future of Siberian oil. Evidence of this is seen in the following question which a *Literaturnaya gazeta* correspondent asked in an interview with Academician Trofimuk, Director of the Institute of Geology and Geophysics of the USSR Academy of Sciences' Siberian Department.

> Question: Andrei Alekseevich, your optimistic estimates of the oil- and gas-bearing structures of West and East Siberia are well known. ....What do you build on your optimism concerning the potentialities of the Siberian underground resources? You are, of course, well aware of different views on the prospects for growth in oil extraction in Siberia....[31]

A Siberian mouthpiece, *Ekonomika i organizatsiya promyshlennogo proizvodstva* (*Economics and Organization of Industrial Production*), also acknowledged in a 1979 editorial that "long-range prognoses for the levels of oil extraction (in Tyumen' province) are open to dispute, in contrast to gas extraction forecasts."[32]

The pro-West Siberians had been more or less reticent about identifying who the pessimists were, and in which institutions they worked. In the late 1970s, however, they were sometimes identified by name. For instance, two Siberian geologists, F. K. Salmanov and I. I. Nesterov, said: "Today those who come out against the search for oil in the North are not only 'individuals' but also the whole body of an institute, for example, of the Leningrad Oil Institute, and responsible geologists in the USSR Ministry of the Oil Industry."[33] In connection with this, it is worth noting that a conference, held in Tyumen' in 1969, discussed the question of determining an optimal oil production level for West Siberia. At that time, the Oil Ministry and its Siberian organization, *Glavtyumenneftegaz*, put forward a figure of 75-80 million tons of oil as an estimate of the optimal level for 1980, while A. T. Shmarev, RSFSR Deputy Geology Minister, submitted a figure of 150 million tons.[34] There was apparently no consensus between them; The "Oil Industry" section of the conference report gave the production level of 70-100 million tons by 1975 and 180-200 million tons by 1980, while the section of "Geological Exploration" put forward the figure of 150-200 million tons by 1975.[35] As we have seen, the 1969 decree envisaged that 100-120 million tons of oil would be extracted in West Siberia by 1975 and 230-260 million tons by 1980. Salmanov and Nesterov further detailed the differences of opinion over the future rate of oil production in West Siberia: for the 1970 target geologists advanced a figure of 30-35 million tons, while oil industry officials put forward a figure of 12 million tons; for 1975 the former envisaged a figure of 150 million tons, while the latter presented a figure of 70-80 million tons; and while geologists considered the output level of 315 million tons by 1980 as realistic, their oil industry colleagues submitted the figure of 240-260 million tons.[36] According to Academician N. Nekrasov, similar debate took place at the time of drawing up the Eleventh Plan.[37]

The two Siberian geologists, Salmanov and Nesterov, having implied that the geologists' prognoses proved to be more realistic, complained that planning organs, however, had turned a deaf ear to them and only listened to other opinions. They argued that the seemingly cautious stance taken by the Oil Ministry was motivated by the well-known logic of Soviet plan target-setting, i.e. "the less you take, the more you lead a peaceful life" (*Pomen'she voz'mesh'--spokoinei prozhivesh.*).[38] Bogomyakov, a Siberian geologist who became Tyumen' obkom First Secretary, criticized the striving for an understated plan as being responsible for the earlier "low" estimates of West Siberia's oil potential.[39] In any case, it is clear that the Oil Ministry and its subordinate organizations were more cautious or "pessimistic" about West Siberia's oil future than the local geologists and their sympathizers.

In the late 1970s and the early 1980s, the Siberian geologists continued to express their belief that the level of oil extraction in West Siberia could not only be maintained for a long time but could also be further enhanced. In 1981, Salmanov, now the chief of Glavtyumengeologiya, was confident that West Siberia had the potential for producing 450-500 million tons of oil and one trillion cubic meters of gas by 1990 as envisaged by the Eleventh Plan Directives.[40] Another geologist, Nesterov, was quoted as saying in 1979 that "we are just beginning the systematic study of the underground resources in the Yamal-Nenets North, where oil may be discovered in reservoirs that are already known. But after all, it also exists at even deeper levels."[41] In the following year, he expressed his unwavering confidence that the scientific substantiation of the potential of the new and deeper formations to which geological prospecting had been extended "makes it possible to state that a second Tyumen' oil and gas region may be discovered...within Tyumen' itself and that West Siberia will retain its role as the country's main base of oil and gas extraction."[42] Of such formations, according to Academician Trofimuk, Paleozoic sediments which exist at deeper strata (three to five kilometers below surface) in West Siberia were the most promising.[43] He also argued that East Siberia contained no less oil and gas reserves than the Ob' region in West Siberia.[44]

In sum, the West Siberians and their supporters throughout the 1970s were confident of the future of West Siberian oil, to say nothing of the region's gas reserves. However, there were wide differences of opinion among industrial organizations and specialists in the Soviet Union on the magnitude of West Siberian oil reserves. In general, the pro-West Siberians were united in criticizing both "blind optimists" for their short-sightedness and "pessimists" for their timidity.[45] Most of those subjected to such criticism were attached to central planning organs and industrial ministries; i.e. Gosplan, both USSR and RSFSR Ministries of Geology, and the Ministry of the Oil Industry.

B. Costs

In the 1960s and the early 1970s, the pro-West Siberians were also busy stressing the cheapness of West Siberian oil and gas. West Siberia's oil industry chief Muravlenko, for instance, asserted in 1969 that the oil produced in the eastern region was already the cheapest in the Soviet Union.[46] Shcherbina, the then Tyumen' Party leader, also declared that "our cost of extracting oil is less than the average branch index."[47] In a similar vein, Siberian economist V. E. Popov argued in 1970 that "one Samotlor deposit in Tyumen' province can produce four times as much oil each year as Azerbaidzhan" and that the state would save a huge sum of money by accelerating the development of the eastern resources.[48]

In the early part of the 1970s, many central officials and academics agreed with the West Siberians about the economic benefits of Siberian oil development. For instance, two central Party officials, N. Yeronin and V. Kremnev, said in 1970 that "the cost (*sebestoimost'*) of extracting one ton of oil (in West Siberia) has been reduced from 11.6 rubles in 1965 to 3.8 rubles, which is lower than the average branch index."[49] In particular, a Gosplan economist, A. Probst, tried to compare systematically the expenditures (*privedennye zatraty*) for producing and transporting various types of fuel to industrial centers in the European part of the country.[50] In terms of production, according to Probst, the cheapest fuels were Ekibastuz and Kansk-Achinsk coal (2.7 and 1.8 rubles, respectively, per ton of standard fuel), and Tyumen' and Central Asian gas (2.2 and 5.4 rubles, respectively); the second cheapest consisted of Tyumen' and Mangyshlak oil (6.2 and 8.3 rubles, respectively) and Kuznets open-cast coal (6.6 rubles); and the third were other coal and shales such as Donets and Moscow coal.[51] In his opinion, development should be concentrated in the first two groups. Oil was cheapest to transport. The cost of sending West Siberian oil equivalent to one ton of standard fuel to the industrial centers was 1.3 rubles in 1971 while that of gas and coal amounted to as high as 6.5 and 15.4 rubles, respectively.[52] Thus, he argued, oil and gas, especially from West Siberia, were the most economic fuels if both production and transport costs were taken into consideration.[53] In 1973, he was still insisting that the largest and most favorable oil and gas deposits were predominantly east of the Urals. Regional variations in average *privedennye zatraty* for oil and gas extraction were estimated to be around 10 rubles per ton of oil and per 1,000 cubic meters of gas. According to him, Tyumen' oil and gas were the cheapest available sources of fuel.[54]

The Gosplan economist even disputed the argument that the development of atomic power would eliminate the advantage of the eastern regions in terms of cost-effectiveness.[55] Probst also argued that the advantages of locating new development projects, based on existing infrastructure, in the European part of the country were gradually disappearing. This was so, firstly, because the existing infrastructure in many places of the European USSR could not support further development without additional investment and, secondly, because by that time a considerable infrastructure had already been created in a number of areas of Siberia, Central Asia and Kazakhstan. Apparently encouraged by such calculations, many pro-West Siberians had also been arguing that West Siberian oil and gas were far more effective than other types of fuel and, in particular, coal. In 1969, Shcherbina had criticized some research institutes for still giving preference to the development of coal production, which he said could not compete with West Siberian hydrocarbons.[56] Time and again, it was Academician Trofimuk and his Siberian colleagues who urged the competitiveness of West Siberian gas.[57]

However, there were still many who advocated further development of "conveniently located reserves" in older regions. They claimed that investment in their respective areas was fully effective as evidenced, for example, by the production costs in the Ukraine, which they said were lower than the national average.[58] According to Mal'tsev, Director of the Perm' Oil Association, the lower-than-average cost of Perm' oil was due to the savings on the cost of transportation. "The closeness of oil refineries to the oilfields considerably reduces expenditures on the transportation of raw materials, oil and oil products," he said.[59] In addition to pointing out the relatively dense network of existing pipelines, others stressed the advantages of other existing infrastructure such as roads and housing, and of labor resources.[60]

What was the attitude of central planning organs and industrial ministries on the issue? In 1973, Oil Minister Shashin endorsed the pro-West Siberian claims by saying that the production cost of West Siberian oil stood at 60 percent of the average figure for the oil industry.[61] He said that capital consumption (*kapitaloemkost'*) had been low in new oil regions in comparison with their older counterparts, but "it is impossible not to invest in the old regions because it will enhance the efficiency of the national economy as a whole through the improvement of the fuel balance in the European Soviet Union."[62] As late as the mid-1970s, G. A. Mirlin, chief of Gosplan's Geology and Mineral Resources Department, put forward a similar argument in the area of geological-exploratory work:

> Although the efficiency of geological-exploratory work for oil and gas in West Siberia is six to eight times higher than the national branch average, it is far more efficient in the European part (of the country) to use fuel extracted from the deposits west of the Urals from the position of the national economy. If you ask me as a geologist, I am feeling that we give Tyumen' small funds. At the same time, however, it is necessary to invest in oil in Komi ASSR, the Urals-Volga, Belorussiya and the Ukraine in order to extract all the oil in the European part of the country.[63]

Commenting on such "pro-European" preference of Gosplan and other central economic organizations in developing the oil industry, Academician Trofimuk was quoted as complaining that "it is easier for Gosplan to turn down a project (*variant*) which is realistic but risky and to advocate one which is of not much merit but does not require capital investment and risk."[64]

In any case, the cost of oil production in West Siberia also began to rise from around the mid-1970s. As early as 1974, Party weekly *Ekonomicheskaya gazeta*, expressing concern that more and more money had to be poured into the oil industry in West Siberia, noted that it would not be entirely right to say that Tyumen' oil was cheap.[65] In 1975, according to a Soviet economist, the cost (*sebestoimost'*) of oil production in West Siberia amounted to 82.6 percent of the branch average.[66] But no Soviet source has since furnished data covering expenditures on oil production in West Siberia. In the case of gas, M. Pervukhin, a senior Gosplan official, revealed in 1976 that expenditure on the extraction of West Siberian gas equivalent to one ton of standard fuel was 6.6 rubles.[67] It was compared to 2.2 rubles for the equivalent production, as given by Probst in 1971. According to Ya. A. Mazover, chief energy economist of Gosplan's Council for Study of Productive Forces, *privedennye zatraty* for extracting and sending West Siberian gas equivalent to one ton of standard fuel to Moscow rose from 9.5-10.2 rubles in the early 1970s to 18 rubles toward the end of the decade.[68] Such a tendency towards increasing cost seems to have been conspicuous in the West Siberian oil industry as well. In 1979, *Ekonomika i organizatsiya promyshlennogo proizvodstva* expressed concern that "capital investments in Tyumen' were recovered within one year in 1974-1975, but now it takes one and a half years to recover them."[69]

According to a Siberian economist, the upward trend of capital expenditures and operating costs was not peculiar to the West Siberian oilfields but was characteristic of the Soviet oil industry as a whole.[70] In fact, other fuel industries, most of them now situated in the eastern part of the country, found themselves confronted with a similar situation in the later years of the 1970s.[71] Nevertheless, many voices had apparently been raised in the Soviet Union against the strategy of eastern development and, especially, against the further development of the West Siberian oil industry. This is suggested by the following question *Literaturnaya gazeta* asked of Academician A. Aganbegyan, Director of the Institute of Economics and Organization of Industrial Production of the USSR Academy of Sciences' Siberian Department:

> Question: .... Siberia is really a storeroom of the most valuable natural resources, but it is common knowledge, after all, that in Siberia everything is more expensive--it is more costly to drill oil wells, to build roads, to erect plants, houses and so forth. Moreover, Siberia is situated fairly far from the most populated areas of the country and transport costs for shipment out of Siberia of oil, coal, timber and other products are great. For the opening up of new regions in Siberia, it is necessary to create infrastructure literally in an empty place....
>
> Therefore, wouldn't it be more advantageous to stake not on the opening up of new regions, but on the development of the already populated, and on the prospecting and extracting of mineral resources nearer at hand? *In other words, I would like a frank answer to a question that troubles many people: Won't the extensive development of Siberia's resources lead to lowering the economic efficiency of our national economy?*[72]

For the oil industry in West Siberia, spiralling expenditures were not the only problem. More importantly, it was confronted with increasingly uncertain prospects for further growth in oil extraction. Against this background, debate over which fuel sources should be given development priority was clearly renewed in the Soviet Union beginning in the second half of the 1970s. For instance, the supporters of a coal-oriented development strategy called attention to the fact that coal was the most abundant fuel resource in the Soviet Union and was competitive economically. In 1974, Academician V. Kirillin who was the Chairman of the USSR State Committee for Science and Technology (*GKNT*), noting that the reserves of coal were many times greater than those of oil and gas, argued that coal, if extracted by modernized open-cast methods, would be comparable in cost to oil and gas.[73] In the following year, Gosplan Deputy Chairman A. Lalayants also stated a preference for the rapid development of the coal industry.[74] There were still many other supporters of coal, most of them researchers who were associated with institutes of Gosplan, GKNT, and the USSR Academy of Sciences.[75] Many who were concerned with the power industry also supported the development of coal resources. For example, Academician A. P. Aleksandrov, President of the USSR Academy of Sciences, stressed that "it is necessary to oust oil and its products from all the main spheres of consumption of energy resources, replacing them with coal and atomic energy."[76] Other specialists associated with electric power have shown their interest in the idea of "power by wire" and in the gasification of cheap eastern coal for power generation.[77] Many of these have also emphasized the importance of the utilization of atomic power in order to free oil and other fuel resources from generating electricity.[78] These specialists found supporters in two Moscow economists, Academician L. A. Melent'ev, who headed the USSR Academy of Sciences' Scientific Council for Complex Problems of Power, and A. A. Makarov, a sector head of the Academy's Institute of High Temperatures. They argued that marginal costs (*zamykayushchie zatraty*) for coal--excluding Kansk-Achinsk coal--and gas doubled in various regions during the period of 1974-1979 while those for oil have increased more than three times. In contrast, they said, marginal costs for electricity increased by only 20 percent "thanks to the extensive utilization of atomic power."[79] They stressed that this showed the efficiency of power engineering in the country's new energy situation which would make possible the replacement of oil and gas by electric power.

Still others advocated the development of gas resources as a substitute for oil. Unlike coal, however, the gas strategy had been a West Siberian programme. Whenever the Soviets talked about gas, they had in mind vast, proved reserves in the northern part of Tyumen' province. It is worth noting that supporters of the further development of Siberian oil and gas had defended it on the basis not only of the relative cheapness of production (minimization of costs) but also of the benefits to the national economy (maximization of benefits). For instance, Academician Aganbegyan gave the following answer to the question referred to earlier:

> Efficiency depends on the relation between results and expenses. What are the results of rising expenditures in Siberia?
>
> Take the West Siberian oil and gas complex. Expenditures are truly astronomical. More than 25 billion rubles in capital investment will be put in during the Tenth Plan period. .... If Tyumen's riches were somewhere near Moscow, expenditures for its development would be 2-2.5 times lower. But, alas, there is only one Tyumen' in our country. But we must know what we get in return for these expenditures.
>
> During the Tenth Plan period, 1,700 million tons of hydrocarbons (in terms of oil) will be extracted in West Siberia. The national-economic effect derived from this may be valued at no less than 150 billion rubles. As you can see, the economic efficiency of investing in the West Siberian oil and gas complex is extremely high despite the huge rise in costs. Expenditures here pay off in approximately one year.[80]

B. Vainshtein and his fellow economists at the Ministry of Construction of Oil and Gas Industry Enterprises similarly argued that the economic benefit of the West Siberian oil and gas complex was exceptionally high in terms of final returns: The net output (*chistaya produktsiya*) of the complex was projected to be up to 90 billion rubles in 1976-1980.[81]

It is not easy for an outsider to know how profitable or efficient fuel development in West Siberia had been. We know almost nothing of the actual cost of production of Siberian oil and how much the Soviets earned by selling it both at home and abroad. In any case, what is interesting is the fact that there had been wide differences of opinion on the issue of economic efficiency of West Siberian oil and gas development, as evidenced in the case of the reserves issue. Broadly speaking, there were two rival arguments concerning the prospects for fuel development in West Siberia. The West Siberians and their supporters as a party to this controversy remained firmly attached to the view that the West Siberian lowland was rich in hydrocarbon resources and their development was highly profitable. They complained that planning organs and central industrial ministries did not often take into account such potentialities and the efficiency of these resources. Such an attitude, in the opinion of Ye. N. Altunin, the head of the Tyumen' Gas Association, had dragged out the settlement of many important questions and created unnecessary difficulties in the development of the complex.[82]

NOTES

1. *Sovetskaya Rossiya*, February 28, 1970.
2. A. A. Yamnov, "Prognozy i otkrytiya," *Ekonomicheskaya gazeta*, No. 2 (1970), p. 6.
3. *Ibid.*
4. *Izvestiya*, March 6, 1965.
5. *Pravda*, April 2, 1965. One ton of oil is approximately equivalent to 1.43 tons of standard fuel (one ton standard fuel = 7,000 kilocalories) and one ton of natural gas 1.18 tons of standard fuel.
6. *Pravda*, August 31, 1968.
7. "Bol'shaya neft' Sibiri," *Ekonomicheskaya gazeta*, No. 22 (1969), p. 12.
8. *Pravda*, July 6, 1969.
9. *Sovetskaya Rossiya*, February 28, 1970.
10. M. Simzen and V. Udovenko, "K vostoku ot Urala," *Ekonomicheskaya gazeta*, No. 16 (1970), p. 19.
11. *Pravda*, March 28, 1971.
12. A. Sidorenko, "Yevropeiskaya chast' strany raskryvaet nedra," *Kommunist*, No. 18 (1970), 61.
13. *Ibid.*
14. *Ibid.*, pp. 61, 62.
15. *Ibid.*, p. 66. At that time, Sidorenko also recommended that three ministries--the oil and gas ministries and his own geology ministry--conduct exploratory work in the old oil and gas regions of the European USSR.
16. *Pravda*, February 25, 1971.
17. *Pravda*, November 16, 1971.
18. For example, see *Pravda*, March 16, 1971; and A. Amirov, A. Alizade, and A. Pirverdyan, "Starym Bakinskim mestorozhdeniyam--novuyu zhizn'," *Ekonomicheskaya gazeta*, No. 29 (1974), p. 10.

19. *Ekonomika neftyanoi promyshlennosti*, No. 6 (1973), 8.

20. V. D. Shashin, "Puti povysheniya effektivnosti neftyanoi promyshlennosti," *Planovoe khozyaistvo*, No. 4 (1973), 21.

21. I. Ognev, "Yevropa-Sibir'," *Ekonomika i organizatsiya promyshlennogo proizvodstva*, No. 4 (1976), 171. At the same time, Krylov supported the enhanced recovery programme in the old oil regions in the European USSR. See *Ekonomicheskaya gazeta*, No. 14 (1974), p. 10.

22. *Pravda*, February 19, 1976.

23. *Ibid.*

24. *Pravda*, June 11, 1975.

25. *Pravda*, August 10, 1977.

26. *Literaturnaya gazeta*, January 18, 1978, p. 10.

27. V. Filanovskii, "Zapadno-Sibirskii neftegazovyi kompleks: rezul'taty i perspektivy," *Planovoe khozyaistvo*, No. 3 (1980), 20.

28. "Osnovnye problemy kompleksnogo razvitiya Zapadnoi Sibiri," *Voprosy ekonomiki*, No. 8 (1978), 21. ( ) added.

29. *Sovetskaya Rossiya*, December 22, 1976.

30. Filanovskii, p. 19. The two Siberian geologists revealed that such skepticism over the availability of West Siberian oil and gas resources dated back to the 1930s. Many specialists did not believe in the presence of West Siberian oil and a "heated debate" started. In 1955, the opponents of Siberian exploration even devised the so-called "line of N. A. Nazarkin," north of which they claimed there were no geological formations likely to contain oil and gas. They included Tyumen' province in this no-oil-region. *Sovetskaya Rossiya*, December 8, 1978.

31. *Literaturnaya gazeta*, January 1, 1981.

32. "Ne chislom, a umeniem," *Ekonomika i organizatsiya promyshlennogo proizvodstva*, No. 2 (1979), 6. ( ) added.

33. *Sovetskaya Rossiya*, December 8, 1978.

34. Ognev, p. 175.

35. *Ibid.*, p. 176.

36. *Sovetskaya Rossiya*, December 8, 1978.

37. *Trud*, July 12, 1979.

38. *Sovetskaya Rossiya*, December 8, 1978; and Ognev, p. 177. It should be taken into account the fact that a low production target may mean less trouble for the extracting ministries but, at the same time, less geological-exploratory assignments and less money for geologists. Moreover, according to Nesterov, the extracting branches

appropriate funds for the development of geological-prospecting work and the extracting ministries, which "are guided only by their own current, narrowly departmental interests," try to reduce appropriations for exploratory and prospecting work. See *Pravda*, July 22, 1979.

39. G. P. Bogomyakov, "Tyumenskii kompleks i ego budushchee," *Ekonomika i organizatsiya promyshlennogo proizvodstva*, No. 5 (1976), 9-11.

40. *Pravda*, February 13, 1981.

41. *Pravda*, May 17, 1979.

42. I. Nesterov, "Neftegazovyi potentsial Zapadnoi Sibiri," *Ekonomicheskaya gazeta*, No. 11 (1980), p. 15.

43. *Izvestiya*, June 2, 1979; and *Sovetskaya Rossiya*, September 11, 1979.

44. A. A. Trofimuk, "Nauka v Sibiri--dlya Sibiri," *Ekonomika i organizatsiya promyshlennogo proizvodstva*, No. 3 (1977), 35-36.

45. Reserves estimation is of course closely connected with investment decisions as the following passage by I. Makarov, Director of the Sverdlovsk Railroad's Tyumen' Division, demonstrates: "When the Tyumen'-Tobolsk Mainline was being planned, it was often called a railway to 'nowhere.' At that time, the potential of the Ob' Basin's oil deposits was still a subject of heated debate.... Quite a few people contended that there would be nothing to haul along the new line. These opinions did not go unheeded. The mainline's carrying capacity was planned at a figure much lower than the present requirements...." See *Pravda*, September 27, 1978.

46. *Pravda*, November 30, 1969.

47. *Ekonomicheskaya gazeta*, No. 6 (1970), p. 5.

48. *Sovetskaya Rossiya*, October 22, 1970.

49. N. Yeronin and V. Kremnev, "Uskorennymi tempami," *Ekonomicheskaya gazeta*, No. 49 (1970), p. 15. ( ) added.

50. A. Probst, "Puti razvitiya toplivnogo khozyaistva SSSR," *Voprosy ekonomiki*, No. 6 (1971), 57; and A. Probst, *Voprosy razmeshcheniya sotsialisticheskoi promyshlennosti* (Moskva, Nauka, 1971), p. 242. On *privedennye zatraty*, see Chapter 3, footnote 15.

51. *Ibid.* All the figures given in parentheses are *privedennye zatraty*.

52. *Ibid.*

53. Probst, "Puti razvitiya toplivnogo khozyaistva SSSR," p. 58.

54. A. Probst, "O dolgosrochnoi perspektive razmeshcheniya proizvodstva," *Voprosy ekonomiki*, No. 5 (1973), 21.

55. *Ibid.*
56. Quoted in Ognev, pp. 155-156.
57. *Pravda*, August 31, 1968; May 23, 1969; and March 28, 1971.
58. *Pravda*, November 16, 1971.
59. *Pravda*, March 16, 1971.
60. *Ekonomicheskaya gazeta*, No. 29 (1974), p. 10.
61. V. Shashin, "Puti povysheniya effektivnosti neftyanoi promyshlennosti," *Planovoe khozyaistvo*, No. 4 (1973), 20.
62. *Ibid.*, p. 19.
63. Quoted in Ognev, pp. 156-158. ( ) added.
64. *Ibid.*, p. 158.
65. *Ekonomicheskaya gazeta*, No. 27 (1974), p. 2.
66. M. M. Brenner, "Chtoby uvelichit' moshch' neftyanogo potoka strany," *Ekonomika i organizatsiya promyshlennogo proizvodstva*, No. 1 (1978), 132.
67. *Literaturnaya gazeta*, February 18, 1976, p. 11.
68. Ya. A. Mazover (ed.), *Problemy razvitiya i razmeshcheniya toplivnykh baz SSSR* (Moskva, Nauka, 1982), p. 35.
69. "Ne chislom, a umeniem," p. 9.
70. L. P. Guzhnovskii, "Neftyanaya i gazovaya promyshlennost'," in V. E. Popov (ed.), *Toplivno-energeticheskii kompleks Sibiri* (Novosibirsk, Nauka, 1978), p. 49.
71. Yu. Yakovets, "Ekonomicheskie rychagi i povyshenie effektivnosti mineral'no-syr'evogo kompleksa," *Planovoe khozyaistvo*, No. 1 (1978), 69-70.
72. *Literaturnaya gazeta*, November 7, 1979, p. 11. Emphasis added.
73. V. Kirillin, "Energetika--problemy i perspektivy," *Kommunist*, No. 1 (1975), 46.
74. A. Lalayants, "Dva obshchestva--dve linii v razvitii toplivno-energeticheskogo kompleksa," *Planovoe khozyaistvo*, No. 4 (1975), 28.
75. For example, see *Sovetskaya Rossiya*, January 13, 1978; *Pravda*, December 16, 1979; and *Trud*, July 24, 1981.
76. *Izvestiya*, April 11, 1979 and February 21, 1981; and "Vstupitel'noe slovo Prezidenta Akademii Nauk SSSR A. P. Aleksandrova," *Vestnik Akademii Nauk SSSR*, No. 5 (1980), 12.
77. For example, see *Pravda*, December 17, 1976.
78. Academicians Kirillin and Aleksandrov and many nuclear scientists such as B. Kadomtsev called for the fast development of atomic power generation. *Izvestiya*, December 3, 1978.

79. L. A. Melent'ev and A. A. Makarov, *Energeticheskii kompleks SSSR* (Moskva, Ekonomika, 1983), pp. 122-123.

80. *Literaturnaya gazeta*, November 7, 1979, p. 11. For a similar argument by him, see also *Sotsialisticheskaya industriya*, May 8, 1981.

81. B. Vainshtein, A. Khaitun, and N. Sokolov, "Effektivnost' neftegazovogo kompleksa Zapadnoi Sibiri," *Voprosy ekonomiki*, No. 10 (1978), 23 and *Razvitie narodnogo khozyaistva Sibiri* (Novosibirsk, Nauka, 1978), p. 181.

82. *Sovetskaya Rossiya*, May 16, 1978.

5

Articulation of Pro-West Siberian Demands

During the 1970s and the early 1980s, major policy changes favoring the accelerated development of West Siberian hydrocarbons were each accompanied by a series of public discussions. Arguments about reserves and costs advanced by the West Siberians and their supporters were in fact part of such promotional efforts. Proceeding from these arguments, the pro-West Siberian elements made various demands and criticisms of existing policy and the activities of central organizations with regard to the eastern energy development. What demands did they make? We are primarily interested in demands with significant all-Union implications, especially demands for the development priority of the West Siberian fuel complex. Such demands often involve national investment priority or reallocation of resources on a large scale. In this case, the stakes are high and thus competition and conflict among those involved are likely to be intense. An article carried in the Party organ *Pravda* bears witness to such a competition for resources at an early stage of the development of West Siberian oil:

> The serious lack of coordination in the construction of pipelines (in West Siberia) turned out to be largely due to the protracted conflict of viewpoints. It is necessary, by the way, to note here that such a delicate matter as the ability to hear out the arguments of opponents, while not running to extremes which only confuse the point of the matter and lead to waste of time, becomes the "cost" of one or other important views and decisions. Here are the two sides of the matter. The Siberians argue: They have explored reserves (*razvedka*) and the extraction of one

> ton of oil will cost a few kopecks in the future, then why spend tens, sometimes hundreds, of rubles for the same ton, searching after oil, for example, at the bottom of the Caspian Sea? Would it not be better to put part of these funds into the further exploration of the Ob' region which is badly in need of them? They are quite rightly answered: During the next five-year plan period, the country is to extract about 2.7 billion tons of oil, of which the share of Tyumen', for all its rapid growth, will amount to no more than 400 millions. Then, the basic commitment still remains with the old regions. But, then, what on earth will provide for growth and extraction there in the absence of explored reserves? That is true. But violent accusations follow as if the Siberians want to "squeeze" everything else with their colossus and to squander other considerable reserves....[1]

In this chapter, we will examine the demands made for the priority development of West Siberian hydrocarbons. Such demands can only be met by the country's top policy-makers. Did the pro-West Siberian elements succeed in pressing their demands on the leadership? We will subsequently see how their manoeuverings were related to "high politics" between Soviet leaders in the energy area.

A. Manoeuvre for Development Priorities, 1968-1970

Since hydrocarbons were first discovered in West Siberia in June 1960, local officials and specialists had made various requests and proposals for the rapid opening up of these resources. For at least a year before the adoption of the 1969 decree the West Siberians and their supporters stepped up promotional campaigns.[2]

1965-1967 The Soviet press had carried a few articles featuring the activities of geologists and oil and gas workers in West Siberia in the first half of the 1960s.[3] It was, however, after 1965 that the press allocated more space for the pro-West Siberians to air their development proposals and suggestions. The first one million tons of Siberian oil were extracted in that year.

In March 1965, A. K. Protozanov, a Tyumen' obkom secretary, stressed that the development of fuel resources in his province would help improve the fuel and power balance of the Urals industrial region.[4] He said that it would be necessary to invest at least two billion rubles into the region in 1965-1970. Despite the huge sum of money needed, he claimed that its economic effect for the national economy would be immense. In July, he argued that Siberia would require about 40 million tons of oil by the end of the 1960s.[5] He said that the exploitation of local oil deposits would relieve oilfields in the European part of the country from the burden of delivering oil to the eastern part and thus help improve the fuel balance of the European area. The secretary then suggested that it would require capital outlays of about 700-750 million rubles to produce 40 million tons of oil in his province. He complained, however, that the authorities had set an unjustifiably low target for oil extraction there. Emphasizing a high return of capital investments due to a high concentration of deposits in Tyumen' province, four of his Siberian colleagues criticized both RSFSR and USSR Gosplan officials for failing to give proper attention to difficult environmental conditions in their area in calculating capital expenditures for the opening up of fuel resources there.[6] They were economist I. Karyagin, Director of the Tyumen' Oil and Gas Research-Design Institute (*Giprotyumenneftegaz*) O. Mezhlumov, Chief geologist of the province's oil association *Tyumenneftegaz* Yu. Shaevskii, and the association's Chief engineer V. Timonin. In June, President of the USSR Academy of Sciences' Siberian Department M. Lavrent'ev and three other Siberian academics called for an in-depth study of underground resources of West Siberia.[7] Academician Lavrent'ev and Corresponding member of the USSR Academy G. Prudenskii stressed the need for recruiting highly qualified technical specialists and economists for the region. Prudenskii concurrently headed the Siberian Department's Institute of Economics and Organization of Industrial Production. In November, meanwhile, Director of the Tyumen' Geology Administration Yu. G. Erv'e, emphasizing that unit capital costs for hydrocarbon production in Tyumen' province were not higher than the national average, also called for more investments in the geological exploration and development of the new oil region.[8] He was at once seconded by his Siberian colleagues.[9] In that year, at least three more articles were contributed by West Siberian geologists G. Ostryi and S. Shupta, economist I. Karyagin, and Party official Protozanov.[10]

In January of the following year, local geologist Ostryi revealed that there were differences of opinion between the USSR Geology Ministry and the Oil Ministry over the necessity of carrying out further exploratory works in search of oil in Tyumen' province.[11] In a contribution to *Ekonomicheskaya gazeta*, he argued that the exploratory work should not only be maintained "in any circumstances" but also be concentrated in the province and away from other regions where "oil prospecting had produced no results." He noted, however, that the Geology Ministry had instead decreased the planned allocations for the works in the province by many millions of rubles. In that same issue, the Party paper urged that three ministries--geology, oil industry and gas industry--together with USSR Gosplan and other organs review such problems jointly. Local Party officials were also active in promoting the pro-West Siberian cause. In a *Pravda* contribution in February, Party secretary Protozanov pointed out the need to build more houses and social amenities, to construct large-diameter trunk pipelines, and to boost electric power capacity.[12] "One of first-priority tasks is to create a powerful construction base," he said. But the planning organs, according to him, had "for some reason" curtailed capital investments for the creation of the base. Finally, he stressed that a comprehensive long-term programme for the opening up of the riches of the West Siberian lowland should be elaborated as soon as possible. In May, his superior B. Ye. Shcherbina came out in his support by calling for more attention to the rapid, complex development of the province.[13] The obkom first secretary emphasized that a general programme would be needed for the complex development of productive forces in West Siberia on a long-term basis. He revealed that despite the shortage of electricity the proposed construction of the *Nizhne-Ob'* thermal power station had been suspended in the face of growing opposition. He called for a prompt solution of transport problems and timely consideration on the question of developing the machine-building industry to meet the needs of the oil and gas industry and the petro-chemical industry in his region. In November, meanwhile, Protozanov repeated his call for a comprehensive programme for the province.[14] He emphasized that the creation of the province's own construction industry should be included as an important element in that programme. In addition, local geologist Erv'e and others--mainly local academics--continued to make demands such as increased material-technical supply to local geologists and improvement of living conditions in the newly opened region.[15]

Many also called for more attention to the development of the neighboring Tomsk province. In January, for instance, Chairman of the Planning Commission of the West Siberian Economic Region Ye. Utrobin urged that in the eastern part of the Ob' area a large oil and gas complex should be created.[16] He stressed that to meet these goals a unified comprehensive development programme should be worked out and a single organ in charge of the complex should be created. In June a scientific conference was held in Tomsk. Participants--mostly officials from geology and fuel-extracting ministries, and local academics--discussed the future of Tomsk province, and its oil and gas deposits which "are located relatively close to the industrial centers of West Siberia."[17] At that time, the province's Party leader Ye. Ligachev called for the fast development of oil- and gas-extracting industries and petrochemical industry in his region.[18]

In 1967, the central press continued to carry articles--at least three during the first two months--relating to the development of the West Siberian oil and gas industries. Starting a feature series, titled "*LG na beregakh Obi*" (LG along the Ob' River), *Literaturnaya gazeta* published in January a travel commentary on Surgut oil-producing area in Tyumen' province.[19] The article turned its attention mainly to the need to build more roads and other infrastructure in the province. Similarly, in a February issue of the paper four economists in Moscow--S. Slavin, A. Ivanchenko, V. Kistanov, and D. Belorusov--stressed that a comprehensive development programme for the region especially with regard to living conditions should be worked out.[20] The contributors--all of them Gosplan's Council for Study of Productive Forces (*SOPS*) members--also called for the creation of a body which would carry out the programme. Belorusov, who headed a section on the question of the West Siberian complex at the council, said at another time: "According to our estimates, West Siberia will produce more than 30 percent of the country's oil and about 40 percent of natural gas by 1980."[21] He went on to emphasize the need to eliminate what he termed "many serious mistakes and miscalculations" committed in the course of development so that the potentialities of the region could be fully realized. In May and June, meanwhile, *Literaturnaya gazeta* once again came out in support of the West Siberians by pointing out various shortcomings such as poor living conditions for oil and gas workers in the region.[22] The paper invited local specialists and academics in Tyumen' province to make known their opinions.[23] To cite some of them:

L. I. Rovnin (Chief geologist, Glavtyumengeologiya): We geologists have opened scores of oil and gas deposits.

But oil industry workers don't keep pace with the geologists. Why?

Yu. P. Batalin (Chief engineer, Glavtyumenneftegazstroi): In connection with our construction works, USSR Gosplan has no definite perspective plan.

V. Yu. Filanovskii (Chief engineer, Glavtyumenneftegaz): There is no comprehensive plan for the development of West Siberia.

G. P. Bogomyakov (Deputy director, ZapSibNIGNI): The Siberian Department of the USSR Academy of Sciences is indifferent to our problems. I would also like to criticize Gosplan's SOPS. All the recent years we have waited until SOPS works out a comprehensive general plan for our region. But we don't yet have such a plan.

At that time, Director of Glavtyumenneftegaz V. Muravlenko made a similar complaint that "USSR Gosplan and the Ministry of the Oil Industry have failed to determine the extent of the development (of the West Siberian resources) even for the next 10-15 years."[24] In answer to such complaints, M. Pervukhin, a collegium member of USSR Gosplan, said that SOPS should finish working out a general programme for the complex development of the West Siberian fuel resources by 1968 on the basis of the proposals by various research institutes and design-making organs.[25] He mentioned that Gosplan Chairman N. K. Baibakov and Oil Minister V. D. Shashin also made an inspection trip to Tyumen' and Tomsk provinces lately. The Gosplan official agreed with *Literaturnaya gazeta* on the need to create in advance necessary living and working conditions for local oil and gas workers. There were at least three more promotional articles published in support of fuel development in the province during the last three months of the year.[26]

1968 Tyumen' obkom secretary Protozanov revealed in early 1968 that over 400 million rubles were to be poured into his province in that year so that the annual production capacity of oil could be raised to up to 11 million tons and that of gas to nine billion cubic meters.[27] He went on to argue that the capacity, however, could be raised even higher, to 120 million tons of oil and tens of billion cubic meters of gas if equipment and qualified labor were introduced and good communication lines were installed in the area. "Unfortunately," he said, "several central departments and ministries do not fully take into account the potential of Tyumen' province. There are still not a few skeptics who make wild guesses: Is it profitable to extract oil and gas in the northern taiga?" Asserting that the cost of extracting hydrocarbons there would be cheaper than the national average in the near future, the secretary made various demands for improvements such as the development of power engineering and the building of houses and other social infrastructure. In February, *Pravda* reported that the Tyumen' province Party Committee held a conference to discuss the rapid opening up of fuel resources in the area.[28] After that time, however, promotional discussions in support of oil and gas development in the province disappeared from the Soviet press for nearly half a year. There were only a couple of correspondent reports about need for swamp transports in the region.[29]

It was two Siberian geologists who broke a long silence to advocate the "comprehensive, long-term development" of the West Siberian oil region. Academician A. A. Trofimuk and his colleague G. P. Bogomyakov, predicting that West Siberian oil deposits would form the main oil-extracting base for the next 20 to 30 years, argued in August that the new oilfields should be developed "strategically on a long-term basis."[30] Emphasizing the need for the comprehensive development of the fuel complex, they urged that not only scholars and Gosplan but also all the related industrial ministries should take part in the drawing up of a programme for its future. Addressing the various problems that confronted the oil industry in north Tyumen' province, meanwhile, Director of the Surgut Oilfield Administration I. Shidlovskii criticized a technology department of the Oil Ministry for not only neglecting to cut down the costs of capital construction in his area but even obstructing the effort to enhance local design-making capacity.[31] He brought similar charges against both USSR and RSFSR State Construction Committees and the Gas Ministry's Chief Construction Administration. Shortly afterwards, Glavtyumenneftegaz's Chief engineer Filanovskii called for a thorough review of the development of the oil riches in West Siberia and for a comprehensive development strategy. In a *Pravda* contribution, he said: "Now the time has come to discuss in detail how and at what cost we can make best use of the enormous wealth, which we have in Siberian oil."[32] Finally, three local specialists--V. Maksimov, M. Musin, and G. Ostryi--discussed in December technological problems in connection with oil industry development in the area.[33] They called for closer coordination among research and design-making institutions.

In Tomsk, a conference was held in July to discuss the prospective economic development of Tomsk province in 1971-

1975.[34] At the meeting, Chairman of Gosplan's Council for Study of Productive Forces (SOPS) and Corresponding Member of the USSR Academy N. Nekrasov gave the figure of 30-32 billion rubles for the development of oil and gas industry and forestry in Siberia in 1971-1980. At the close of the conference, participants recommended the rapid opening up of oil and gas resources in the province and the development of machine-building and other supporting industries there. Jointly sponsored by the Tomsk province Party Committee and the province's Executive Committee (*oblispolkom*), *Ekonomicheskaya gazeta*, Gosplan's SOPS, the State Committee for Science and Technology, the Siberian Department of the USSR Academy, the Planning Commission of the West Siberian Economic Region, the meeting was attended by Tomsk obkom First Secretary Ye. Ligachev, USSR Geology Minister Academician A. V. Sidorenko, chief of USSR Gosplan's Oil and Gas Industry Department P. P. Galonskii, Corresponding Member of the USSR Academy A. G. Aganbegyan, Vice President of the Academy's Siberian Department Academician A. A. Trofimuk, and Deputy Gas Minister Yu. I. Bokserman. Predicting that the province could extract 17-20 million tons of oil a year in the near future, local Party boss Ligachev reiterated the demands made at the conference.[35] He had made similar requests in February of 1968 after a year-long silence.[36]

1969 In the early part of 1969, the pro-West Siberians did not make any significant demands in the Soviet press. In May, however, two promotional conferences were held in Siberia. Both meetings, officially described as discussing the problems of the "development and location of productive forces" in Siberia, and in Tyumen' province in particular, devoted their attention almost entirely to the country's "fuel and power balance" and to the contribution of the eastern region.[37] Speaking at the first of these gatherings, held in Novosibirsk by the USSR Academy of Sciences' Siberian Department, Tyumen' Party leader Shcherbina emphasized that "it is necessary to define the new conception of the future development of productive forces in Siberia."[38] The "new conception" was further elaborated at an ensuing conference, held in Tyumen', which called for a "comprehensive, long-term and interdepartmental programme" (*kompleksnaya, perspektivnaya, mezhvedomstvennaya programma*) for the region.[39] More than 1,000 people from central and local research institutions, government ministries, Party organs and local administrative and economic organizations attended. It was the first time that such large-scale meetings had been held to discuss the development of the province.

It seems that much of the controversy that arose at the Tyumen' conference pertained to the proposed scope and speed of the development of West Siberia. There, Tyumen' Party boss Shcherbina revealed that certain organizations were continuing to put forward their own proposals, according to which, he said, only an insignificant amount of funds would be invested in the Tyumen' region.[40] He insisted that a proposal introduced by the Siberians "three years ago" should be adopted without any revision so that West Siberia would be developed as a region specializing in the oil, gas and related industries. As noted in the previous chapter, debates took place at the conference about the future optimum level of oil production in West Siberia.[41] According to obkom secretary Protozanov, there were similar debates between some participants over two differing plan proposals for the construction of railways in the region.[42] At that time, four eminent academics--Nekrasov, Trofimuk, Aganbegyan and N. V. Cherskii--advocated the exploitation of Siberian energy sources, and particularly natural gas in Tyumen' province.[43] In an article published shortly afterwards, Academician Nekrasov also said that "in our view, the regions of East and West Siberia should be at the top of the (development) list."[44] "At present," he argued, "special attention should be given to determining long-range prospects, and to scientific projections of the rational location of productive forces in our country and the economic development of large individual regions. In particular, the time has come to start thinking about Siberia in the year 2000 and about its role and place in the further growth of the economic might of the Soviet Union."[45]

During the second half of 1969, the pro-West Siberians, apparently in anticipation of an impending decision on West Siberian development, engaged extensively in public discussions. Emphasizing the economic benefit of opening up West Siberian oil and gas resources, Corresponding Member of the USSR Academy Aganbegyan urged that industries such as petrochemicals be set up in the energy-rich Siberian regions.[46] He was echoed by two Gosplan economists, V. Kistanov and S. Tokarev, who suggested that industries with high power requirements be built in Siberia.[47] According to them, many such industries including chemical and metallurgical plants, continued to be built in the European USSR. Meanwhile, Tyumen' obkom Secretary Protozanov stressed the acuteness of the transportation problems in the region and said that "transportation problems in the industrial Ob' region must be considered as an integral whole, in terms of their relation to the development and correct utilization of West Siberia's productive forces."[48] In November, Glavtyumenneftegaz Director Muravlenko pointed out that the construction of infrastructure such as railroads, pipelines and power stations had lagged behind the growth of oil production in West Siberia.[49] Many more articles by the pro-West Siberians appeared in the Soviet press during this period.[50]

1970 Against this background, the 1969 decree was made public in *Pravda* on January 15, 1970.[51] Commenting on the decision, Tyumen' Party leader Shcherbina expressed satisfaction that it "will open a new perspective in the transformation of this richly endowed territory."[52] Elsewhere, he praised the decree as a measure ensuring the comprehensive opening up of oil resources in his province. "The decision," he said, "covers a wide range of economic, technical and social problems, connected with the creation of the largest complex of the national economy."[53] Academician Trofimuk, without directly referring to the decision, declared in January that "the underground resources of the West Siberian lowland are now the main base for further rapid development in the extraction of oil and gas."[54]

Several central officials also commented favorably on the potentialities of the development of West Siberian oil. At the time of the announcement of the decree, A. A. Yamnov, head of the geology sector of the Party Central Committee's Heavy Industry Department, said that the oilfields in West Siberia were considered the largest of their kind in the world.[55] He went on to express his conviction that there was most likely a new huge oil- and gas-bearing basin to the east of Tyumen'. Later that year, two other central Party officials commented that the decree provided West Siberia with a concrete programme of operations both for the immediate and for the more distant future.[56] These were N. Yeronin, head of the oil industry sector of the CC Heavy Industry Department, and V. Kremnev. Meanwhile, Oil Minister Shashin welcomed the decree as a "special decree." In an interview following the announcement of the decree, the country's chief oil industry manager said that bright prospects were in store for the oil industry in West Siberia.[57] He added that the decree made possible the comprehensive development of the newly opened eastern oil region.

In late February, a large-scale scientific conference was held in Novosibirsk to discuss "problems connected with the fulfillment of the decree."[58] By mid-1970, according to V. Maksimov, a section head of Tyumen' obkom, more than a score of industrial ministries and departments, and enterprises from almost all the republics of the Soviet Union were participating in the West Siberian undertaking.[59] Similarly, N. V. Lukbyanenok, Chairman of Tomsk province Soviet Executive Committee, remarked in an article that "the scope of oil-extracting, construction and geological prospecting works in the north of (Tomsk) province have grown, especially following the adoption of the decree."[60]

To sum up, the proponents of West Siberian development had taken up the promotion of their cause in a press campaign as early as 1968. It seems that a decision to accelerate the development of West Siberia had already been made in principle by the time of the convocation of the Siberian conferences in mid-1969. However, it would seem from the debates at the Tyumen' conference that the Soviets had not yet reached an agreement on the rate of exploitation of West Siberian oil and gas resources. From that time, the pro-West Siberians stepped up their campaign in the Soviet press. It should be noted that during this period two Party organs, *Pravda* and *Ekonomicheskaya gazeta*, were generous in allowing the pro-West Siberians space for their campaign. These central papers also carried many articles by their own correspondents resident in West Siberia. In 1968, for instance, two correspondents of *Ekonomicheskaya gazeta* reported on various problems, including that of capital investment in the development of the oil and gas industry in West Siberia.[61] In one article, they reported that departmentalism had hampered the building of the necessary infrastructure. Two *Pravda* correspondents, E. Kiselev and I. Titov, while praising Siberian oil workers for what they had "managed to do in Samotlor this year (1969)," also turned their attention to the difficulties that had confronted them.[62] Another *Pravda* reporter, A. Murzin, also closely surveyed various aspects of West Siberian developments in 1970.[63]

What demands had the pro-West Siberians made? Many had pressed for more funds, for advanced instead of outmoded technology, for new methods of building instead of old-fashioned ones, and so on. Chief engineer Filanovskii of Glavtyumenneftegaz, for instance, complained that "Glavtyumenneftegaz, to which about 150 million rubles a year in capital investments are allocated, has virtually no right to spend even one ruble on the financing of research work."[64] The Tyumen' conference included in its recommendations for the region the intensification of the search for oil and gas, the acceleration of the construction of pipelines, and further extension of electrification.[65] At this early stage of development, imbalances in housing and other construction directed to social needs were also one of the main complaints on the part of the West Siberians.[66]

Many of the demands were still more far-reaching. The advocates of West Siberian development did not limit their demands to the development of the extraction industries. They also wanted to see the whole cycle of production carried out in the Siberian region. Thus, as noted above, Aganbegyan and others suggested that those industries with high consumption of energy should be built in the energy-rich eastern regions. Academician Nekrasov said in 1969 that oil refineries should be built in the eastern part of the country close to the source of raw materials. In 1970, Tyumen' Party leader Shcherbina revealed that Gosplan's SOPS, of which Academician Nekrasov was the head, had proposed the setting up of energy-consuming enterprises in West Siberia. "But in Gosplan," he complained, "they apparently do not give much consideration to this recommendation."[67] A Siberian economist, V. E. Popov, pointed out that the attitudes of industrial ministries in Moscow towards the expansion of their enterprises evinced a "pro-European" inclination.[68] At the same time, many pro-West Siberian elements made far more important demands; i.e. the demands that the region be developed into the country's main base for the fuel industry, that a comprehensive long-term development programme be elaborated to this end, and that organizations be set up charged with the development of the region. In short, they wanted to see the status of West Siberia significantly enhanced in terms of national development priorities. When the Tyumen' conference recommended the comprehensive development of the region, it actually called, above anything else, for a substantial increase in the allocation of funds and materials to West Siberia. The conference also called for the creation of an organization to be entrusted with full responsibility for West Siberian development.[69] Before the announcement of the 1969 decree, V. P. Maksimov, chief of a section of the Tyumen' State Oil and Gas Research-Design Institute (*Giprotyumenneftegaz*), and two of his Siberian colleagues stated that "in our opinion, clear coordination of all the research and design work in West Siberia should be fully achieved."[70] Meanwhile, two Siberian geologists--Academician Trofimuk and Bogomyakov--urged the participation of all the appropriate departments and agencies in the development of Siberian oil and gas, and economist Aganbegyan advocated the creation of a specialized regional planning institute.[71] In 1970, Tyumen' Party boss Shcherbina put forward a more concrete organizational proposal to enable the fullest implementation of the 1969 decree. He suggested the creation of a department within Gosplan, which would be charged with the development of the oil-producing Tyumen' province, a central research institute for the study of problems of the North, and an academic institute in Tyumen' to deal with the complex economic problems there.[72]

B. Demands for Further Development, 1976-1978

Similar manoeuverings by the advocates of the West Siberian undertaking were made in the ensuing years. Such campaigns were carried out in a more organized way after 1976. Until then, public discussions on the part of the pro-West Siberians appeared to be rather isolated, individual affairs.

1971-1974 In 1971, a year after the announcement of the 1969 decree, the Soviet press continued to carry articles--mostly of a mobilizational nature--relating to the construction of the oil industry in West Siberia. In March, Academician Trofimuk expressed his usual optimism that West Siberia would give 700-800 million tons of oil a year in the future.[73] In that month, he and his colleagues--Yu. G. Erv'e, I. I. Nesterov, and Ye. N. Altunin--argued for the exploitation of what they termed the world's largest gas deposits in Urengoi along with the Medvezh'e deposits which were planned to be developed in 1971-1975.[74] Oil Minister Shashin was also optimistic about the prospect of West Siberian oil development. Noting that a total of 67 large oil deposits had been opened there, he said that "we consider this is only the beginning."[75] Meanwhile, mass-circulation *Sovetskaya Rossiya* treated various problems of West Siberian development in its February issue. In this issue, engineer-turned section chief of Tyumen' obkom V. P. Maksimov and others discussed drilling and related problems.[76] One of the problems still confronting West Siberian development was the unsatisfactory coordination between the industrial ministries and departments involved. Aganbegyan, in his speech to a special session of the USSR Academy of Sciences in Novosibirsk in April, called for a systematic approach to the construction of large industrial complexes, especially in Siberia.[77] Thus far, according to him, the various parts of such a complex were being built by the relevant ministries with little coordination with each other.

In 1972-1973, there were not many articles about the development of West Siberia, but some of those which did appear struck a more impatient note. In the area of oil production, Muravlenko, head of Glavtyumenneftegaz, singled out the construction of oil and gas pipelines, power transmission lines and roads as the most urgent problems. According to him, "the Ministry of the Oil Industry, engaging itself energetically in the problem of developing the new oil- and gas-extracting base in West Siberia in the current five-year plan period, in our view, so far pays very little attention to long-term problems" such as pipelines and roads.[78] In addition to this, many called attention to the unsatisfactory housing and living conditions in these environmentally harsh regions.[79] But insufficient oil exploration proved to be the most serious concern on the part of both West Siberians and central officials. Thus, Muravlenko complained about the insufficiency of prospecting work being done in West Siberia: "A certain slump in the exploration of new large oil deposits has begun to show lately. In essence, the volume of prospecting work does not grow and preparation of explored deposits for exploitation is carried out insufficiently. Oil prospecting works in the regions located north of the Middle Ob' are especially falling behind."[80] In November, Tyumen' Party leader Shcherbina criticized the geologists for not moving their prospecting work further to the north.[81] Earlier, Oil Minister Shashin expressed similar concern that the USSR Ministry of Geology was not carrying out sufficient prospecting and exploratory work in the new regions of West Siberia.[82] Against this background, a meeting on oil exploration was held in Tyumen' in late 1973 which Shcherbina and Shashin both attended.[83] Among the participants were also Party Central Committee Secretary V. I. Dolgikh and Gosplan's Deputy Chairman A. M. Lalayants.

It was during 1974-1975 that serious doubts were voiced about the prospects of the oil industry in West Siberia. In January 1974, a meeting of oil industry officials and enterprise managers was held in Moscow. Shcherbina, who had been made the Minister of Construction of Oil and Gas Industry Enterprises, attended the meeting along with Gosplan Deputy Chairman V. E. Dymshits and Gas Minister S. A. Orudzhev.[84] There is no doubt that former

Tyumen' leader Shcherbina and many others continued to favor the accelerated development of West Siberian hydrocarbons.[85] During this period, however, arguments in a number of Soviet publications came out in favor of the enhanced recovery of oil in the old oil regions.[86] This coincided with the growing concern over the rising costs of exploring for and producing oil in West Siberia.[87] As a result of such problems, some set their eyes on the quest for maritime oil sources as a possible alternative to the further development of West Siberia.[88] Others began to point to the advantages of developing coal and other fuel sources.[89] Such arguments may be viewed as a counteroffensive against the priority development of West Siberian hydrocarbons as the country was about to adopt a new five-year plan.

1975-1976 Meanwhile, the pro-West Siberians began to concentrate their efforts on a publicity campaign. One of their main concerns at this time was related to the worsening situation of oil reserves in West Siberia. In 1974, Academician Trofimuk continued to express his concern over the increasing disproportion between the prospecting and exploratory drilling on the one hand and the development drilling on the other. In his opinion, the balance in favor of the latter caused the unsatisfactory reserves situation in the eastern region.[90] But he had to wait another year for support for his argument. Early in the following year, I. Nesterov, Director of the West Siberian Geological-Prospecting and Oil Research Institute (ZapsibNIGNI), specified three regions in West Siberia as being the most promising prospective oil regions.[91] He urged that both all-Union and RSFSR Geology Ministries ought to "invest as generously as possible in the exploration of the underground resources in West Siberia."[92] In June, geologist-turned Tyumen' Party leader G. P. Bogomyakov was quoted as warning that if new oil deposits were not opened, a sharp fall in oil production in West Siberia would be unavoidable.[93] He criticized Gosplan for "not doing any timely thinking as to what will happen in two or three years if Tyumen' suddenly not only is unable to 'cover' other regions but also slows down its own growth."[94] He complained that neither Gosplan nor the Oil Ministry had any clear plan for developing "enormous new" oil areas in West Siberia to replace Tyumen' in case the latter failed to produce enough oil. In February 1976, F. Salmanov, Chief geologist of Glavtyumengeologiya, also called for more geological-exploratory work in search of oil resources in West

Siberia. Pointing out that the extent to which the geology of Tyumen' province had been studied was only about five percent that of Tatar ASSR or Bashkir ASSR in the Urals-Volga region, he insisted on the necessity of drilling 70 to 80 million meters of exploratory wells in West Siberia.[95] He revealed that only six million meters had been drilled so far in the West Siberian region. The Siberian geologist urged the utmost speed in prospecting for new deposits and in the further exploration of known deposits so that predicted reserves should become industrial reserves without unnecessary delay. In the long run, he said, exploratory drilling ought to reach a level of 1.5 to 2 million meters of wells per year. He added that it would be necessary to take into consideration the increased cost of preparing oil reserves as a result of the northwards movement of prospecting operations. The Siberian geologist was echoed by Oil Minister Shashin when the latter also expressed concern over the diminution of oil reserves. In a contribution to *Ekonomicheskaya gazeta*, he said that exploratory work should proceed first of all in the Middle Ob' and the northern part of Tyumen' province.[96] The minister then called on the USSR Ministry of Geology to play a more decisive role in the exploration of oil reserves.

During these years, pro-West Siberian elements also complained about other problems which arose in the course of the development of the oil and gas industry in the region. In early 1976, shortly before the convocation of the Twenty-fifth Party Congress, R. I. Kuzovatkin, Director of the Nizhnevartovsk Oil and Gas Extraction Administration (*Nizhnevartovskneft'*) in West Siberia, complained that construction work was not satisfactory in the Samotlor oilfields.[97] In 1975, Yu. P. Batalin, First Deputy Minister of Construction of Oil and Gas Industry Enterprises who had formerly worked as a chief engineer in West Siberia, was quoted as stressing the need for the commitment of more funds and advanced technology to the Siberian oilfields.[98] Particularly serious problems had arisen in connection with housing and the construction of social infrastructure, as Tyumen' Party boss Bogomyakov had complained.[99] As of late 1974, according to two Gosplan officials, V. Varlamov and I. Panfilov, the programme of the Ninth Five-Year Plan for building social infrastructure in West Siberia had been only 20-30 percent realized during the first three and a half years.[100]

Many attributed such disproportions in part to the lack of a unified approach to the development of West Siberian resources. According to *Pravda* correspondent A.

Murzin, there was a comprehensive plan for the development of the region which had been worked out at one time (*v svoe vremya*) by the combined forces of institutes, ministries and departments.[101] Revealing that little consideration had been given to this work, he urged reconsideration of this plan in order to effectively deal with the various problems confronting the West Siberian complex. In addition, Academician Nekrasov advocated the setting up of regional councils of enterprise managers in territorial industrial complexes to help facilitate coordination among the organizations involved in them.[102] Such a surge of demands and complaints during this period was apparently the result of efforts by the pro-West Siberians to influence the national plan then being worked out for the coming five-year plan period.

1976-1977 Arguments in support of the West Siberian cause largely disappeared from the Soviet press in the period following the Twenty-fifth Congress in February-March 1976. There is every indication that the pro-West Siberians at that time failed in their efforts to promote the cause of the accelerated development of Siberian hydrocarbons. As we have seen, the Congress endorsed Kosygin's proposal for a more balanced energy approach with relatively more emphasis given to coal. Capital investment in Tyumen' province did not grow much during the period of 1976-1977.[103] As will be seen later, Kosygin seems to have commanded a majority on economic issues in the Politburo at the time of the Congress and successfully defeated the pro-West Siberians who were clearly backed by Brezhnev. In any case, there appeared in mid-1976 a very informative article by I. Ognev, correspondent of the Siberian mouthpiece, *Ekonomika i organizatsiya promyshlennogo proizvodstva*, on the differences of opinion which had occurred between the West Siberians--mainly geologists--on the one hand and central planning organs and industrial ministries on the other from the early days of oil prospecting and exploration in West Siberia.[104] He reported that Gosplan's position on oil exploration was that further development of old oil regions in the European USSR was no less advantageous for the national economy than the opening up of oil reserves in the remote eastern regions.[105]

From late 1976 onwards, the pro-West Siberians once again took a concerted offensive against many central economic bodies allegedly less enthusiastic about a further commitment to West Siberian development. In their published articles, they pointed to a variety of problems confronting the fuel complex and asked for more funds and resources to help tackle them. At that time, Glavtyumenneftegaz Director Muravlenko summed up three problems as being the most pressing for the complex:

> In our view,...for the more rational development of the oil and gas deposits of the West Siberian lowland, at least three tasks should be carried out. Firstly, it is necessary to further consolidate the technical base of geologists so that they discover new underground resources more rapidly. Secondly, along with well-known deposits, it is necessary also to develop less significant ones.... Thirdly, the necessary amount of housing, public-service and cultural institutions should be built.[106]

Commenting on the issue of the fuel reserves situation, G. Shmal', a Tyumen' obkom secretary, repeated the previous pro-West Siberian demand that it would be necessary to drill 70 million meters of exploratory wells in West Siberia for an accurate assessment of the oil and gas resources there.[107] Stressing that the efficiency of capital investment in oil and gas prospecting in West Siberia was six to eight times higher than the national average, he complained that the RSFSR Ministry of Geology did not pay any attention to the needs of Tyumen' geologists. As for gas reserves, according to him, it was the opinion of many central ministry officials that it was not even worthwhile prospecting for gas deposits because sufficiently explored reserves already existed.

In early 1977, Erv'e, head of Glavtyumengeologiya, revealed that in the previous year for the first time in the last 15 years the target for the growth of oil reserves in West Siberia had not been fulfilled. He went on to blame the failure on various constraints which forced prospectors to concentrate their efforts in the already developed areas, rather than on the deep exploratory drilling of new regions.[108] Earlier that year, *Pravda* in an editorial had acknowledged the need for the acceleration of the search for new oil and gas deposits.[109] In August, two of its correspondents, S. Vtorushin and A. Murzin, also reported on the unsatisfactory discovery rate of oil reserves in the region:

> ...for each square kilometer of territory in the province, only five meters of well have been drilled. This is twenty times less than in Tatariya or Bashkiriya.

> ...there is no doubt that the interior of these areas (new oil regions such as Yamal-Nenets national region) offers promise. Recently this opinion was again unanimously expressed by the country's leading oil geologists, meeting in Tyumen'.[110]

They pointed to the complacency of central planning and industrial organizations and the supply bottlenecks faced by Siberian geologists as being the main causes of the worsening oil reserves situation there.[111]

Meanwhile, local oil industry officials were also voicing their demands. In late 1976, Director of the Nizhnevartovsk Oil and Gas Extraction Administration Kuzovatkin said:

> If we compare the capacities of the existing construction organizations in Nizhnevartovsk district and those now being formed with the volume of construction-and-installation work planned for the new five-year plan...and take into account unfinished construction, it is clear that without outside help the plan for preparing the deposits probably cannot be fulfilled.
>
> .... During the last five-year plan period, (oil) extraction (in the district) was 34 percent above plan, but capital investments realized were only 12 percent over plan. There was 117 million rubles' worth of unfinished construction at the end of the five-year period. The preparation of deposits is four years behind schedule.[112]

He also complained that there were chronic delays in the completion of new housing, which was necessary due to the rapid growth of the population in many new oil regions of West Siberia.[113] On this matter, his superior Muravlenko once said that appropriations for housing had been allocated, but that contractor organizations of the USSR Ministry of Industrial Construction and of the USSR Ministry of Construction of Oil and Gas Industry Enterprises did not have sufficient capacity.[114]

In early 1977, the two *Pravda* correspondents, Vtorushin and Murzin, also reported on the problems connected with the transportation of West Siberian gas. Pointing out that long-distance gas transportation required a huge quantity of pipelines, they recommended that large gas-processing and gas-consuming enterprises be built as close as possible to the gas deposits.[115] Their argument went as follows:

> The idea of using some Tyumen' gas in the North is nothing new. However, until now it has had many opponents. Their main argument is that it is difficult to build in the North. Therefore, they say,... gas should be piped to the Urals and the European regions, where large-capacity power stations will be erected. In arguing their point, the "opponents" for some reason forget that, if they are to operate, these power stations will need not only fuel but large amounts of land and enormous quantities of water. In the populated regions of the Center, all of these are limited. .... But in northern Tyumen' province, there is no lack of water.[116]

In a similar vein, two Moscow economists argued that highly energy-intensive and non-labor-intensive types of industrial production could be effectively located in Siberia.[117] They were A. A. Beschinskii and R. Ya. Vitebskii, senior members of a research institute of the USSR Ministry of Power and Electrification.

Perhaps the most outspoken article on the problems of developing the West Siberian oilfields was published in November 1977 by L. P. Guzhnovskii, head of the Tyumen' Department of Economic Research of the Institute of Economics and Organization of Industrial Production of the USSR Academy of Sciences' Siberian Department.[118] He revealed that there had been substantial disagreements over the country's oil development policy. In particular, these were concerned with the balance of investment between West Siberia and the European oilfields, and with a variety of technical issues connected with the development of the West Siberian oil industry. On the subject of capital investments in the West Siberian oil industry, he said:

> In 1971-1975 the annual plans for the extraction of oil in West Siberia were considerably higher than the five-year plan's assignments. Some deposits were put into operation before industrial exploration had been completed or adequate plans for extraction had been drawn up. The outfitting of deposits lagged behind the pace of (development) drilling operations. The interregional redistribution of oil extraction was not accompanied by analogous changes in the capital

> investments put into the industry's public-service infrastructure.[119]

He then went on to attack the policy of enhanced recovery in the old oilfields of the European USSR:

> During recent years, efforts have been made to maintain previous levels of oil extraction at certain large oil deposits in several regions of the European part of the country: in this, they saw the rational direction of the further development of oil extraction. It seems to us that this tendency runs counter to the national economy's task of obtaining the planned volume of oil with the least expenditure of manpower and material resources. If one proceeds from such a way of carrying out the task, then the determination of the level of oil production for certain regions or deposits, divorced from optimization of the development of the whole branch, may not be considered as optimal. In particular, the least efficient method of stabilizing extraction or slowing its decline is to sink additional wells at existing deposits, especially when the deposits are in the later stages of exploitation. Nonetheless, this method of sinking wells is being employed in the European regions.
>
> The decline in extraction from old deposits can be compensated for with smaller capital investments by prospecting and working deposits in new oil regions. The concentration of effort on maintaining extraction levels in the Urals-Volga regions is highly questionable. The possibility cannot be ruled out that the Urals-Volga will get in the way of West Siberia and other new regions, as was the case of Azerbaidzhan in 1948-1950 in relation to the Urals-Volga.[120]

In the same issue, three of his colleagues emphasized that the preparation of oil deposits for extraction was especially urgent in West Siberia. Blaming the violation of the proper ratio in the growth rates of exploratory drilling and development drilling for a lag in the preparation of industrial reserves in West Siberia, L. I. Churikov, head of a laboratory at the Tyumen' State Oil and Gas Research-Design Institute (*Giprotyumenneftegaz*), and his colleagues demanded that the volume of exploratory drilling in Tyumen' should be increased by several times.[121]

1978 The renewed manoeuverings by the pro-West Siberian elements were followed by the Party Central Committee's December plenum in 1977. It was at this meeting that Brezhnev announced the programme for the crash development of West Siberian oil. On January 26, 1978, an enlarged conference of oil industry officials was summoned to adopt new 1978 targets that would comply with the revised national economic plan adopted at the plenum.

Welcoming the plenum decision, Tyumen' Party leader Bogomyakov said that:

> Well-founded displeasure (*nedovol'stvo*) has been voiced lately over the lag in the preparation of oil reserves for industrial development. What happened? The underground resources are the same. If scientists' forecasts have changed at all, they have become more optimistic. But inadequate exploration of reserves is holding up the planning of extraction.
>
> The reason is perfectly obvious. During the last 10 years, oil extraction has grown by leaps and bounds, but as for the volume of exploratory drilling, to use a songwriter's figurative expression, "as it was, so it remains." At one time Tyumen' geologists kept knocking on the doors of the RSFSR and USSR Ministries of Geology and the Union and republic Gosplan, trying to show them that they should not be content with the high yields from reserves and that the volume of exploratory work should be increased. But the pace fell off, time slipped by, and now we have to accomplish this task with the help of additional resources and efforts.[122]

Tomsk obkom First Secretary Ligachev earlier revealed that in accordance with the plenum decision the volume of geological-exploratory work and oil extraction in his province would be increased by almost two times in 1978 in comparison with that of the previous year.[123] Meanwhile, Academician Trofimuk stressed that "it is quite possible to markedly step up prospecting and exploratory work--without reducing extraction."[124] Academician Nekrasov, also commenting on the December decision, emphasized that West Siberia "is now the main fuel and power base of the country."[125]

A number of Soviet newspapers and journals at that time were engaged in a public campaign in support of the decision.[126] Of the correspondents of the central papers, four were perhaps the most active in reporting various problems of West Siberian development. They were S.

Vtorushin and A. Murzin of *Pravda*, and V. Kozlov and E. Shatokhin of *Izvestiya*. As part of the campaign, a "round-table" conference was summoned in Tyumen' in June on the initiative of the Propaganda Department of the Party Central Committee and Tyumen' obkom. Jointly organized by five journals including *Ekonomika i organizatsiya promyshlennogo proizvodstva*, the meeting discussed the "problems of the comprehensive development of West Siberia."[127] The Party organ, *Ekonomicheskaya gazeta*, later linked the three-day meeting with the recommendations and instructions given by Brezhnev during his trip to Siberia and the Soviet Far East earlier that year.[128]

At the conference, the participants, mainly scholars and energy specialists, discussed a number of problems, ranging from drilling to organizational coordination, associated with the development of the West Siberian complex.[129] Aganbegyan stressed at the meeting that a programme for the development of West Siberia should be multipurpose (*mnogotselevyi*). He argued that, in addition to the creation of the country's main fuel base, the programme should also aim to establish a major petrochemical and power-engineering base, and to set up major energy-intensive production units there. In other words, it should aim at the all-round industrialization of the region. He noted two main problems which stood in the way of further development of the region. One was that of disproportions which had arisen between various branches of the regional economy--for example, the lag in transport and road construction, and in the building of infrastructure and housing. The other was the problem of coordination of the activities of the various ministries and departments involved in the region.[130]

Various solutions to the problem of coordination were suggested. At the conference, for instance, economist B. Vainshtein called for the formulation of a programme to deal with the specific problems of the economic and social development of the West Siberian complex.[131] Others like M. I. Piskotin, Chief editor of *Sovetskoe gosudarstvo i pravo*, supported the creation of a regional organization to facilitate coordination.[132] In fact, both Siberians and central officials had raised similar demands following the Twenty-fifth Party Congress. Even under ideal circumstances, according to G. Sudobin, Deputy Minister of Construction of Oil and Gas Industry Enterprises, the problem of coordination would inevitably arise. He noted the case of pipeline construction in West Siberia where more than 16 ministries and departments along with the three largest construction administrations (*glavki*) of his ministry were involved.[133] In an effort to deal with such problems, Kuzovatkin, head of the Nizhnevartovsk Oil and Gas Extraction Administration, had proposed in 1976 that the Oil Ministry and the local Soviets take charge of the construction of industry and of social infrastructure in their own areas:

> In our view, when large oil and gas complexes are created in the undeveloped regions of West Siberia, the local Soviets should from the very start assume the function of general client (*zakazchik*), administer appropriations for the construction of housing and of cultural and service facilities, and conduct all-round planning for such construction. The plans should be coordinated with production development and population growth.
>
> Since oil and gas extraction is and will remain the chief function of oil districts, we think that the Oil Ministry should be the general client for the construction of all industrial facilities and warehouses. It should be given the power to resolve problems relating to the construction of all important production facilities in the region. To this end, the other ministries involved should transfer funds to the Oil Ministry.
>
> ....
>
> Logically, Gosplan should set up territorial planning agencies in the rapidly developing oil regions of West Siberia to unite and direct the efforts of all the enterprises there.[134]

Similarly, a *Pravda* correspondent reported a local proposal for efficient management of the construction of the Tobolsk Petrochemical Complex:

> A model for the management of the construction project was worked out at the initiative of local specialists. Management is supposed to consist of two levels. The upper level would include authorized representatives of the client, the contracting ministries, the USSR State Committee for Material and Technical Supply (*Gossnab SSSR*) and the USSR State Committee on Construction (*Gosstroi SSSR*). This body (to be located in Moscow or Tyumen'), which would be headed by a special representative of Gosplan, would be vested with the broadest authority. The higher level

> would resolve all fundamental questions relating to the development of the Tobolsk complex, supervise cooperation among ministries, and adjust the areas of the builders' efforts. If such a body had existed, neither the transportation "bottleneck" nor others like it would have arisen at the construction project. Now there are many such problems.
>
> ....
>
> The Siberians propose that the lower-level management agency for the complex be set up in Tobolsk. The best idea would be for this body to be headed by the petrochemical combine's general director, since all the other organizations that have come into being there serve this enterprise.[135]

In Moscow, Academician Nekrasov agreed that West Siberia, and other such territorial-production complexes, would need a single boss (*edinyi khozyain*) who would assume the function of a coordinator.[136] But some Gosplan officials seem to have been less enthusiastic about the idea of establishing a supra-departmental organization in West Siberia. In answer to a question by a *Literaturnaya gazeta* correspondent on the necessity of creating such organs in territorial complexes, for example, M. G. Pervukhin, a senior Gosplan official, replied:

> .... I think that it is not necessary to set up special organs for the management of territorial-production complexes. We have branch administration of the national economy. The head of a construction site or an enterprise is not allowed to receive instructions from both its own ministry and a territorial administration. Instructions may contradict each other. Nothing good comes of it. The elimination of imbalances, the synchronization of the construction of interrelated enterprises, should be achieved by way of establishing industrial centers (*Gosstroi SSSR*'s business), by drawing up project lists (*titul'nye spiski*) in annual plans (Gosplan's task), and by strict implementation of these projects and plans by ministries. Party and Soviet organs will be engaged in coordination on the spot.[137]

In sum, the pro-West Siberians conducted a public campaign for the accelerated development of hydrocarbons in West Siberia in a more or less concerted manner during the mid-1970s. They carried on the campaign most actively during the period from late 1976 through 1977. The priority development of West Siberian oil was reaffirmed by the decision of December 1977. But as for their calls for a comprehensive programme for the complex and an organization in charge of its management, these demands were yet to be satisfied.

C. Recurring Demands for Priority, 1979-1981

In July 1979, Academician Nekrasov revealed that discussions were under way concerning the optimum level of oil and gas production for West Siberia in the Eleventh Five-Year Plan period (1981-1985).[138] Earlier that year, *Ekonomika i organizatsiya promyshlennogo proizvodstva*, revealing that long-range forecasts for oil extraction in Tyumen' province were still open to dispute (in contrast to gas-extraction prognoses), said in an editorial:

> Some organizations predict that the rates of output growth will decline substantially as early as the Twelfth Five-Year Plan. But province Party officials think that oil extraction can rise to a rate of 30-35 million tons annually. According to the adherents of this view, the level of oil extraction is limited not by its natural reserves, but by the country's economic resources. The volume of Tyumen' oil extraction will depend on whether the country can provide Tyumen' with pipes, drilling tools, machines, construction materials, finances, and so forth.[139]

The editorial stressed the importance of accurately determining the optimum level of oil production for the coming plan period:

> Without exaggeration, the accurate determination of future prospects is one of the key problems in developing the Tyumen' complex. It is extremely important to answer the question: How much oil will the complex produce in 1985--30, 50 or 70 million tons more than in 1980? It should not be forgotten that past underestimations of current production volumes have caused the Tyumen' workers many extra difficulties.
>
> An initial figure--the level of extraction--determines the volume of drilling and of construction-and-installation work. .... For the Tyumen' workers,

> it is important to have a clear picture of the future (production levels), with a year-by-year breakdown. Unfortunately, today they do not even know the main figures for 1981, to say nothing of those for years towards the end of the Eleventh or Twelfth Five-Year Plan.[140]

Apparently in support of the maximum development of West Siberian oil, Nesterov, head of the West Siberian Geological-Prospecting and Oil Research Institute (*ZapsibNIGNI*), reiterated in July of that year his claim that there were rich oil deposits to be tapped in many northern regions of West Siberia.[141] He called for more materials and equipment for prospecting and exploratory work there. Earlier, he was also quoted as saying that "if we are to replenish oil reserves, the volume of exploratory drilling must be sharply increased."[142] Similar demands were voiced by many others. V. Bidzhakov, Chief geologist of the Tomsk Territorial Administration of Geology, claiming that there was no doubt about the great potentialities of oil in his area, called for more geological works there.[143] In early 1980, Nesterov once again advanced his arguments for more exploratory drilling in West Siberia, and at that time he was seconded by Filanovskii, head of Gosplan's Oil and Gas Industry Department who was formerly chief engineer of Glavtyumenneftegaz.[144] Similar demands were also made by Party and economic officials in gas-extracting areas of West Siberia.[145] Finally, Academician Nekrasov lent his support to the argument by saying that "the preparation of new industrial reserves of gas and especially of oil is the most important problem for the development of the West Siberian oil and gas complex in the Eleventh Five-Year Plan and in the more distant future."[146]

In connection with production, the Siberian journal *Ekonomika i organizatsiya promyshlennogo proizvodstva* in the editorial quoted above singled out transportation and capital construction as the main problems confronting the West Siberian complex.[147] In the same issue, Glavtyumenneftegaz's Director Arzhanov also discussed a variety of problems ranging from the shortage of skilled drilling workers to the inadequacy of housing. Local gas officials were also active at this time in making their voices heard. For instance, Altunin, Tyumen' obkom Secretary who was formerly director of the Tyumen' Gas Industry Association (*Tyumengazprom*), said in an interview that more than four billion rubles had been invested in the gas industry in Tyumen' province, but "this is still not enough."[148]

He pointed out that the capacity of construction organizations was inadequate, and added that power supply and transportation would be the two main areas impeding the achievement of planned gas production. In June, G. Sulimenkov who succeeded Altunin as Director of Tyumengazprom said that the most important problem to be solved by the Siberian gas industry was the development of infrastructure, i.e. transportation, power supply, compressor stations and housing.[149] In Moscow, meanwhile, Gosplan's oil chief Filanovskii and others, calling attention to technical and economic problems facing future oil production in West Siberia, began to emphasize the potential of gas in the northern part of the region.[150] Two Moscow academics, Academician L. Melent'ev and energy economist A. Makarov, also argued in 1980 that "in the next five to eight years, it will be possible to substitute natural gas for oil as fuel."[151]

The pro-West Siberians wanted to have a development programme for the complex in order to deal with such problems as the preparation of reserves and capital construction in a more balanced long-term manner. By the late 1970s, many of them had still criticized the lack of any comprehensive programme as a serious obstacle in the development of the complex. Siberian economist Aganbegyan was quoted as saying in 1979 that weak aspects of the previous stage of the development had shown the extent to which it had lacked a long-range programme.[152] He urged that if the repetition of past mistakes was to be avoided, Tyumen' officials must provide such a programme without delay. According to Gosplan's oil and gas industry chief Filanovskii, local officials had actually called for the introduction of a programme as such:

> From the very beginning of organizing the extraction of oil and gas, when it became clear that West Siberia had large resources of hydrocarbon raw materials, local Party and Soviet organs time and again directed attention to the question of working out a long-term (over 15-20 years) comprehensive plan for development of the West Siberian complex.[153]

More recently, the Siberian Department of the USSR Academy of Sciences proposed such a plan. Just in time to coincide with Brezhnev's Siberian tour in early 1978, it made public a programme, entitled "The Comprehensive Development of Siberia's Natural Resources."[154] This programme was made up of 24 special-purpose programmes, which encompassed the core problems of making comprehensive use of the mineral, land and other resources of the region. Of these special programmes, according to Academician Trofimuk, the most important was the "West Siberian Oil and Gas Programme," which he said dealt with such questions as the optimum level of oil and gas extraction and their rational utilization.[155] In the following year, he stated that the West Siberian programme would help eliminate disproportions between the fast rate of oil extraction and the slow preparation of reserves in the area.[156]

The West Siberian programme was discussed extensively at two ensuing meetings. An enlarged meeting of the USSR Gosplan was held in December 1979 at which participants discussed "the most important problems of the development of productive forces in Siberia and of the accelerated introduction of scientific works of the Siberian Department of the USSR Academy of Sciences."[157] The meeting was attended by Gosplan Chairman N. K. Baibakov, RSFSR Gosplan Chairman N. I. Meslennikov, Academician G. I. Marchuk, Oil Minister N. A. Mal'tsev, and many other officials and scholars. At the meeting, Academician Marchuk who headed the Siberian Department of the USSR Academy of Sciences stressed that the Siberian Programme had been worked out by all the interested parties--local government and Party officials, and heads of economic enterprises and research institutes in Siberia.[158] In connection with the West Siberian subprogramme, Oil Minister Mal'tsev, who had succeeded the late Minister Shashin, agreed with Academician Trofimuk that exploratory drilling in West Siberia had been far from sufficient.[159] Academician A. P. Aleksandrov, President of the USSR Academy of Sciences, also supported the sharp increase in geological-exploratory work for oil and gas in Siberia.[160]

This meeting was followed in June 1980 by an all-Union conference in Novosibirsk on the development of the productive forces of Siberia.[161] Convened on the heels of the June plenum of the Party Central Committee, the conference dealt primarily with the accelerated development of the oil industry in West Siberia and the further growth of oil reserves there.[162] At that time, it was stressed that it was the first time since 1969 that such a large-scale meeting had been held to discuss the development of Siberian resources.[163] The participants included Academician Marchuk, now Deputy Chairman of the USSR Council of Ministers and Chairman of the State Committee for Science and Technology, and Academicians Trofimuk, D. K. Belyaev, Aganbegyan and Nekrasov.[164] Many regional Party leaders, central ministry officials and central planning officials also attended the meeting. The Soviet press at that time noted that the conference focused on those problems confronting the Siberian Programme.[165] Later, Academician V. Koptyug, newly-appointed President of the USSR Academy's Siberian Department, said that the Siberian Programme "has found its expression in the joint decree of the RSFSR Gosplan, RSFSR State Committee on Construction, and the Siberian Department, 'On Proposals for Development of Scientific-Technical Progress in the RSFSR'," and also in the recommendations made recently at the all-Union conference on the development of the productive forces of Siberia.[166] In 1981, Aganbegyan revealed that the West Siberian Programme along with two other subprogrammes of the Siberian Programme would be implemented during the Eleventh Five-Year Plan period, in accordance with the Directives of the Twenty-sixth Party Congress.[167]

With reference to the Siberian Programme, Academician Trofimuk advocated the necessity of new organizational devices in order to achieve the effective coordination of the activities of all the ministries and departments involved in the development of Siberian resources.[168] As we have seen, poor organizational coordination had been pointed to as one of the major problems in the development of the West Siberian oil and gas complex. In the management of the Soviet economy, it is an often heard refrain that "narrow departmentalism" frequently gain the upper hand.[169] The West Siberian development had been no exception to this rule. According to Aganbegyan, departmental fragmentation was so pervasive that even such organizations as Glavtyumenneftegaz and Glavtyumengeologiya, for example, were often unable to find a common language, even though they were involved in a common task.[170] In this connection, Gosplan's oil and gas industry head Filanovskii even went so far as to question the validity of the branch principle in industrial management, i.e. the exclusive management of each of the industrial branches by a relevant functional ministry and department:

> ...the problem of organizing effective management in the West Siberian oil and gas complex arises. In the first stage (of West Siberian development), branch management of the complex produced positive results and enabled the task of the accelerated development of the oil and gas industries, of power engineering, and of transport to be settled. At the present stage,

this principle has already outlived itself and causes numerous undesirable phenomena.[171]

What kind of organizational devices did the pro-West Siberians propose to create at that time? The two *Pravda* correspondents, S. Vtorushin and V. Sevastyanov, wrote as follows:

> Who will manage the complex? .... At present, local Party organs have to a great extent assumed the role of coordinators. But they have neither the authority nor the capability to solve large-scale inter-branch (*mezhotraslevyi*) problems. .... Economic problems often divert Party workers from other tasks that are no less important. The Tyumen' territorial-production complex requires an inter-departmental (*mezhvedomstvennyi*) coordinating agency endowed with broad powers. What body should be in charge of it? It seems to us that the higher the level of its competence is, the greater the benefits it will bring. It is important that this agency for the management of the complex have broad planning and financial authority.[172]

For the success of the Siberian Programme, Academician Trofimuk said that it would be necessary to create a coordinating council with full legal authority.[173] His colleague Aganbegyan also put forward some proposals related to the implementation of its regional subprogrammes:

> What organizational forms for the implementation of these regional programmes would one like to see? Some experience is available. When the programme for the Urals-Kuznetsk combine was completed, a government bureau was set up under the direction of V. V. Kuibyshev. Centralized management (*tsentralizovannoe rukovodstvo*) of the construction of the Baikal-Amur Mainline Railroad is being implemented successfully. It would be a good idea to manage the fulfillment of regional programmes in a similar fashion; the USSR Council of Ministers should have agents at the local level to resolve inter-branch problems.[174]

Earlier that year, Academician Nekrasov had made a similar suggestion for the development of the West Siberian complex:

> ...it is necessary to create a higher organ in charge of the management of the development of the productive forces of the complex. A state interdepartmental commission of the USSR Council of Ministers could become such an organ. In the 1930s during the formation of the Urals-Kuznetsk combine, a state interdepartmental commission was created which worked under the leadership of V. V. Kuibyshev, a member of Politburo *TsK VKP* (*b*) (the all-Union Communist Party [Bolsheviks]) and Chairman of the USSR Gosplan. The commission included prominent scholars, heads of People's Commissariats and of departments of local Party and Soviet organs. This commission coordinated the work of all the organizations, which were engaged in the solution of the combine's problems, determined the basic directions of the development and location of all the units in the territory of the complex, of scientific-research and design-survey works.[175]

Finally, in January 1981 a *Pravda* editorial ran as follows:

> Who should manage the territorial-production complex? Today, when the discussion is going on about the draft resolution of CC CPSU to be put before the Twenty-sixth Party Congress, not a few letters connected with this problem have been received by this editorial office. Some of them suggest the setting up of a body of the authorized agents of USSR Gosplan (*sistema upolnomochennykh Gosplana SSSR*) who are provided with appropriate rights, others (support) an interministerial coordinating council.[176]

It was against this background that Brezhnev in his speech to the Twenty-sixth Party Congress revealed the creation of two high-level coordinating organs concerned with the development of the West Siberian complex. According to the Party leader,

> Another urgent task is to overcome the lack of coordination between the actions of various departments. There was talk at the Twenty-fifth CPSU Congress about the need to create a system for the administration of groups of similar and interrelated branches. For this purpose, the USSR Gosplan has set up comprehensive interbranch (*mezhotraslevye*) subdivisions. The USSR Council of Ministers' Commission on Questions of the Development of the West Siberian Oil

> and Gas Complex, as well as an interdepartmental territorial commission of the USSR Gosplan, with headquarters in Tyumen', were formed recently. These are steps in the right direction. They are a help in improving the management of territorial-production complexes and in doing a better job of taking account of regional and branch interests (*regional'nye i otraslevye interesy*) and combining them. This work must be continued.[177]

The Gosplan commission was located in the West Siberian province. It was the first time in the history of the central planning organ that one of its divisions had been set up in a locality away from Moscow. V. Kuramin, former head of the Chief Tyumen' Administration for the Construction of Oil and Gas Industry Enterprises, was appointed as its chief. As for the Council of Ministers' commission, V. E. Dymshits, a deputy chairman of the Council, had been named to concurrently serve as its head.[178]

The pro-West Siberians expressed satisfaction over the results of the Twenty-sixth Party Congress. At the Congress, Tyumen' Party leader Bogomyakov said that particular importance would be attached to the acceleration of prospecting and exploratory work in order to prepare 500 million tons of oil and more than 500 billion cubic meters of gas for extraction by 1990.[179] B. Trofimov, a section chief of Tyumen' obkom, calling attention to the policy emphasis on West Siberian gas stressed by Brezhnev at the Congress, announced that the volume of capital investments in the oil and gas industry in West Siberia during the Eleventh Five-Year Plan period would exceed 55 billion rubles--more than twice the volume invested in the previous plan period.[180] In August of that year, a conference was held in the Party Central Committee to discuss questions related to the acceleration of the development of the gas industry and gas transportation in West Siberia.[181]

We have thus far examined various demands and complaints voiced by the proponents of the development of the West Siberian complex in connection with the three major policy changes effected in their favor, i.e. in 1969, 1977 and 1981. What were these demands and complaints? They complained about chronic supply bottlenecks and called for more effective implementation of existing policy. They also urged that special attention be paid to pressing regional problems such as housing and the construction of social infrastructure in the oil and gas regions of West

Siberia. At the same time, they made more far-reaching demands, most important of which was the demand for development priority. Perhaps the word most frequently used by the pro-West Siberian elements during the period was *"kompleksnyi,"* which can be variously translated as "comprehensive," "all-round," or "balanced." As early as 1966, for instance, they called for the "comprehensive development" of the region. In the name of comprehensive development, they wanted the central government to grant a special status to the West Siberian complex in resource allocation and other matters in preference to other industries and regions. Each of the policy shifts bearing upon the future of West Siberia demonstrated the success of the pro-West Siberians in pressing for their demands. In the area of resource allocation, the policy changes were each accompanied by sharp increases in capital investment in the complex. The proponents of the creation of the West Siberian complex also had long advocated an organization for the efficient management of the complex and they saw two commissions set up for the purpose. The pro-West Siberians were not the only ones who had been calling for the establishment of such organizations for a region or complex. For example, B. V. Isaev, First Secretary of Pavlodar obkom, had insisted that "the experience of creating our industrial complex (coal and electric power) shows that a territorial production complex needs a single boss."[182] It was, however, the proponents of the West Siberian hydrocarbon development who succeeded in persuading the central authorities to institute such organizations. Speaking at the Twenty-sixth Party Congress, Tyumen' Party leader Bogomyakov welcomed the creation of the USSR Council of Ministers' West Siberian commission. He remarked that it was improving the coordination of the activities of industrial ministries involved in the development of the complex.[183]

At the same time, it should be noted that those who supported the creation of a special organization for the West Siberian complex had to wait for at least a decade before their demand was met. As early as 1969 a scientific conference, held in Tyumen', recommended the setting up of an organization which would be charged with full responsibility for the development of hydrocarbon resources in West Siberia. At that time Shcherbina, the then Tyumen' Party leader, and others also called for the establishment of an agency within Gosplan and research institutes for the region.[184] This may indeed demonstrate that many of the pro-West Siberian demands--and the press campaigns in which these demands were expressed--had been initiated by the

West Siberians and their supporters. George Breslauer makes an interesting observation concerning the behavior of Tyumen' Party leader Bogomyakov, one of the most outspoken advocates of West Siberian development. Bogomyakov "signs articles that are strikingly iconoclastic, in ways different from all the other secretaries (in other RSFSR provinces)."[185] In other words, according to Breslauer, the Tyumen' leader interprets many development issues, including those connected with the allocation of resources, in terms of political conflict and resorts to the airing of debate in the media as a means of overcoming opposition to desired change. In fact, many other pro-West Siberians also resorted to similar tactics; for example, West Siberian geologists had few scruples about naming some of the so-called "pessimists" and "optimists" whom they criticized for standing in the way of accelerated geological-exploratory work in West Siberia. Another example may be provided by a correspondent of the Siberian mouthpiece, *Ekonomika i organizatsiya promyshlennogo proizvodstva*, who wrote an unusually outspoken article interpreting the issues related to the opening up of fuel resources in West Siberia in terms of conflicts of interests.[186]

The public discussions conducted by the pro-West Siberian elements show a certain pattern. In each policy debate, they made known their demands long before the change in policy in their favor came about. In the case of the 1969 decision, they discussed the opportunities presented by the newly opened oilfields in West Siberia and put forward policy proposals and recommendations through public discussions and promotional gatherings for several years prior to the decision. Likewise, for at least one year before the announcement of the 1977 decision, they were also engaged in promotional manoeuverings. In connection with the crash West Siberian development decision adopted at the Twenty-sixth Party Congress in 1981, the pro-West Siberian elements had been involved in public arguments in an organized way since at least 1979. It is important to note that many of the arguments they put forward shortly before the announcements of the policy changes appear to have been made in anticipation of impending formal decisions. As we have seen, two promotional gatherings were held in Siberia in May 1969, about half a year before the announcement of a formal decision on West Siberian oil development. Apparently in anticipation of the decision, the pro-West Siberians had stepped up their publicity campaigns. Similarly, a large-scale meeting was organized in Siberia in June 1980, about half a year before the convocation of the Twenty-sixth Party Congress, at which Brezhnev announced his West Siberia-based gas policy.[187] With regard to the December 1977 decision, one of the most outspoken articles on the problems of developing the West Siberian complex appeared in the November issue of a Siberian journal that year.[188] Its author, a local oil economist, openly criticized the existing policy of enhanced oil recovery in the old oilfields of the European USSR, which had been supported by USSR Gosplan Chairman Baibakov. Such a bold attack on existing policy would be inconceivable in the Soviet system unless a new policy position had already been adopted at the top. Finally, on each of these occasions, the formal decision was followed soon after by mobilizational campaigns.

In short, from these cases the following stages in Soviet energy policy formation may be discerned: (1) policy proposals (with public discussions as one form of such proposals) --> (2) decision in principle (or at least favorable responses from the leadership) --> (3) public discussions in anticipation of the adoption of the decision --> (4) formal decision --> (5) mobilizational discussions in support of the decision. In Chapter 4, we have examined the competing arguments concerning the development of West Siberian oil. In the cases considered here, the media controversy between the rival parties begins to disappear from view at stage (3). From that point public discussions become more one-sided. As for the pro-West Siberian public discussions, they also became more mobilizational in nature at stages (3) and (5) and seemed primarily intended to generate support for the new decision. In addition, promotional gatherings were mostly organized at these stages.[189]

What is important to identify here is that "decision in principle" had been preceded by "public discussions." In the case of the pro-West Siberian manoeuverings, public discussions in support of West Siberian development (stage 1) appeared long before the adoption of the formal decisions (stage 4). In the next chapter, we will examine the relationship between the pro-West Siberian public discussions and the leadership more closely.

NOTES

1. *Pravda*, February 16, 1970. ( ) added.
2. Broadly speaking, their promotional discussions

may be viewed as a continuation of old controversies about the rapid opening up of the country's eastern regions. Many observe that such controversies date back to the 1950s. V. Holubnychy argues that "just prior to and probably during the 21st Party congress (1959) there must have developed the first big fight between the proponents of further heavy investment in Siberia and those who advocated an emphasis on the European parts of the USSR." Vsevolod Holubnychy, "Spatial Efficiency in the Soviet Economy," in V. N. Bandera and Z. L. Melnyk (eds.), *The Soviet Economy in Regional Perspective* (New York, Praeger, 1973), p. 14. According to Robert North, rivalries have long been manifest concerning the development priorities of eastern resources including oil, the degree of processing in and out of the eastern region, the nature and location of supply bases and the choice of transport modes. Robert N. North, "Soviet Northern Development: The Case of NW Siberia," *Soviet Studies*, XXIV (October 1972), 171-199; and Robert N. North, *Transport in Western Siberia: Tsarist and Soviet Development* (Vancouver, University of British Columbia Press and the Center for Transportation Studies, 1979).

3. For example, see *Pravda*, December 4 and 14, 1964; *Literaturnaya gazeta*, December 12, 1964; and *Trud*, December 24, 1964 and February 19, 1965.

4. *Izvestiya*, March 6, 1965.

5. *Ibid.*, July 13, 1965.

6. *Pravda*, April 2, 1965.

7. M. Lavrent'ev and others, "Zapadno-Sibirskaya nizmennosti," *Ekonomicheskaya gazeta*, No. 24 (1965), p. 13.

8. Yu. Erv'e, "Bogatstva Tyumenskogo Severa," *Ekonomicheskaya gazeta*, No. 44 (1965), p. 35.

9. V. Tkachenko and others, "S chego nachinat' osvoenie Tyumenskoi kladovoi?," *Ekonomicheskaya gazeta*, No. 46 (1965), p. 17.

10. *Trud*, September 3 and 4, 1965; *Pravda*, December 19, 1965; and *Izvestiya*, December 29, 1965.

11. G. Ostryi, "Puti k Sibirskoi nefti," *Ekonomicheskaya gazeta*, No. 4 (1966), p. 17.

12. *Pravda*, February 27, 1966.

13. *Ibid.*, May 27, 1966.

14. A. Protozanov, "Perspektivy i zaboty Tyumeni," *Ekonomicheskaya gazeta*, No. 47 (1966), pp. 4-5.

15. Yu. Erv'e, "Pokoryayutsya nedra Sibiri," *Ekonomicheskaya gazeta*, No. 14 (1966), p. 11; and *Sovetskaya Rossiya*, August 14 and September 17, 1966.

16. Ye. Utrobin, "Vsei moshch'yu industrii," *Ekonomicheskaya gazeta*, No. 4 (1966), pp. 16-17.

17. "Nefti i gaz: Tomskoi zemli," *Ekonomicheskaya gazeta*, No. 32 (1966), pp. 19-20; and *Pravda*, September 23, 1966.
18. *Izvestiya*, June 30, 1966.
19. *Literaturnaya gazeta*, January 18, 1967.
20. *Ibid.*, February 22, 1967, p. 10.
21. *Trud*, January 5, 1967.
22. *Literaturnaya gazeta*, May 10, May 17, and June 7, 1967.
23. *Ibid.*, June 7, 1967.
24. *Sovetskaya Rossiya*, June 15, 1967. ( ) added.
25. *Literaturnaya gazeta*, December 13, 1967.
26. *Stroitel'naya gazeta*, October 8, 1967; *Izvestiya*, October 21, 1967; and *Trud*, December 23, 1967.
27. *Izvestiya*, February 11, 1968.
28. *Pravda*, February 26, 1968.
29. A. Nikitin and Ye. Vostrukhov, "Lyudi, boloto, tekhnika," *Ekonomicheskaya gazeta*, No. 25 (1968), pp. 16-17; and R. Urmantsev, "Na Tyumenskom meridiane," *Trud*, August 15, 1968.
30. *Pravda*, August 31, 1968.
31. *Sovetskaya Rossiya*, September 21, 1968.
32. *Pravda*, October 11, 1968.
33. *Ibid.*, December 17, 1968.
34. "Zemlya Tomskaya v budushchei pyatiletke," *Ekonomicheskaya gazeta*, No. 33 (1968), pp. 23-26; and *Pravda*, August 17, 1968.
35. Ye. Ligachev, "Segodnya i v perspektive," *Ekonomicheskaya gazeta*, No. 29 (1968), p. 5.
36. Ye. Ligachev, "Effektivnee ispol'zovat' bogatstvo Zapadno-Sibirskoi nizmennosti," *Ekonomicheskaya gazeta*, No. 8 (1968), pp. 6-7. In 1967, there were three articles which discussed the development of underground resources, especially natural gas, in Tomsk province. See *Izvestiya*, January 26, 1967; Ye. Vostrukhov, "Vasyuganskii koeffitsient," *Ekonomicheskaya gazeta*, No. 26 (1967), p. 33; and *Pravda*, September 22, 1967.
37. *Literaturnaya gazeta*, June 4, 1969, p. 10.
38. *Izvestiya*, May 27, 1969.
39. "Bol'shaya neft' Sibiri," *Ekonomicheskaya gazeta*, No. 22 (1969), p. 12.
40. Quoted in I. Ognev, "Yevropa-Sibir'," *Ekonomika i organizatsiya promyshlennogo proizvodstva*, No. 4 (1976), 155.
41. See Chapter 4, Section A.
42. *Izvestiya*, September 5, 1969. See also Chapter 4, footnote 45.

43. *Pravda*, May 23, 1969.
44. *Ibid.*, July 6, 1969. ( ) added.
45. *Ibid.*
46. *Trud*, September 2, 1969.
47. *Pravda*, October 15, 1969.
48. *Izvestiya*, September 5, 1969.
49. *Pravda*, November 30, 1969.
50. For example, see V. Belov and G. Ostryi, *Pravda*, August 20, 1969; M. A. Lavrent'ev and others, *Komsomol'skaya pravda*, October 25, 1969; A. M. Alekseev, Yu. T. Movsesyan, and L. I. Sevastyanov, "Dinamicheskaya model' razvitiya i razmeshcheniya neftedobyvayushchei promyshlennosti, stroitel'noi bazy i gorodov v raionakh Zapadno-Sibirskoi nizmennosti," *Izvestiya Sibirskogo otdeleniya AN SSSR*, seriya obshchestvennykh nauk, No. 11 (1969), 21-27.
51. The announcement was made more than a month after it had been adopted. On January 12, three days before the announcement of the decree, a meeting of heads of enterprises and organizations of the Oil Ministry had been held, at which Oil Minister V. D. Shashin had reported on the results of the December 1969 Party Central Committee plenum. *Pravda*, January 13, 1970.
52. *Sovetskaya Rossiya*, February 28, 1970.
53. B. Ye. Shcherbina, "Novye rubezhi Tyumenskikh neftyanikov," *Ekonomicheskaya gazeta*, No. 6 (1970), p. 5.
54. A. A. Trofimuk, "Da," bogaty!," *Ekonomicheskaya gazeta*, No. 3 (1970), p. 22.
55. A. A. Yamnov, "Prognozy i otkrytiya," *Ekonomicheskaya gazeta*, No. 2 (1970), p. 6.
56. N. Yeronin and V. Kremnev, "Uskorennymi tempami," *Ekonomicheskaya gazeta*, No. 49 (1970), p. 15.
57. "Neftyanye bogatstva Zapadnoi Sibiri--na sluzhbu narodnomu khozyaistvu," *Ekonomicheskaya gazeta*, No. 4 (1970), pp. 6-7. See also his contributions to *Pravda*, December 25, 1970; and *Trud*, December 25, 1970.
58. *Pravda*, February 27, 1970.
59. *Izvestiya*, June 7, 1970.
60. *Sovetskaya Rossiya*, September 3, 1970. ( ) added.
61. A. Nikitin and Ye. Vostrukhov, "Lyudi, boloto, technika," *Ekonomicheskaya gazeta*, No. 25 (1968), pp. 16-17; and "Inertsiya 'pervoi palatki'," *Ekonomicheskaya gazeta*, No. 26 (1968), pp. 14-15.
62. *Pravda*, September 2, 1969.
63. For example, see *Pravda*, February 12, 16, and 24; and March 8, 1970.
64. *Pravda*, October 11, 1968.

65. *Ekonomicheskaya gazeta*, No. 22 (1969), p. 13.
66. For example, see *Trud*, September 2, 1969.
67. *Ekonomicheskaya gazeta*, No. 6 (1970), p. 6.
68. *Sovetskaya Rossiya*, October 22, 1970.
69. *Literaturnaya gazeta*, June 4, 1969.
70. *Pravda*, December 17, 1968.
71. *Pravda*, August 31, 1968; and *Trud*, September 2, 1969.
72. *Ekonomicheskaya gazeta*, No. 6 (1970), p. 6.
73. *Sovetskaya Rossiya*, March 21, 1971.
74. *Pravda*, March 28, 1971.
75. *Literaturnaya gazeta*, January 2, 1971, p. 10.
76. *Sovetskaya Rossiya*, February 3, 1971.
77. "Ob investitsionnykh programmakh perspektivnogo razvitiya raionov Sibiri i Srednei Azii," *Ekonomika i organizatsiya promyshlennogo proizvodstva*, No. 6 (1971), 9.
78. V. I. Muravlenko, "Chto volnuet neftyanikov Zapadnoi Sibiri," *Ekonomicheskaya gazeta*, No. 20 (1973), p. 15.
79. For example, see *Trud*, November 11, 1973.
80. Muravlenko, "Chto volnuet neftyanikov Zapadnoi Sibiri." He had also expressed similar concern in the previous year. *Izvestiya*, July 18, 1972.
81. *Pravda*, November 23, 1973.
82. V. Shashin, "Puti povysheniya effektivnosti neftyanoi promyshlennosti," *Planovoe khozyaistvo*, No. 4 (1973), 21.
83. *Pravda*, November 23, 1973.
84. *Ibid.*, January 22, 1974.
85. In 1975, Shcherbina advocated the fast opening up of West Siberian gas resources as a mighty helpmate of oil. *Pravda*, June 12, 1975.
86. See, for example, *Pravda*, December 1, 1973; and *Ekonomicheskaya gazeta*, No. 11 (1974), pp. 7-8; No. 14 (1974), p. 10; No. 23 (1974), p. 10; and No. 29 (1974), p. 10.
87. For example, see *Ekonomicheskaya gazeta*, No. 27 (1974), pp. 1-2; A. Lalayants, "Dva obshchestva--dve linii v razvitii toplivno-energeticheskogo kompleksa," *Planovoe khozyaistvo*, No. 4 (1975), 20-31; and Yu. Bokserman, "Puti povysheniya effektivnosti transporta topliva," *Planovoe khozyaistvo*, No. 2 (1975), 20-29.
88. For instance, see an article by A. Geodekyan, Deputy Director of the Institute of Oceanology of the USSR Academy of Sciences, in *Pravda*, May 29, 1974.
89. For example, see V. Kirillin, "Energetika--problemy i perspektivy," *Kommunist*, No. 1 (1975), 43-51. The

article was one of the speeches delivered at an annual meeting of the USSR Academy of Sciences in November 1974. *Vestnik Akademii Nauk SSSR*, No. 2 (1975), 3-31.

90. *Sotsialisticheskaya industriya*, September 13, 1974.

91. *Pravda*, February 19, 1975.

92. *Ibid.*

93. *Pravda*, June 11, 1975.

94. *Ibid.*

95. *Ibid.*, February 19, 1976.

96. V. D. Shashin, "Gorizonty neftyanoi industrii," *Ekonomicheskaya gazeta*, No. 22 (1976), p. 4.

97. *Pravda*, January 28, 1976.

98. *Ibid.*, June 11, 1975.

99. "Tyumenskii kompleks: segodnya i v perspektive," *Ekonomicheskaya gazeta*, No. 19 (1975), p. 6.

100. V. Varlamov and I. Panfilov, "Osnovnye napravleniya formirovaniya territorial'no-proizvodstvennogo kompleksa Zapadno-Sibirskoi ravniny," *Planovoe khozyaistvo*, No. 10 (1974), 58.

101. *Pravda*, June 11, 1975.

102. *Trud*, December 19, 1975.

103. See Chapter 3, footnote 73.

104. Ognev, pp. 154-180.

105. *Ibid.*, pp. 156-158.

106. "Zapadnaya Sibir'--glavnaya neftedobyvayushchaya baza strany," *Ekonomicheskaya gazeta*, No. 16 (1977), p. 13.

107. *Sovetskaya Rossiya*, December 22, 1976. See also footnote 95 of the present chapter.

108. *Sovetskaya Rossiya*, March 24, 1977.

109. "Geologiya i industriya," *Pravda*, January 14, 1977.

110. *Pravda*, August 10, 1977. ( ) added.

111. *Ibid.*

112. R. I. Kuzovatkin, "Front i tyl Samotlora," *Ekonomika i organizatsiya promyshlennogo proizvodstva*, No. 6 (1976), 80-81. ( ) added.

113. *Ibid.*, pp. 83-84.

114. *Ekonomicheskaya gazeta*, No. 16 (1977), p. 13.

115. *Pravda*, February 26 and 27, 1977.

116. *Ibid.*, February 26, 1977.

117. A. Beschinskii and R. Vitebskii, "Energetika i razmeshchenie promyshlennogo proizvodstva," *Voprosy ekonomiki*, No. 5 (1977), 35-46, esp. 40.

118. L. P. Guzhnovskii, "Sibirskii vklad v neftyanoe mogushchestvo strany," *Ekonomika i organizatsiya promyshlennogo proizvodstva*, No. 6 (1977), 35-43.

119. *Ibid.*, pp. 35-36. ( ) added.
120. *Ibid.*, pp. 36-37.
121. L. I. Churikov, N. A. Sesin, and V. A. Dyukanov, "Geologorazvedka i neft'," *Ekonomika i organizatsiya promyshlennogo proizvodstva*, No. 6 (1977), 43-46.
122. *Literaturnaya gazeta*, January 18, 1978.
123. *Pravda*, December 18, 1977.
124. *Literaturnaya gazeta*, January 18, 1978.
125. *Trud*, February 21, 1978.
126. For example, see "K Severu ot Tyumeni," *Kommunist*, No. 8 (1978), 33-42; *Pravda*, June 5, June 10, July 14, and October 17, 1978; *Izvestiya*, January 18, February 17, February 24, and April 19, 1978; *Sovetskaya Rossiya*, May 16, 1978; *Sotsialisticheskaya industriya*, April 12, 1978; and *Trud*, April 11, 1978.
127. The journals represented at the meeting were *Planovoe khozyaistvo* (No. 9, 1978), *Voprosy filosofii*, (No. 9, 1978), *Voprosy ekonomiki* (No. 8, 1978), *Ekonomika i organizatsiya promyshlennogo proizvodstva*, (No. 2, 1979), and *Sovetskoe gosudarstvo i pravo*.
128. *Ekonomicheskaya gazeta*, No. 25 (1978), p. 3.
129. For instance, see "Osnovnye problemy kompleksnogo razvitiya Zapadnoi Sibiri," *Voprosy ekonomiki*, No. 8 (1978), 15-37; and "Kompleksnoe razvitie proizvoditel'nykh sil Zapadnoi Sibiri--v tsentre vnimaniya uchenykh i prakticheskikh rabotnikov," *Planovoe khozyaistvo*, No. 9 (1978), 97-114.
130. "Kompleksnoe razvitie...," *Planovoe khozyaistvo*, No. 9 (1978), 98.
131. "Osnovnye problemy...," *Voprosy ekonomiki*, No. 8 (1978), 23.
132. *Ibid.*, pp. 19f.
133. *Trud*, February 21, 1978.
134. Kuzovatkin, *Ekonomika i organizatsiya promyshlennogo proizvodstva*, No. 6 (1976), 86-87.
135. *Pravda*, January 16, 1978.
136. *Trud*, May 27, 1978.
137. *Literaturnaya gazeta*, February 18, 1976, p. 11.
138. *Trud*, July 12, 1979.
139. "Ne chislom, a umeniem," *Ekonomika i organizatsiya promyshlennogo proizvodstva*, No. 2 (1979), 6.
140. *Ibid.* ( ) added.
141. *Pravda*, July 22, 1979.
142. *Ibid.*, May 17, 1979.
143. *Sovetskaya Rossiya*, September 11, 1979.
144. I. Nesterov, "Neftegazovyi potentsial Zapadnoi Sibiri," *Ekonomicheskaya gazeta*, No. 11 (1980), p. 15; and

V. Filanovskii, "Zapadno-Sibirskii neftegazovyi kompleks: rezul'taty i perspektivy," *Planovoe khozyaistvo*, No. 3 (1980), 21.

145. For example, see V. Strizhov and R. Dadashev, "Ekonomika severnogo gazopromysla," *Ekonomicheskaya gazeta*, No. 25 (1980); and V. Kozlov and others, *Trud*, August 26, 1980.

146. *Trud*, July 12, 1979.

147. "Ne chislom, a umeniem," pp. 5 and 11.

148. Ye. N. Altunin, "Strategiyu vydirat' segodnya," *Ekonomika i organizatsiya promyshlennogo proizvodstva*, No. 2 (1979), 15.

149. *Sovetskaya Rossiya*, June 28, 1979.

150. Filanovskii, "Zapadno-Sibirskii neftegazovyi kompleks," pp. 23-24.

151. L. Melent'ev and A. Makarov, "Perspektivnoe razvitie toplivno-energeticheskogo kompleksa," *Planovoe khozyaistvo*, No. 4 (1980), 91.

152. *Pravda*, May 17, 1979.

153. Filanovskii, "Zapadno-Sibirskii neftegazovyi kompleks," p. 25.

154. On the Siberian Programme, see an interview given in 1978 by Academician G. I. Marchuk, Chairman of the Siberian Department of the USSR Academy of Sciences. *Literaturnaya gazeta*, May 1, 1978. According to Academician Trofimuk, the Programme was worked out in response to a CC CPSU resolution, "O deyatel'nosti SO AN SSSR," *Izvestiya*, March 31, 1978.

155. *Izvestiya*, March 31, 1978.

156. *Trud*, January 11, 1979. See also the following articles contributed by the academician. *Sovetskaya Rossiya*, August 9, 1979; and "Kompleksnaya programma 'Sibir'," *Ekonomicheskaya gazeta*, No. 30 (1979), p. 6.

157. "Uskorennoe razvitie proizvoditel'nykh sil Sibiri--vazhneishaya narodnokhozyaistvennaya zadacha," *Planovoe khozyaistvo*, No. 3 (1980), 120. Brezhnev had remarked at the November plenum of the Party Central Committee in 1978 that Gosplan would soon draw up a long-term national economic plan. Speaking at an ensuing CC plenum, held just a year later, the Party leader stressed the necessity of a long-term energy plan. *Pravda*, November 28, 1979.

158. "Uskorennoe razvitie...," *Planovoe khozyaistvo*, No. 3 (1980), 122.

159. *Ibid.*, p. 123.

160. *Ibid.*, p. 124.

161. "Materialy k vsesoyuznoi konferentsii po razvitiyu proizvoditel'nykh sil Sibiri," *Izvestiya Sibirskogo*

otdeleniya Akademi Nauk SSSR, seriya obshchestvennykh nauk, No. 6 (1980), 10.

162. *Izvestiya*, June 29, 1980. In April 1980, it was also reported, a conference was held in the CC CPSU to discuss stepping up capital construction in the oil and gas region of West Siberia. *Pravda*, April 15, 1980.

163. *Izvestiya*, June 29, 1980.

164. "Nauchnaya konferentsiya," *Ekonomicheskaya gazeta*, No. 25 (1980), p. 16.

165. For example, see *Ibid.* and *Trud*, August 21, 1980.

166. *Trud*, August 21, 1980.

167. *Sotsialisticheskaya industriya*, May 8, 1981.

168. *Sovetskaya Rossiya*, August 9, 1979.

169. For example, see *Pravda*, May 17, 1979.

170. *Sotsialisticheskaya industriya*, May 8, 1981.

171. Filanovskii, "Zapadno-Sibirskii neftegazovyi kompleks,"p. 24. ( ) added.

172. *Pravda*, May 17, 1979.

173. *Trud*, January 11, 1979.

174. *Pravda*, December 7, 1979.

175. *Trud*, July 12, 1979. ( ) added.

176. "Vozvoditsya kompleks," *Pravda*, January 29, 1981. ( ) added.

177. *Pravda*, February 24, 1981.

178. "The Government of the USSR," *Radio Liberty Research*, RL 338/82 (August 20, 1982), p. 3.

179. *Pravda*, February 27, 1981.

180. B. Trofimov, "Formirovanie Tyumenskogo neftegazovogo kompleksa," *Planovoe khozyaistvo*, No. 9 (1981), 85.

181. *Izvestiya*, August 15, 1981.

182. *Pravda*, July 3, 1977. ( ) added.

183. *Ibid.*, February 27, 1981.

184. See footnotes 69-72 of the present chapter.

185. George W. Breslauer, "Is There A Generation Gap in the Soviet Political Establishment?: Demand Articulation by RSFSR Provincial Party First Secretaries," *Soviet Studies*, XXXVI (January 1984), 20. ( ) added.

186. See footnote 104 of the present chapter.

187. See footnote 161 of the present chapter.

188. See footnote 118 of the present chapter.

189. Khaim Groys, an emigre who formerly worked at a power engineering institute in the Soviet Union, testifies that the Soviet authorities, after making a decision, used to refer the issue to public debate to determine the best

ways of implementing it. (Personal communication in October 1982. He is currently working at Radio Liberty in Munich, West Germany.)

6

The Soviet Leadership on West Siberian Oil

We have seen that a media controversy had raged on the issue of energy strategy in the Soviet Union during the 1970s. Disagreement was not simply between the advocates of West Siberian development and their opponents, but also between two Soviet leaders--L. I. Brezhnev, the then Party General Secretary, and A. N. Kosygin, ex-Chairman of the USSR Council of Ministers. As noted earlier, each identified himself with an alternative policy orientation: The government leader espoused a more balanced approach in the exploitation of energy sources with relatively greater emphasis placed on non-hydrocarbons; the Party boss preferred the priority development of the oil and gas resources of West Siberia. This chapter will examine what conception each of the two Soviet leaders had of the West Siberian development and what role the advocates of West Siberian oil played in influencing the policy position of the leadership. If media debate in the Soviet Union functions to give the leadership necessary information to formulate policy, a contending party in the debate can be said to be influential to the degree that the leadership adopts a policy position along lines suggested by that party.

At the time of the announcement of the West Siberian oil programme of 1969, neither leader added any comments about it. About a year later, however, Kosygin declared in his speech to the Twenty-fourth Party Congress that "the extraction of oil will be developed on a large scale in the major new deposits of Tyumen' and Mangyshlak, where it is envisaged that 75 percent of the total increment in oil extraction will be obtained."[1] Brezhnev also stressed in his Congress report that "one of the main tasks of the five-year plan is the pacesetting (*operezhayushchye*) and more efficient development of the fuel and power complex."[2] He called, among other things, for an increase in the share of oil and gas in the country's fuel balance. He referred to "the programme for the development of the huge oil-bearing region in West Siberia" as one of the most successfully "coordinated efforts by many branches and economic regions" in the recent years.[3]

The Party leader had long taken a positive attitude towards the development of the natural resources, especially fuel and power, situated in the eastern part of the country. As early as 1966, he had declared that the further development of Siberia and the Soviet Far East had become a "problem of great economic and political significance."[4] It is clear that he had paid close attention to West Siberian fuel development. In general, however, it appears that Kosygin as the country's chief economic administrator played a role more salient than that of any other Soviet leader in energy affairs up to at least the middle of the 1970s. Brezhnev, for all his interest in these matters, and especially in the West Siberian programme, seems to have been less involved in them. In many of his public speeches, the Party leader had made only a few general comments on energy affairs in comparison to his detailed treatment of agriculture and other issues.[5] By contrast, Kosygin paid uninterrupted attention to energy matters. In 1972, he called for a more effective use of fuel, pointing out that there was an unjustifiably high consumption of fuel and power at industrial enterprises and in public services.[6] As for West Siberian oil and gas, the government chief noted that oil and gas from Tyumen' together with that from other new fields would meet the fuel requirements of the country's central and western regions.[7] In 1974, he expressed his satisfaction with the performance of the oil and gas industry in West Siberia:

> The Twenty-fourth Congress of the CPSU set the task of considerably increasing oil and gas extraction in West Siberia. In the past 10 years, large fuel production bases have been newly created on the basis of the discovery of the richest deposits--mainly in Tyumen' province. It is now safe to say that Tyumen' province will yield nearly four times as much oil in 1974 as in 1970, and that gas output will increase 2.6 times.
>
> .... The target set by the Twenty-fourth Congress of the Party will be overfulfilled.[8]

He made an inspection tour of Tyumen' and other fuel-extracting regions in the eastern part of the country almost every year during the first half of the 1970s.[9]

Oil and gas, however, were not the only things to attract the attention of the country's top economic manager. In 1972, for instance, Kosygin said that atomic power stations were acquiring practical significance and were being built on a large scale. At that time, he emphasized that the economic efficiency of atomic power stations had "become fully competitive with that of thermal power stations in regions remote from cheap fuel sources."[10] At the Twenty-fourth Party Congress, the premier announced a programme for the construction of atomic power stations with a total capacity of 30 million kilowatts over a period of 10-12 years, which he said would "reduce capital investments in the development of the coal industry by three billion rubles."[11] As to the coal industry, he showed no more than a passing interest in it, merely commenting that its production would continue to grow alongside that of oil and gas, and this growth would chiefly be achieved by the introduction of open-cast mining.[12]

In the course of time, however, the government leader became more cautious about the prospects of the country's fuel and power supply. Calling for more "careful and rational" utilization of natural resources, he said in a speech in 1974 that "our country is endowed with everything necessary so that the Soviet economy could develop dynamically. .... Our resources are great. But they are not unlimited."[13] He made the remarks about three weeks after Party leader Brezhnev had commented on the same topic in a tone of optimism: "Our country is a country of incalculable wealth and inexhaustible possibilities. The matter is only correctly to use these riches and possibilities in a proprietary way (*po-khozyaiski*)."[14] It may be incautious to estimate differences of view between the two Soviet leaders concerning the country's natural resource potentials solely on the basis of such brief quotations as above, but at least they seem to show that at that time Kosygin was more wary of the country's energy future than was Brezhnev.

As a consequence of this position, Kosygin initiated in 1976 his "balanced" energy policy with emphasis on the rapid development of coal as a substitute for oil and gas. In 1977, he described the situation of the Soviet oil and gas industry as follows:

> The resources of oil and gas in the European part of the USSR are declining, and the centers of oil and gas extraction are shifting to the remote northern and eastern regions where the production conditions are more difficult. The outlays for prospecting, development and industrial exploitation, as well as maintaining extraction levels and transport, are rising substantially. The need for pipes, compressors and special construction machinery is growing. The Soviet Union has been compelled to increase investments and build several gas and oil pipelines from the northern regions of Tyumen' to the Center, each of which is twice as long as the Orenburg pipelines. All this naturally affects the growth rate of oil output.
>
> In these complicated conditions for developing the fuel industries, we are planning a set of measures to ensure a more rational and economic use of available fuel resources.[15]

He then reiterated such measures as had already been enunciated the previous year: to raise the share of hard fuels, mainly eastern coal, in the production of electric power and heat; to develop atomic power stations in the energy-poor European USSR; to reduce consumption of oil as a fuel; and so forth.[16]

At that time, Brezhnev's interest in the energy matter was still peripheral in comparison with the keen attention he paid to agriculture. But the Party leader clearly endorsed the pro-coal policy as he said that "the increase in oil production will bring hardly anything, if a considerable amount of oil will be burnt as fuel instead of being utilized to obtain more valuable kinds of fuel and petrochemical products, and to increase export resources."[17] When Brezhnev initiated the crash West Siberian oil programme in 1977, *Pravda* included the following passage in a shortened version of his speech delivered at the December plenum of the Party Central Committee that year:

> Coal, whose production is to rise to 746 million tons in 1978, has occupied and will continue to take an important place in the fuel and power balance of the country. .... Hydro and atomic power will also be developed at an exceptionally rapid speed.[18]

At the November 1979 Party plenum, Brezhnev repeated the need to develop the coal industry and atomic power engineering.[19]

Despite the announcement of the pro-oil policy, meanwhile, Kosygin continued to express his preference for a balanced energy approach. In 1978, the government head argued that "the rise in the share of nuclear power and coal in the fuel and power balance will make it possible to save vast quantities of gas and oil, which are irreplaceable sources of chemical raw materials."[20] He pointed out that unique deposits of coal would make it possible to provide for an effective restructuring of the country's fuel balance.[21] In 1979, the government leader still emphasized the need to develop atomic power stations and cheap coal in the Eleventh Plan period:

> This year, considerable work is to be done to draw up the plan for the Eleventh Five-Year Plan period and the main guidelines for the economic and social development of the USSR up to the year 1990.
>
> .... In the new five-year plan period, the further development of fuel and power complexes is to be carried out to a considerable extent. .... It is of particular importance to make use of the opportunities offered by nuclear power. .... This will not only provide a major saving on fossil fuels but also get rid of the need to transport tremendous quantities of fuel from the eastern regions to the European part of the country.
>
> In addition, it is planned to rapidly develop extremely rich deposits of cheap coals, mined by the open-cast method in the eastern regions of the country....[22]

In that same year, however, Kosygin also expressed high approval for the achievement of the oil industry in West Siberia, praising the Party for its economic development policy:

> As in other spheres of economic affairs, new phenomena are clearly traceable in the allocation of the productive forces: growth in scale, acceleration of the speed and intensification of the comprehensiveness of the development of new areas, the bringing into being of new ways of organizing the process. A striking example is the development of the oil industry in recent years. Not so long ago the Volga region, where the main development took place in the 1950s, was still the main oil region. It took more than two decades to reach an annual oil production there of 100

> million tons. In West Siberia, where the opening up of new oilfields began in the 1960s, and proceeded in much more difficult natural and economic conditions, that level was achieved in 10 years. At the present time, more than one billion tons of oil and an enormous quantity of gas have been extracted in West Siberia. The basis for these results was a firm fusion of the genuine heroism of the workers of West Siberia, boldness of technical thinking and the wisdom of the Party's economic policy.
>
> The building of a powerful base for the extraction of oil and gas in West Siberia in the past 10-15 years was the biggest shift in the distribution of productive forces in the whole history of our economic development. Its significance for our economy can hardly be overrated. The growth in production of these important raw materials in the present five-year period and in the longer term will come exclusively from the Siberian fields.[23]

In 1978, the government chief revealed that the exploration and development of the natural resources of West Siberia had been one of the major tasks in which he and his subordinates in the USSR Council of Ministers had been engaged.[24]

Does this mean that the two leaders achieved a consensus in energy strategy? We cannot rule out this possibility since there was at least a semblance of agreement between them as evidenced by their recognition of each other's policy positions as shown above. It would be unthinkable that the government chief had worked out energy policy on his own, without any consultation with the Party leadership, when in 1976 he announced the shift towards a greater emphasis on coal. When Brezhnev switched to the pro-oil policy the following year, he did not then deny the need to develop other types of energy sources to ease the burden on the oil industry. In the course of time, he even coopted many of Kosygin's policy proposals in the area. In general, Kosygin was reticent about the crash development policy of West Siberian oil and gas in the latter part of the 1970s. At the same time, however, there are no indications that he challenged the "wisdom" of the policy reversal implemented by Brezhnev. More importantly, the government leader also made a trip to Tyumen' and other industrial centers in Siberia in March 1978, a week before Brezhnev started a similar tour of the eastern region apparently as part of his campaign to rally support for his Siberian oil programme.[25] If we accept that there was a consensus between the two leaders, the series of changes in Soviet energy policy may be interpreted more as a concerted reaction to the worsening energy problems of the country during the period than as the result of differences between energy conceptions of the two leaders.

But there is also a strong possibility that the two leaders were at loggerheads with each other in energy affairs. The very evidence that has been employed to uphold the notion of leadership consensus can be used to support the opposite. The recognition by one of the leaders of the need to develop those fuel and power industries that the other favored may have been nothing more than a manoeuvre in a subtle political game. When Brezhnev, for instance, stressed the urgency of West Siberian oil development in 1977, he did not make any special mention of coal and other types of energy sources. His speech given before the December plenum of that year reads as follows: "We have developed and will develop the extraction of coal and atomic energy, and will construct hydroelectric power stations. But looking at things realistically, we certainly have to admit that the decisive role in supplying fuel and power ...will remain with oil and gas, first of all from Tyumen'."[26] But a *Pravda* editorial, carried about a week later to feature the plenum decision, emphasized the importance of non-hydrocarbon fuel sources in a separate paragraph.[27]

The following may be taken to serve as good evidence of basic disagreements between Brezhnev and Kosygin over energy strategy. An important rationale for the rapid development of West Siberian oil and gas resources was that the cost of developing them could be justified in consideration of the high energy prices on the world market. Thus Brezhnev stressed in 1977 that the fuel and power sector "has paramount importance both for the development of our economy, for the economy of socialist countries and for foreign trade."[28] In 1981, he was more concrete in his assertion that the West Siberian fuel programme would benefit the country by exporting oil and gas to the capitalist countries: West Siberia has gas reserves so gigantic that "for many years they can provide for both the country's domestic requirements and its export needs, including exports to capitalist countries."[29] In fact, the Party leader had over a period of many years taken a position in favor of expanded economic relations with Western capitalist countries. For instance, he said at the Twenty-fourth Party

Congress in 1971 that "the improvement of the system of foreign economic relations is an important reserve for increasing the economic efficiency of the national economy."[30] It was at the Twenty-fifth Party Congress in particular that the Party leader evinced a good deal of enthusiasm for attracting foreign capital and technology as well as consumer goods.[31] In the area of energy policy, he had long been identified with the policy of attracting Western capital through the so-called compensation deals (*kompensatsionnye sdelki*) such as the pipe-for-gas barter with West Germany.[32] In May 1978, Brezhnev himself visited West Germany and signed long-term economic agreements with the Bonn government in which the Soviet Union was to supply natural gas and other raw materials to West Germany in return for German credit.[33] About a month before Moscow and Bonn signed a second agreement in July 1980, N. A. Tikhonov, the then First Deputy Chairman of the USSR Council of Ministers, reportedly told German officials that a debate was going on over whether to export new gas or keep it within the Soviet bloc.[34] This could easily have been a bluff, i.e. a negotiating move to pressure the Germans to pay a better price.

According to a Western sovietologist, however, "some members of the Politburo (indeed) have opposed such barter deals in the past, basing their case on the risks inherent in mortgaging the Soviet patrimony to foreigners."[35] He implied that it was Kosygin in particular who was opposed to Brezhnev's compensation deals. If the above assertion is right, it may be used to support the notion of leadership disagreements over energy strategy. In fact, Kosygin had said in 1975 that Soviet economic relations with the United States were held back by the discriminatory nature of the American trade laws adopted in December 1974. He said that "in the light of the long-term interests of the two countries, we regard this as a reverse (*zigzag*) in our relations."[36] At the Twenty-fifth Party Congress, however, he noted that the rapid growth in the fuel and power base had ensured the satisfaction of the requirements of the country's economy and also the "fulfillment, in the main, of contract commitments for the supply of fuel to foreign countries."[37] He believed that compensation agreements would provide the long-term pattern for cooperation with Western industrial countries.[38] At that time, he may have had in mind West Germany and other West European countries rather than the United States. In any case, the government leader remained reticent on the subject after this time.

Based on an interview, with a former Soviet journalist who contributed to Soviet publications on the subject of energy before emigrating to the West, Lilita Dzirkals and others argue that "the appearance of a disagreement between Brezhnev and Kosygin over basic strategy in energy development was real enough, although unrelated to any power struggle between them."[39] Many Western specialists believe that the two Soviet leaders often disagreed with each other over many other policy issues. Since the mid-1970s, according to George Breslauer, they differed with each other in their approaches to the problems of agriculture, overall investment priorities, and economic management.[40] He contends that Brezhnev was increasingly impatient to "secure a quick improvement in economic performance that would bolster his authority."[41] But Kosygin as the country's chief administrator would have espoused a more orthodox, balanced policy--with support from elements in his government bureaucracy. If the above interpretation is right, it is rather unlikely that the two leaders were in harmony on such a major policy issue as energy. In any case, it can be concluded from their policy pronouncements that Brezhnev was more determined to develop oil and gas resources in West Siberia than Kosygin.

What then persuaded the General Secretary to come out in favor of the crash development of West Siberian oil and gas? During his tour of Siberia and the Soviet Far East in the spring of 1978, he said that the December Central Committee plenum of the previous year discussed various "bottlenecks" (*uzkie mesta*) and difficulties that confronted the Soviet industry.[42] It was just before this tour that he announced the crash development policy of West Siberian oil and gas. It seems that at that time the Party leader viewed the problem of the oil industry not as a shortage of reserves but as a question of construction bottlenecks, supply difficulties, and investment requirements. If this is true, it was just what the supporters of West Siberian energy development had long emphasized. They certainly found an unexpected supporter in the U.S. Central Intelligence Agency (CIA) when it published reports concerning prospects for Soviet oil production in mid-1977. The CIA predicted that Soviet oil production would peak in 1980, then begin to decline sharply, so that the Soviet Union would soon become a net oil importer.[43] It added that the output plans for West Siberia in 1980 did not appear attainable because of extensive drilling requirements and other related problems. Marshall Goldman observes that "there are indications that the report proved to be a major factor in prodding the Soviet authorities into action."[44] Another important factor which encouraged Brezhnev to support the crash West Siberian oil and gas development would be the crucial role of hydrocarbons in Soviet exports. In 1977, for instance, oil was a source of 52 percent of Soviet hard currency earnings and 28 percent of its overall trade earnings.[45] As was noted earlier, the Party leader had given great importance to trade especially with Western industrial countries. No doubt he firmly believed that the cost of developing West Siberian oil and gas could be fully recovered. Again, this is another rationale put forward by the pro-West Siberian elements. In June 1978, for example, Siberian economist A. Aganbegyan claimed that the hydrocarbons extracted in Tyumen' province during the Tenth Plan period would be valued at more than 100 billion rubles as the "world" price of oil was about 70-80 rubles per ton.[46] More recently, a group of Soviet energy specialists even argued that the size of the country's foreign currency earnings depends on the volume of oil output. According to them, capital investments in the (West Siberian) oil and gas complex can thus determine the volume of the Soviet foreign trade turnover.[47]

In the wake of the 1977 decision, Tyumen' Party leader Bogomyakov revealed that there had been a controversy over the future course of oil and gas development in West Siberia:

> What next (after 1980)? How to increase (oil and gas) output? This question, undoubtedly, alarmed many. Concerning the future, there were not a few contradictory opinions until recently. (But) instructions of the December plenum of the CC CPSU (1977) clearly defined the place of the Tyumen' complex in satisfying the country's need for oil and gas.[48]

The above passage again shows that the pro-West Siberians succeeded in persuading the General Secretary. In view of Brezhnev's previous preference for West Siberian oil and gas, it must have been easier for them to convince him of the benefit to be obtained by the further development of Siberian oil and gas resources.

Brezhnev's role in energy policy-making became conspicuous from that time on and this became a factor in the pro-West Siberians' favor. Until then, energy priorities had been Kosygin's bailiwick. But it was no longer the government leader but the General Secretary who thereafter made any important alterations in Soviet energy policy. At the Twenty-sixth Party Congress, Brezhnev gave primary consideration to energy policy before turning to any other sector including agriculture, which had long enjoyed top-priority attention in the Soviet Union.[49] He stressed at the October 1980 Party plenum that the Politburo supported his proposal for the accelerated development of the oil and gas industry in West Siberia.[50] He affirmed at the 1981 Party Congress that his West Siberian programme was supported by the Party Central Committee, urging that the Congress also endorse it.[51] Meanwhile, the ailing Soviet premier retired from his post in October 1980 and died two months later. He was succeeded by N. A. Tikhonov, one of Brezhnev's close associates. The new premier fully accepted Brezhnev's gas programme:

> The Eleventh Five-Year Plan is the first stage in carrying out the energy programme of the USSR, which has been *worked out at the initiative of Leonid I. Brezhnev*. Prime significance is attached in it to the accelerated development of the gas industry, above all in West Siberia with its reliable raw material base. It is planned that the entire increment in gas production will come from West Siberia during the new five-year plan.[52]

At the same time as the involvement of the Party leader in energy policy-making was becoming more prominent, the role of the Party in this area apparently also became more conspicuous. In April 1980, for instance, a conference was held in the Central Committee to discuss stepping up capital construction in the oil and gas regions of West Siberia.[53] V. I. Dolgikh, Central Committee Secretary, made a keynote speech at the meeting.[54] Two provincial Party leaders, Tyumen' obkom First Secretary G. P. Bogomyakov and his Tomsk counterpart Ye. K. Ligachev, were present. Also of relevance here is the manner in which Tyumen' leader Bogomyakov, speaking at the Twenty-sixth Party Congress, emphasized the Party involvement in the West Siberian oil and gas programme:

> The questions connected with (the fulfillment of Party decisions for the development of oil and gas resources in Tyumen' province) have been discussed more than once at Central Committee plenums, in the Politburo, and in the Secretariat. The secretaries of the Party

> Central Committee and Central Committee departments have systematically and exactingly supervised the carrying out of the tasks.[55]

The West Siberian leader was certainly trying to use the forum to put pressure on opponents of West Siberia.

NOTES

1. A. N. Kosygin, "Direktivy XXIV s'ezda KPSS po pyatiletnemu planu razvitiya narodnogo khozyaistva SSSR na 1971-1975 gody," *Pravda*, April 7, 1971.

2. L. I. Brezhnev, "Otchetnyi doklad TsK KPSS XXIV s'ezdu KPSS," *Pravda*, March 31, 1971.

3. *Ibid.*

4. L. I. Brezhnev, "Otchetnyi doklad TsK KPSS XXIII s'ezdu KPSS" (March 29, 1966), in L. I. Brezhnev, *Leninskim kursom: rechi i statei*, Vol. 1 (Moskva, Politizdat, 1970), p. 315.

5. For example, see his speeches made at the Twenty-fourth Party Congress and on the occasion of the 50th anniversary of the foundation of the Soviet Union. *Pravda*, March 31, 1971; and L. I. Brezhnev, "O pyatidesyatiletii SSSR," (December 21, 1972), in L. I. Brezhnev, *Ob osnovnykh voprosakh ekonomicheskoi politiki KPSS na sovremennom etape, rechi i doklady*, Vol. 2 (Moskva, Politizdat, 1979), pp. 132ff.

6. A. N. Kosygin, "50 let nerushimogo soyuza i druzhby narodov sovetskikh sotsialisticheskikh respublik," in A. N. Kosygin, *K velikoi tseli: izbrannye rechi i stat'i*, Vol. 2 (Moskva, Politizdat, 1979), p. 206.

7. *Ibid.*

8. A. N. Kosygin, "Moguchaya postup' velikoi strany," (June 12, 1974), in *K velikoi tseli*, Vol. 2, p. 258.

9. For example, see *Pravda*, January 5, 1968; and *Izvestiya*, January 11, 1973; March 12, 1974; and March 4, 1975.

10. A. N. Kosygin, "Sotsial'no-ekonomicheskoe razvitie sovetskogo mnogonatsional'nogo gosudarstva," *Kommunist*, No. 17 (1972), 20.

11. Kosygin, "Direktivy XXIV s'ezda KPSS...."

12. Kosygin, "Moguchaya postup' velikoi strany," pp. 258-259.

13. *Pravda*, November 3, 1974.

14. *Ibid.*, October 12, 1974.

15. A. N. Kosygin, "Kursom bratskogo sotrudnichestva," (June 21, 1977), in *K velikoi tseli*, Vol. 2, p. 506.

16. *Ibid.*, p. 507.

17. L. I. Brezhnev, "Otchet TsK KPSS i ocherednye zadachi partii v oblasti vnutrennei i vneshnei politiki," (February 24, 1976), in *Materialy XXV s'ezda KPSS* (Moskva, Politizdat, 1976), p. 59.

18. *Pravda*, December 18, 1977.

19. See Chapter 3, footnote 55.

20. A. N. Kosygin, "Tvorcheskaya sila velikikh idei oktyabrya," (November 4, 1978) in *K velikoi tseli*, Vol. 2, pp. 623-624.

21. *Ibid.*, p. 623.

22. *Izvestiya*, March 2, 1979.

23. A. N. Kosygin, "Kurs na effektivnost'--vazhneishee zveno ekonomicheskoi politiki partii," *Planovoe khozyaistvo*, No. 7 (1979), 11-12.

24. A. N. Kosygin, "O proekte zakona o Sovete Ministrov SSSR," (July 5, 1978) in *K velikoi tseli*, Vol. 2, pp. 600-601.

25. On Kosygin's trip, see *Izvestiya*, March 24-25, 1978. On Brezhnev's Siberian tour, see *Pravda*, March 29, April 10, and April 15, 1978.

26. See Chapter 3, footnote 44.

27. See footnote 18 of the present chapter.

28. L. I. Brezhnev, "Iz vystupleniya na plenume TsK KPSS," (December 13, 1977) in L. I. Brezhnev, *Ob osnovnykh voprosakh...*, Vol. 2, p. 452.

29. L. I. Brezhnev, "Otchet TsK KPSS XXVI s'ezdu KPSS i ocherednye zadachi partii v oblasti vnutrennei i vneshnei politiki," (February 23, 1981) *Pravda*, February 24, 1981.

30. *Pravda*, March 31, 1971.

31. Brezhnev, "Otchet TsK KPSS i...," in *Materialy XXV s'ezda KPSS*, pp. 56-58. He discussed the subject in a subsection of his speech, entitled "The development of foreign economic relations." No such subsection existed in his previous Congress reports.

32. For example, see N. A. Tikhonov, "Segodnya FRG--eto odin iz nashikh krupnykh partnerov v delovom vzaimovygodnom sotrudnichestve s zapadom," (1976) in N. A. Tikhonov, *Izbrannye rechi i stat'i* (Moskva, Politizdat, 1980), pp. 227-228.

33. *Pravda*, May 7, 1978.

34. *Financial Times*, July 3, 1980.

35. R. D. Anderson, Jr., "Soviet Decision-Making and

Poland," *Problems of Communism*, XXXI (March-April 1982), 35. ( ) added.

36. A. N. Kosygin, "Leninskii kurs partii," (June 11, 1975) in *K velikoi tseli*, Vol. 2, p. 370.

37. A. N. Kosygin, "Osnovnye napravleniya razvitiya narodnogo khozyaistva SSSR na 1976-1980 gody," (March 1, 1976) in *Materialy XXV s'ezda KPSS* (Moskva, Politizdat, 1976), p. 115.

38. *Ibid.*, p. 136.

39. Lilita Dzirkals, Thane Gustafson, and A. Ross Johnson, *The Media and Intra-Elite Communication in the USSR* (Santa Monica, Ca., Rand Corporation, 1982), pp. 73-74.

40. George W. Breslauer, *Khrushchev and Brezhnev as Leaders: Building Authority in Soviet Politics* (London, George Allen & Unwin, 1982), Chapters 13-14.

41. *Ibid.*, p. 233.

42. *Pravda*, April 7, 1978.

43. Central Intelligence Agency, *Prospects for Soviet Oil Production*, ER 77-10270 (April 1977); and Central Intelligence Agency, Directorate of Intelligence, *Prospects for Soviet Oil Production: A Supplemental Analysis*, ER 77-10425 (July 1977).

44. Marshall Goldman, *The Enigma of Soviet Petroleum: Half-empty or Half-full?* (London, George Allen & Unwin, 1980), p. 178. Officially, however, the Soviets continued to criticize the CIA reports. For example, see *Novoe vremya*, No. 52 (1977), 19; *Soviet News*, July 12, 1977 and November 21, 1978; and *Sotsialisticheskaya industriya*, August 31, 1979.

45. Marshall Goldman, "The Changing Role of Raw Material Exports and Soviet Foreign Trade," in U.S. Congress, Joint Economic Committee, *Soviet Economy in A Time of Change*, Vol. 1 (Washington, D.C., 1979), p. 188.

46. A. G. Aganbegyan, *Ekonomika i organizatsiya promyshlennogo proizvodstva*, No.3 (1979), 8. Also see Chapter 4, footnotes 80-81.

47. A. M. Golubnichii, V. P. Gur'ev, V. T. Permyakov, and N. A. Sesin, "Voprosy sovershenstvovaniya planirovaniya na novom etape razvitiya neftyanoi promyshlennosti Zapadnoi Sibiri," in S. N. Starovoitov (ed.), *Problemy razvitiya Zapadno-Sibirskogo neftegazovogo kompleksa* (Novosibirsk, Nauka, 1983), p. 95.

48. *Literaturnaya gazeta*, January 18, 1978. ( ) added.

49. Brezhnev, "Otchet TsK KPSS XXVI s'ezdu KPSS i...," *Pravda*, February 24,1981.

50. *Pravda*, October 22, 1980.

51. Brezhnev, "Otchet TsK KPSS XXVI s'ezdu KPSS i...."

52. N. A. Tikhonov, "Osnovnye napravleniya ekonomicheskogo i sotsial'nogo razvitiya SSSR na 1981-1985 gody i na period do 1990 goda," *Pravda*, February 28, 1981. Emphasis added.

53. *Pravda*, April 15, 1980; and *Sotsialisticheskaya industriya*, April 15, 1980.

54. Dolgikh seems to have been more involved in energy affairs than anyone else. On his view of the Soviet energy situation, see V. I. Dolgikh, "Povyshat' uroven' rukovodstva predpriyatiyami toplivno-energeticheskogo kompleksa," *Partiinaya zhizn'*, No. 1 (1980), 15-23.

55. *Pravda*, February 27, 1981. ( ) added.

7

The Formation of a Pro-West Siberian Policy Coalition

Many of those engaged in the energy sector of the Soviet economy argued for the priority development of West Siberian oil and gas resources. It was the Siberians themselves who vigorously promoted the further development of the energy potential of their region. At the same time, not a few officials and academics in Moscow publicly expressed support for the development of West Siberia as the country's main fuel base. Who, precisely, were these people? What institutional interests, if any, did they represent? In this chapter, we will examine those who participated in public discussions on the West Siberian side. As will be seen, the pro-West Siberian elements had formed themselves into a policy grouping or coalition in the course of public discussions. In this coalition were represented various interests both in Siberia and in Moscow. It appears to have been a more or less loose alliance--especially if we include the pro-West Siberian supporters in Moscow in it--but one stable over time.

A. 1968-1970

On the basis of the arguments and demands put forward both before and after the 1969 decree in support of the accelerated opening up of West Siberian oil, we can draw up the following list (Table 7.1) of pro-West Siberian alignments. In West Siberia, regional Party officials lobbied vigorously for the development of oil and gas resources in their region. Tyumen' obkom First Secretary B. Ye. Shcherbina was one of the most outspoken advocates of the development of his province. In the Soviet press of that time articles may also be found by Party officials such as

Table 7.1: Major Proponents of West Siberian Oil and Gas Development, 1968-1970

	In Siberia	In Moscow
Party Apparatuses	Shcherbina, B. Ye. Ligachev, Ye. K. Protozanov, A. K. Maksimov, V. P.	Yamnov, A. A. Yeronin, N. M. Kremnev, V. I.
Government Agencies	Utrobin, Ye. Lukbyanenok, N.	Shashin, V. D.
Industrial Enterprises	Muravlenko, V. I. Shidlovskii, I. Altunin, Ye. N. Erv'e, Yu. G. Rovnin, L. I. Filanovskii, V. Yu. Batalin, Yu. P.	
Research Institutions	Trofimuk, A. A. Aganbegyan, A. G. Bogomyakov, G. P. Belov, V. Ostryi, G. Nesterov, I. I. Popov, V. E. Simzen, M. Udovenko, V.	Nekrasov, N. N. Kistanov, V. Tokarev, S. Probst, A. Slavin, S. Ivanchenko, A. Belorusov, D.
Media Organs		Nikitin, A Vostrukhov, Ye. Kiselev, E. Titov, I. Murzin, A.

Ye. Ligachev, Tomsk obkom First Secretary; A. Protozanov, Second Secretary of the Tyumen' obkom; and V. P. Maksimov, a section chief of the Tyumen' province Party. In 1971, Maksimov and his counterpart in the Tomsk province Party, G. G. Veselkov, took part in a meeting for the discussion of development problems in their respective regions.[1] There were also local government officials, oil and gas industry enterprise managers, and engineers, who aligned themselves in support of the development of hydrocarbon resources in their region. We have seen that N. V. Lukbyanenok, Chairman of the Tomsk Province Executive Committee (*oblispolkom*), highly praised the 1969 decision. Other enthusiastic Siberians included Ye. Utrobin, Chairman of the Planning Commission of the West Siberian Economic Region; V. I. Muravlenko, Director of Glavtyumenneftegaz who time and again stressed the need for the commitment of more resources and advanced technology to West Siberian oil development; I. Shidlovskii, Director of the Surgut Oilfield Administration; Ye. N. Altunin, Director of Tyumengazprom; Yu. G. Erv'e, Director of Glavtyumengeologiya who reportedly first discovered West Siberian oil[2]; L. I. Rovnin, Chief geologist of Glavtyumengeologiya; V. Yu. Filanovskii, Chief engineer of Glavtyumenneftegaz; and Yu. P. Batalin, Chief engineer of Glavtyumenneftegazstroi.

There were also many Siberian academics and specialists who eagerly defended the West Siberian undertaking. Perhaps one of the most outspoken advocates of West Siberian oil and gas development was Academician A. A. Trofimuk. He served as Director of the Institute of Geology and Geophysics of the USSR Academy of Sciences' Siberian Department and concurrently as the Department's First Vice Chairman. A. G. Aganbegyan, Corresponding Member of the USSR Academy of Sciences, headed the Institute of Economics and Organization of Industrial Production of the Academy's Siberian Department, a quasi-consulting firm which publishes the journal *Ekonomika i organizatsiya promyshlennogo proizvodstva*. His predecessor G. Prudenskii and Academician M. Lavrent'ev, Chairman of the Academy's Siberian Department, had also argued for hydrocarbon development in West Siberia. G. P. Bogomyakov as Deputy Director of the West Siberian Geological-Prospecting and Oil Research Institute (*ZapsibNIGNI*) had been equally active in advocating the rapid opening up of new oil deposits in the eastern region. Another outspoken geologist I. I. Nesterov headed a section of the same institute. Amongst the Siberians, there were also economists and engineers such as V. E. Popov, Chief of the Long-Term Economic Forecast Laboratory of Aganbegyan's economic institute; economists I. Karyagin, M. Simzen, and V. Udovenko; and O. Mezhlumov, Director of the State Tyumen' Oil and Gas Research-Design Institute (*Giprotyumenneftegaz*) and his colleagues V. Belov and G. Ostryi.

During this early period of the West Siberian development, at least three central Party officials with responsibility for the oil and gas industries also made known their support for the undertaking. They were A. A. Yamnov, chief of the Party Central Committee Heavy Industry Department's geology sector; N. M. Yeronin, chief of the Department's oil industry sector; and V. I. Kremnev who had worked with Yeronin. On the government side, Oil Minister V. D. Shashin was no doubt enthusiastic about the West Siberian oil programme, at least judging from his public statements in the early part of the 1970s.

In addition, there were several pro-West Siberian academics in Moscow. Academician N. N. Nekrasov was certainly the most prominent of these. Educated in the Siberian city of Irkutsk, he headed Gosplan's Council for Study of Productive Forces (*SOPS*). A. Probst and five other economists who came out in support of the West Siberian development--V. Kistanov, S. Tokarev, S. Slavin, A. Ivanchenko, and D. Belorusov--were leading members of the council. According to V. Holubnychy, the council had inclined in favor of the rapid development of the country's eastern part since the late 1950s.[3] At the same time, there were correspondents of *Pravda*, *Literaturnaya gazeta*, and other central press organs whose articles clearly expressed support for the pro-West Siberian cause. Among them were A. Nikitin and Ye. Vostrukhov--both correspondents of *Ekonomicheskaya gazeta*--and three *Pravda* correspondents, E. Kiselev, I. Titov, and A. Murzin.

In the previous chapters, we have examined how these individuals put forward promotional arguments supporting what was to become the line of the 1969 decision. Cooperation among them can also be observed in the way they presented their arguments. For instance, academics both in Moscow and Siberia frequently contributed articles to *Pravda* under joint authorship. Siberian academics published their promotional articles in collaboration with local managers and specialists as well. In addition, large-scale gatherings gave the pro-West Siberians an opportunity to exchange views and find allies. It is instructive in this connection to list the names of prominent participants in such meetings. At the Novosibirsk conference, for example, the participants included Academician Lavrent'ev, Chairman of the USSR Academy's Siberian Department and concurrently Vice President of the Academy; Academicians Nekrasov, Trofimuk, L. A. Melent'ev who headed the Academy's Scientific Council for Complex Problems of Power, and L. V. Kantorovich who was well known as a reform-minded mathematical economist in Siberia; and Corresponding Member of the Academy Aganbegyan.[4] At the ensuing Tyumen' conference, Nekrasov, Trofimuk, Aganbegyan, and the Academy's Corresponding Member T. Zaslavskaya participated along with many senior government officials such as Deputy Oil Minister R. Mingareev.[5] Academics Lavrent'ev, Trofimuk, and Aganbegyan, and local enterprise directors Muravlenko, Erv'e, and Batalin also figured amongst those attending a scientific session summoned following the announcement of the 1969 decree.[6] Party and government officials from both Moscow and Siberia also participated in this session. From the above, it would appear highly likely that many of these leading pro-West Siberians had been acquainted with one another for a considerable time.

In short, the pro-West Siberian elements appear to have been closely connected with one another in their promotional efforts during the period--both horizontally in Siberia and vertically between Moscow and the locality. They coalesced into an informal alliance. It is instructive, by the way, to consider the names of some of the 18 Lenin Prize winners of the early 1970s, who received the award for their part in the discovery and development of West Siberian oil and gas resources.[7] These include I. I. Nesterov, section head of ZapsibNIGNI, F. K. Salmanov, head of the Pravdinsk Oil Exploratory Expedition in West Siberia, both honored for their role in the opening up of large-scale oil deposits in the Middle Ob'; G. P. Bogomyakov, for the exploration of gas deposits in the northern part of West Siberia, who was recommended along with several other West Siberian geologists for the prize a month before by RSFSR Geology Minister L. I. Rovnin, former chief geologist of Glavtyumengeologiya.[8]; and V. P. Maksimov, the Tyumen' obkom section head who was formerly a section chief of Giprotyumenneftegaz, S. A. Orudzhev, First Deputy Oil Minister, and V. Yu. Filanovskii, former Chief engineer of Glavtyumenneftegaz, all for their technological contribution to the development of the oil industry in Tyumen' province. As we have seen, Filanovskii was the author of an important article in support of the West Siberian cause during this period. He was soon transferred to a post with the USSR Gosplan. Many of the prize winners, including Filanovskii, were active in promoting the West Siberian cause in this early stage of West Siberian development and had become the core elements of the pro-West Siberian forces.

B. 1976-1978

During the period of 1976-1978, the advocates of West Siberian development renewed concerted efforts to promote their cause. By that time, Tyumen' obkom was under the leadership of G. P. Bogomyakov, who had succeed B. Ye. Shcherbina as First Secretary in December 1973. Shcherbina himself had become Minister of Construction of Oil and Gas Industry Enterprises (Minneftegazstroi) in 1973.[9]

Bogomyakov had occupied the post of Second Secretary of the obkom since 1971. In his new position as First Secretary, he was actively engaged in promotional arguments during the first half of the 1970s. Following the December 1977 Party plenum, he revealed that there was much discussion over the course to be taken in Soviet energy policy, and particularly regarding West Siberia. Tyumen' obkom Secretary G. I. Shmal' wrote articles also relating to this debate in 1976. Similarly, Ye. K. Ligachev, Tomsk obkom First Secretary, revealed that, of all the important economic problems discussed at the plenum, that of "the further development of the fuel-power branches, the oil and gas industries in particular, occupied an especial place."[10]

For the last two years before the adoption of the 1977 crash programme, perhaps the most outspoken proponents of West Siberian development were local industry officials and academics. In addition to Muravlenko and Erv'e, Director

Table 7.2: Main Advocates of the Continued Development of West Siberian Oil and Gas, 1976-1978

	In Siberia	In Moscow
Party Apparatuses	Bogomyakov, G. P. Ligachev, Ye. K. Shmal', G. I. Maksimov, V. P.	Brezhnev, L. I.
Government Agencies		Shashin, V. D. Shcherbina, B. Ye. Orudzhev, S. Batalin, Yu. P.
Industrial Enterprises	Muravlenko, V. I. Kuzovatkin, R. I. Erv'e, Yu. G. Salmanov, F. K.	
Research Institutions	Trofimuk, A. A. Aganbegyan, A. G. Guzhnovskii, L. P. Nesterov, I. I. Churikov, L. I.	Nekrasov, N. N. Beschinskii, A. Vitebskii, R. Ya.
Media Organs	Ognev, I.	Bogatko, S. Vtorushin, S. Murzin, A. Sevastyanov, V. Kozlov, V. Shatokhin, E.

R. I. Kuzovatkin of the Nizhnevartovsk Oil and Gas Extraction Administration and Chief geologist F. K. Salmanov of Glavtyumengeologiya were also important industrial figures in West Siberia who were actively engaged in pro-West Siberian arguments. Meanwhile, academics such as Trofimuk and Aganbegyan were backing them in support of hydrocarbon development in West Siberia. Trofimuk even argued that it was wrong to have tried to replace oil with coal at the time of the world energy crisis. In his opinion, coal was more costly than oil in production and "we have so far extracted only half of the oil reserves from the underground" which could be obtained by utilizing advancement in technology.[11] In addition, new faces from Siberian academic circles participated in the discussions. These included I. I. Nesterov, Corresponding Member of the USSR Academy of Sciences and now Director of the West Siberian Geological-Prospecting and Oil Research Institute; L. P. Guzhnovskii, head of the Tyumen' Department of Economic Research of Aganbegyan's economic institute; and L. I. Churikov, head of a laboratory at the Tyumen' State Oil and Gas Research-Design Institute. To these names, finally, that of I. Ognev, correspondent of *Ekonomika i organizatsiya promyshlennogo proizvodstva*, should also be added.

In Moscow, economists and specialists also continued to show support for oil and gas development in West Siberia. For instance, A. E. Probst, chief theoretician of Gosplan's Council for Study of Productive Forces (*SOPS*), was active in advocating the priority development of West Siberian oil and gas. Following the December 1977 Party Central Committee plenum Academician Nekrasov and other central specialists also wrote extensively about the West Siberian issue. In 1977 meanwhile, articles on West Siberian development problems by newspaper correspondents--A. Murzin, S. Vtorushin and V. Sevastyanov of *Pravda*, and V. Kozlov and E. Shatokhin of *Izvestiya*--appeared frequently in the press. It should be noted that *Pravda* itself carried an editorial in January 1977 advocating the stepping-up of the search for oil and gas resources in West Siberia.

Last but not least, both Party and government officials in Moscow failed to make any significant public commitments to oil and gas in West Siberia until Brezhnev finally came out in favor of West Siberian oil and gas development.[12] Only Oil Minister Shashin called for a stepping-up of geological exploration for oil in West Siberia in 1976. Apart from him, a small number of government officials such as Minister of Construction of Oil and Gas

Industry Enterprises Shcherbina, his deputy Yu. P. Batalin, Gas Minister S. A. Orudzhev, and some Gosplan officials called attention to various problems confronting the West Siberian fuel complex, but these appear to be isolated cases. Central Committee Secretary V. I. Dolgikh and other Party officials did not make known their positions on the energy matter. Despite the absence of public commitment on the part of Party officials in Moscow, however, the central Party apparatus seems to have been deeply involved in the West Siberian undertaking. Two West Siberian geologists bear witness to this: According to Salmanov and Nesterov, the planned deceleration of drilling works in search of oil and gas in Tyumen' province in the early 1970s was reversed after the "intervention of the Tyumen' obkom with the help of the CPSU Central Committee."[13] It was also at the initiative of the Central Committee and Tyumen' obkom that a round-table meeting was held in Tyumen' in June 1978, six months after Brezhnev's decision for the crash development of West Siberian hydrocarbons. Along with Tyumen' leader Bogomyakov, R. I. Kosolapov, Chief editor of Party organ *Kommunist*, and N. B. Bikkenin, a Central Committee section head, attended the meeting. The appearance of such an important personage as Kosolapov in this remote region may signify the importance the Party leadership attached to West Siberia at that time.

At the meeting, the above participants were joined by a score or so of local specialists and academics involved in the oil and gas industry in West Siberia, and by many leading researchers and government specialists from Moscow. Some of the more important figures from the center included Ya. A. Mazover, head of a sector of Gosplan's Council for Study of Productive Forces; V. S. Varlamov, deputy head of a Gosplan sub-department in charge of territorial planning; V. S. Vainshtein, department head of the Institute of Economics and Management of the Ministry of Construction of Oil and Gas Industry Enterprises; N. M. Nikolaevskii, department head of the Oil Ministry's all-Union Oil Research Institute; R. Ya. Vitebskii, senior research associate at the Ministry of Power and Electrification's State Research-Design and Surveying Institute for Power-Engineering Systems and Electric Power Networks (*Energoset'proekt*); V. P. Krasovskii, head of a department of the USSR Academy of Sciences' Institute of Economics; and N. G. Feitel'man, senior research associate at the same institute. For Siberian participants such as Aganbegyan, the meeting certainly provided a good opportunity to persuade their colleagues from Moscow to support their cause. In fact, Kosolapov,

Chief editor of *Kommunist*, commented at the close of the meeting that it was necessary not only to draw the attention of the public and the central press to the problems of the region but also to provide workers and officials of Tyumen' province with the opportunity to write about their problems.[14] A statement of this kind must have been the origin of the unusual freedom enjoyed by many Siberians and, especially, Tyumen' Party leader Bogomyakov.

So far, we have examined another case of the formation of an alliance around a particular issue of accelerated West Siberian development. At the center of the alliance were the Siberians themselves, many of them highly outspoken and actively promoting and communicating their case to the central authorities. In this process, some central officials and specialists took the step of rendering their support to the Siberians. This time the top leader himself gave his approval to the pro-West Siberian claims.

C. 1979-1981

The pro-West Siberians again concentrated their promotional efforts just before the Twenty-sixth Party Congress. As before, Tyumen' Party leader Bogomyakov and his colleagues had long been busy persuading the central authorities of the oil and gas potential of their region. By the time the Congress was held in early 1981, Ye. N. Altunin had been transferred from the managerial post of the Tyumen' Gas Industry Association (Tyumengazprom) to the secretaryship of Tyumen obkom. G. Lutoshkin, the other Tyumen' obkom Secretary, and B. Trofimov, department head for industry in the same obkom, had also been active in advocating West Siberian interests. Among the local proponents of West Siberian development at this time there were now new chief directors of local enterprises: F. G. Arzhanov and R. Bulgakov who in turn became the head of Glavtyumenneftegaz succeeding the late Muravlenko; G. Sulimenkov, Director of Tyumengazprom; and F. K. Salmanov, Director of Glavtyumengeologiya. Also joining the pro-West Siberian chorus were V. Strizhov, Director of the Nadym Gas Extraction Administration in West Siberia; Yu. Topchev, Chief engineer of Tyumengazprom; V. Bidzhakov, Chief geologist of the Tomsk Territorial Administration of Geology; and lastly V. Kuramin, Chairman of Gosplan's Interdepartmental Territorial Commission on Problems of the West Siberian Oil and Gas Complex (ZapSibMVTK), and his subordinate V. Filatov. Amongst outspoken local academics, there were

Table 7.3: Major Advocates of West Siberian Oil and Gas Development, 1979-1981

	In Siberia	In Moscow
Party Apparatuses	Bogomyakov, G. P. Altunin, Ye. N. Lutoshkin, G. Trofimov, B.	Brezhnev, L. I.
Government Agencies	Kuramin, V.	Filanovskii, V. Yu. Marchuk, G. I.
Industrial Enterprises	Arzhanov, F. G. Bulgakov, R. Sulimenkov, G. Salmanov, F. K. Bidzhakov, V. Strizhov, V. Topchev, Yu.	
Research Institutions	Trofimuk, A. A. Aganbegyan, A. G. Nesterov, I. I.	Nekrasov, N. N. Melent'ev, L. Makarov, A.
Media	*EKO*	Vtorushin, S. Sevastyanov, V. Ognev, I.

still familiar faces of Academicians Trofimuk and Aganbegyan, and the USSR Academy of Sciences' Corresponding Member Nesterov. Finally, the Siberian mouthpiece *Ekonomika i organizatsiya promyshlennogo proizvodstva* (*EKO*) added its voice to those of the pro-West Siberians when in the spring of 1979 it carried an editorial in favor of the West Siberian oil and gas development.

In Moscow, meanwhile, Filanovskii, now the head of Gosplan's Oil and Gas Industry Department, also wrote articles which advocated the further development of West Siberian hydrocarbon resources. Academician G. I. Marchuk, Deputy Chairman of the USSR Council of Ministers and concurrently Chairman of the State Committee for Science and Technology, actively supported the Siberian Programme which included a projected development programme for West Siberia. Succeeding Academician Lavrent'ev, Marchuk was formerly Chairman of the USSR Academy's Siberian Department, which worked out the programme. In the academic circles, two energy authorities, Academician L. A. Melent'ev and economist A. A. Makarov, along with Academician Nekrasov, supported the strategy of the development of natural gas deposits in West Siberia. Academician Melent'ev was Chairman of the USSR Academy's Scientific Council for Complex Problems of Power and concurrently Director of the Institute of High Temperatures of the Academy. His associate Makarov headed a section of this institute. Meanwhile, the two *Pravda* correspondents, S. Vtorushin and V. Sevastyanov, also continued to write in support of the development of the West Siberian fuel complex. Finally, I. Ognev who formerly worked for *Ekonomika i organizatsiya promyshlennogo proizvodstva* continued to cover the West Siberian undertaking now as a correspondent of *Sovetskaya Rossiya.*

No high-ranking Party figures except Brezhnev, however, ever publicly committed themselves to hydrocarbon development in West Siberia. V. I. Dolgikh, Central Committee Secretary in charge of industry, appears to have been more involved in energy affairs than anyone else. But he had so far failed to make known his attitude toward the West Siberian energy issue. In an article published in 1980 Dolgikh, who eventually became a candidate member of the Politburo, admitted the need to more than double the volume of drilling in West Siberia by 1985.[15] At the same time, he advocated the introduction of advanced methods in the Urals-Volga and many other old oil regions, pointing out that there were still huge reserves there. He also cautioned against the use of gas as a fuel on the grounds that gas would be almost 10 times more efficient economically when used as a chemical feedstock than when used as a boiler fuel.[16] In any case, the advocates of West Siberian fuel development had the unquestioned backing of the General Secretary by the late 1970s, as evidenced by his policy announcements in 1977 and 1981, and this gave life to their activities. The Siberians themselves appear to have achieved a greater degree of coordination in their promotional efforts by the late 1970s. During this period, they had clearly established a stable relationship with their sympathizers in Moscow. Many West Siberians were also promoted during this period to posts in central organizations. When an enlarged meeting of Gosplan was summoned in late 1979, the pro-West Siberians found additional supporters in Oil Minister N. A. Mal'tsev, who had succeeded the late Oil Minister Shashin, and Academician A. P. Aleksandrov, who was President of the USSR Academy of Sciences. At an ensuing scientific conference, held in Novosibirsk in June of the following year, the academician and many other participants of the earlier Gosplan meeting also took part.

To sum up, a pro-West Siberian policy alliance was formed in the process of promotional activities on the part of the West Siberians and their supporters during the 1960s and the 1970s. The alliance was concerned with the development priority to be accorded the West Siberian oil and gas industry complex. What interests were represented in this policy coalition? As identified before, regional interests formed the backbone of the alignment. Local enterprise managers, engineers, academics, and local Party and government officials pressed for the accelerated development of the fuel complex. First Party Secretaries Shcherbina and, later, Bogomyakov turned out to be the most outspoken advocates of the interests of their region. There were also local enterprise managers such as Muravlenko and Salmanov who were no less critical than the regional Party leaders of the central planning organs and industrial ministries in Moscow for failure to take measures they considered essential to the operation of their enterprises. Muravlenko, Director of Glavtyumenneftegaz from 1965, became known as one of the most outspoken critics of the central industrial organizations.[17] Salmanov was as outspoken as Muravlenko in the field of geological exploration for oil and gas in West Siberia. Neither of these had any scruples about criticizing even their superior ministries in Moscow. This was especially the case with Salmanov.

There are also the Siberian academics to be considered. Academician Trofimuk was certainly the most optimistic of all Soviet oil industry officials and specialists about the oil potential of the country and especially of its eastern part. He called for an ever more rapid exploitation of oil and gas resources not only because he considered that even by the end of the present century only a small fraction of Soviet reserves would be expended but also because he thought that the future would see the development of new energy sources making the present ones obsolete.[18] His concern about the disproportion between exploratory and development drilling in West Siberia was shared by Nesterov and other local specialists. These local specialists, including Academician Aganbegyan, all belonged to the Siberian Department of the USSR Academy of Sciences. The Siberians, according to W. C. Wilde, greatly benefited from the establishment of the department; in many instances local Party and government leaders were able to "rely upon local economic and other scientific institutes for both practical aid in administering their territories and learned support in pressing their interests in Moscow."[19] He observes that the department became a "champion of eastern development" in the course of a controversy of the early 1970s over regional economic policies in general.[20] Explaining the activities of the Siberian Department, its Chairman Marchuk once said that it had cooperated closely with many all-Union industrial ministries in working out various programmes for Siberian development.[21] Along with its many house organs, one of its institutes publishes the popular forum journal, *Ekonomika i organizatsiya promyshlennogo proizvodstva*. In 1979 in an interview with its chief editor, Academician Aganbegyan, a *Literaturnaya gazeta* correspondent observed that the periodical "in recent years has become a mass-circulation economic journal in our country with a circulation of more than 60,000 copies."[22]

In the course of promotional arguments published in the Siberian journal and in many national-circulation newspapers and other publications, connections were established between the local people in Siberia on the one hand and central officials and academics in Moscow on the other. At the time of the adoption of the 1969 decree, Tyumen' Party officials appeared to have supporters in the central Party apparatus. Although such support was not publicly expressed by Party Central Committee officials prior to two previous pro-West Siberian policy shifts, there is no doubt that the Party leadership rendered active support to West Siberian development. It was the Party leader himself who initiated the crash development policies of West Siberian oil and gas in 1977 and 1981. If Siberian academics were influential in the making of policies which affected the future of their region, their influence would have depended on the degree to which Soviet leaders followed the advice they provided. Thane Gustafson observes that during the time that Academician M. A. Lavrent'ev enjoyed direct support from Khrushchev, the Siberian Department which he then headed "enjoyed relatively greater latitude than it does today."[23] The Siberian academics similarly enjoyed Brezhnev's patronage in the late 1970s. In his speech before Siberian academics in Novosibirsk during his Siberian tour in 1978, the Party leader said the following:

> I would like to stress in our conversation today that we expect even more questions of the practical use of science in solving fuel and power problems and in geological prospecting, petrochemical engineering, machine building and other fields. We must carry this work further so that the active role of scientists will help us to resolve questions of uniting science with practice, and thereby to facilitate growth in the

> country's productive forces. I think that Comrade Marchuk, Chairman of the Siberian Department, will agree with this and, with his characteristic energy, will think about how this task can be realized in more practical and more effective ways.[24]

These remarks would seem to show not only how influential Siberian academics had been in industrial policy-making, but also how much the Party had been involved in the West Siberian development in the Brezhnev era.

On the government side, there were also figures who expressed sympathy for the West Siberians at one time or another. Of these, the most outspoken were Minister of Construction of Oil and Gas Industry Enterprises Shcherbina, his first deputy Batalin, Deputy Geology Minister Erv'e, RSFSR Geology Minister Rovnin, and Gosplan's oil and gas industry chief Filanovskii. All happened to be of West Siberian origin. Academician Marchuk later went to Moscow to take up the post of the deputy chairmanship of the USSR Council of Ministers and concurrently the chairmanship of the State Committee for Science and Technology, a body deeply involved in the technical aspects of the country's fuel and power problems. The Oil Minister Shashin and his successor Mal'tsev also supported the further development of the oil industry in the northern part of West Siberia, but of course this support needs to be considered in the context of their concerns as ministers for the entire Soviet oil industry. They were equally responsible for oil production in old oil regions in the European part of the country. Mal'tsev himself was a former oil industry enterprise director in the Urals-Volga area and had long called for more investment there. There were also a number of academic and semi-academic institutes in Moscow, which dealt with the development of the country's productive forces. Perhaps, of these, the institute with the most publicized pro-West Siberian attitudes was Gosplan's Council for Study of Productive Forces (*SOPS*). Most of the central academics and specialists who spoke in favor of the West Siberian energy undertaking were in fact members of this council. V. S. Varlamov, deputy head of a sub-department of Gosplan, revealed in 1978 that the council was also working out a long-term development programme for West Siberia as well as other territorial production complexes.[25]

Last but not least, there were press correspondents residing in West Siberia who were engaged in reporting the achievements and problems of the fuel complex. Especially active were correspondents from the Party organ *Pravda*--

E. Kiselev, A. Murzin, and S. Vtorushin. The Party weekly *Ekonomicheskaya gazeta* once remarked that "a control post of *Ekonomicheskaya gazeta*, set up in connection with the building of the Pavlodar-Ekibastuz complex, has signalled more than once" what measures should be taken to best implement a development programme for it, i.e. to eliminate various disproportions in the building of the complex and to facilitate its development.[26] In the area of economic development policy, *Pravda* and other important national papers certainly perform a similar function of reporting various shortcomings and difficulties standing in the way of policy implementation and giving necessary instructions. What signals or instructions should be given and to whom they should be addressed will be decided at the top, presumably at the level of the Party's Central Committee. In this process, correspondents from central papers may provide an important means of communicating the grievances and demands of the local people to the center.

We have so far shown that various interests, both in Siberia and in Moscow, were represented in the West Siberian energy coalition. They turned out to be more or less stable over time. This stability may in part have been due to the persistence of particular problems in the development of energy resources in West Siberia, and to the continuous need on the part of the West Siberians to compete for appropriations for the region. To an equal degree, the stability of the pro-West Siberian coalition may be ascribed to the lengthy tenure of office of the leading figures of the participant interests and to the pattern of their recruitment, as the following biographical data show.[27]

Table 7.4: Leading Figures of the Pro-West Siberian Policy Coalition

Siberian Party Apparatuses: Many of local Party members were recruited from Siberia and from the appropriate industries in the region.

Shcherbina, B. Ye.
Born in 1919/Ukrainian/Rail engineer,
Secretary, Kharkov City Party Committee (1950-1951),
Second Secretary, Irkutsk obkom (1951-1961),
First Secretary, Tyumen' obkom (1961-1973),
Minister, Minneftegazstroi SSSR (1973-1984),
Deputy Chairman, USSR Council of Ministers (1984-)

(Continued)

Table 7.4 (Cont.)

Bogomyakov, G. P.
Born in 1930/Geologist,
Deputy Director, ZapsibNIGNI (1964-1967),
Second Secretary, Tyumen' obkom (1971-1973),
First Secretary, Tyumen' obkom (1973-)

Protozanov, A. K.
Secretary, Tyumen' obkom (as of 1959),
Chairman, Tyumen' oblispolkom (as of 1967),
Second Secretary, Tyumen' obkom (as of 1967)

Shmal', G. I.
Second Secretary, Tyumen' obkom (as of 1974)

Altunin, Ye. N.
Director, Tyumengazprom (as of 1981),
Secretary, Tyumen' obkom (as of 1981)

Maksimov, V. P.
Section head, Giprotyumenneftegaz (as of 1970),
Section head, Tyumen' obkom (as of 1971)

Trofimov, B.
Section head, Tyumen' obkom (as of 1981)

Lutoshkin, G. D.
Secretary, Tyumen' obkom (as of 1982)

Ligachev, Ye. K.
Born in 1920/Russian
Deputy head, CC CPSU Department, Bureau for RSFSR (1961-1965),
First Secretary, Tomsk obkom (1965-1983),
Secretary, CC CPSU (1983-1985),
Full Member, Politburo, CC CPSU (1983-)

Siberian Government Agencies:

Utrobin, Ye.
Chairman, Planning Commission of the West Siberian Economic Region (as of 1966)

Lukbyanenok, N.
Chairman, Tomsk oblispolkom (1967-1977)

Siberian Industrial Enterprises: West Siberian industrial enterprise managers and engineers were mostly promoted within the same organizations in the region.

Table 7.4 (Cont.)

Muravlenko, V. I.
Born in 1912/Krasnodar Territory/Oil engineer, Vice Chairman, Kuibyshev & Middle Volga Regional Economic Councils (*sovnarkhozy*) (1960-1965), Director, Glavtyumenneftegaz (1965-1977), Died (1977)

Arzhanov, F.
Chief engineer, Glavtyumenneftegaz (as of 1975), Director, Glavtyumenneftegaz (as of 1978)

Bulgakov, R.
Director, Glavtyumenneftegaz (as of 1981)

Kuzovatkin, R. I.
Director, Nizhnevartovsk Oil and Gas Extraction Administration (under Glavtyumenneftegaz) (as of 1976), Deputy Minister, USSR Minnefteprom & concurrently Director, Glavtyumenneftegaz (as of 1983)

Graifer, V. I.
Deputy Minister, USSR Minnefteprom & concurrently Director, Glavtyumenneftegaz (as of 1985)

Filanovskii, V. Yu.
Chief engineer, Glavtyumenneftegaz (as of 1967), Chief, Gosplan's Oil and Gas Industry Department (as of 1981), First Deputy Minister, USSR Minnefteprom (as of 1985)

Altunin, Ye. N.
See Siberian Party Apparatuses.

Sulimenkov, G.
Director, Tyumengazprom (as of 1979)

Chernomyrdin, V. S.
Director, Tyumengazprom (as of 1984), Minister, USSR Mingazprom (as of 1985)

Erv'e, Yu. G.
Director, Glavtyumengeologiya (as of 1977), Deputy Minister, USSR Mingeo (as of 1978)

Rovnin, L. I.
Chief geologist, Glavtyumengeologiya (as of 1967), Minister, RSFSR Mingeo (1970-)

Table 7.4 (Cont.)

Salmanov, F. K.
Chief, Pravdinsk Oil Exploratory Expedition (as of 1970),
Chief geologist, Glavtyumengeologiya (as of 1976),
Director, Glavtyumengeologiya (1978-)

Kuramin, V.
Director, Glavtyumenneftegazstroi (as of 1980),
Chairman, Gosplan's Interdepartmental Territorial Commission on Problems of the West Siberian Oil and Gas Complex & concurrently a department head, USSR Gosplan (as of 1981),
Deputy Minister, USSR Minneftegazstroi (as of 1984)

Batalin, Yu. P.
Born in 1927/Engineer,
Chief engineer, Glavtyumenneftegazstroi (1965-1970),
Deputy Minister, USSR Mingazprom (1970-1972),
Deputy Minister & First Deputy Minister, USSR Minneftegazstroi (1972-1983),
Deputy Chairman, USSR Council of Ministers (1983-)

Siberian Research Institutions:

Trofimuk, A. A.
Born in 1911/Oil geologist,
Member, USSR Academy of Sciences (1958-),
Worked in the Urals-Volga oil region,
Deputy Chairman, the Academy's Siberian Department (as of 1971),
Director, Institute of Geology and Geophysics of the Siberian Department (as of 1971),
First Deputy Chairman, the Academy's Siberian Department (as of 1978)

Aganbegyan, A. G.
Born in 1932/Tbilisi/ Economist,
Corresponding Member, USSR Academy of Sciences (1964-1974),
Director, Institute of Economics and Organization of Industrial Production & concurrently
Head, Scientific Council for Construction of the Baikal-Amur Railroad, USSR Academy of Sciences (1967-1985),
Member, USSR Academy of Sciences (1974-),
Chairman, the Academy's Commission on Productive Forces (1985-)

Table 7.4 (Cont.)

Marchuk, G. I.
Born in 1925/Orenburg/Physicist-Mathematician,
Member, USSR Academy of Sciences (1968-),
Chairman, Siberian Department of the USSR Academy of Sciences & concurrently
Vice President, USSR Academy of Sciences (1975-1980),
Deputy Chairman, USSR Council of Ministers & concurrently
Chairman, State Committee for Science and Technology (1980-)

Nesterov, I. I.
Geologist,
Section head, ZapsibNIGNI (as of 1970),
Deputy Director, ZapsibNIGNI (as of 1971),
Corresponding Member, USSR Academy of Sciences (as of 1978),
Director, ZapsibNIGNI (as of 1975)

Popov, V. E.
Head, Long-term Economic Forecast Laboratory, Institute of Economics and Organization of Industrial Production, Siberian Department of the USSR Academy of Sciences (as of 1970)

Guzhnovskii, L. P.
Chief, Tyumen' Department of Economic Research, Institute of Economics and Organization of Industrial Production, the USSR Academy's Siberian Department (as of 1976)

Bogomyakov, G. P.
See Siberian Party Apparatuses.

Maksimov, V. P.
See Siberian Party Apparatuses.

Siberian Media Organs:

Ognev, I.
Correspondent, *Ekonomika i organizatsiya promyshlennogo proizvodstva* (as of 1976),
Correspondent resident in West Siberia, *Sovetskaya Rossiya* (as of 1984)

Central Party Apparatuses:

Yamnov, A. A.
Chief, Geology sector of the Party Central Committee Heavy Industry Department (as of 1970)

Table 7.4 (Cont.)

Yeronin, N. M.
Chief, Oil industry sector of the Party Central Committee Heavy Industry Department (as of 1970)

Kremnev, V. I.
Worked in the oil industry sector, CC CPSU,
Edited *Sibirskaya neft'* in collaboration with Tyumenneftegaz Director V. I. Muravlenko (1977),
First Deputy Minister, USSR Minnefteprom (as of 1977)

Central Government Agencies:

Shashin, V. D.
Born in 1916/Baku/Oil engineer,
Director, Tatar Oil and Gas Extraction Administration and other oil industry enterprises,
Head, Chief Oil and Gas Industry Administration, RSFSR Economic Council (1960-1965),
Minister, USSR Minnefteprom (1965-1977),
Died (1977)

(Maltsev, N. A.)
Director, Perm' Oil and Gas Extraction Administration (as of 1971),
First Deputy Minister, USSR Minnefteprom (1972-1977),
Minister, USSR Minnefteprom (1977-1985)

(Dinkov, V. A.)
Minister, USSR Mingazprom (-1985),
Minister, USSR Minnefteprom (as of 1985)

Orudzhev, S. A.
Born in 1912/Baku/Oil engineer,
First Deputy Minister, USSR Minnefteprom (as of 1970),
Minister, USSR Mingazprom (1972-1981),
Died (1981)

Chernomyrdin, V. S.
See Siberian Industrial Enterprises.

Marchuk, G. I.
See Siberian Research Institutions.

Shcherbina, B. Ye.
See Siberian Party Apparatuses.

Batalin, Yu. P.
See Siberian Industrial Enterprises.

Table 7.4 (Cont.)

Filanovskii, V. Yu.
See Siberian Industrial Enterprises.

Erv'e, Yu. G.
See Siberian Industrial Enterprises.

Rovnin, L. I.
See Siberian Industrial Enterprises.

Kuramin, V.
See Siberian Industrial Enterprises.

Central Research Institutions:

Nekrasov, N. N.
Educated at Irkutsk/Economist,
Member, USSR Academy of Sciences,
Chairman, Council for Study of Productive Forces (*SOPS*), USSR Gosplan (as of 1978),
Chairman, Commission for Study of Productive Forces and Natural Resources, USSR Academy of Sciences (as of 1980)

Mazover, Ya. A.
Chief of the fuel sector, USSR Gosplan's SOPS (as of 1980)

Probst, A.
Member, USSR Gosplan's SOPS

Tokarev, S. P.
Member, USSR Gosplan's SOPS

Central Media Organs:

Vtorushin, S.
Pravda's West Siberian correspondent (as of 1970 & 1977)

Murzin, A.
Pravda's West Siberian correspondent (as of 1970 & 1977)

Shatokhin, E.
Izvestiya's West Siberian correspondent (as of 1973 & 1978)

From the above, it is clear that most of the leading figures in the West Siberian coalition enjoyed a long tenure of office in their respective organizations. Many leading academics, for instance, were at the head of their institutes for the whole period of our study. The same feature is characteristic of the career patterns of Muravlenko and other economic officials both in West Siberia and in Moscow. Less prominent figures worked for a long time within particular institutions and other organizations, being promoted to higher positions within the same institutions and organizations. Such tendencies were more conspicuous at the regional level. When inter-organizational transfers were made, they tended to be largely confined to the same region, i.e. within West Siberia. In this connection, it is pertinent to note the practice of recruiting local Party officials from among local specialists and economic officials. Higher up, the practice of moving cadres in the Party apparatus to high positions in government ministries and departments, and vice versa, was employed frequently in the oil and gas industries in the 1970s. Tyumen' Party leader Shcherbina, for example, was appointed head of a central industrial ministry, apparently in an effort to facilitate coordination between Party and government in the area of energy policy. Similarly, the cooptation of many local officials to the center, as was the case with Shcherbina and several others, provided a good opportunity for the West Siberians to establish contact with the central authorities. Throughout the whole period under consideration, all such tendencies certainly furthered the process of pro-West Siberian coalition-building within the Soviet political establishment.

NOTES

1. *Sovetskaya Rossiya*, February 3, 1971.
2. A. A. Yamnov, "Prognozy i otkrytiya," *Ekonomicheskaya gazeta*, No. 2 (1970), p. 6.
3. V. Holubnychy, "Spatial Efficiency in the Soviet Economy," in V. N. Bandera and Z. L. Melnyk (eds.), *The Soviet Economy in Regional Perspective* (New York, Praeger, 1973), pp. 17-18.
4. *Pravda*, May 26, 1969.
5. *Ekonomicheskaya gazeta*, No. 22 (1969), p. 12.
6. *Pravda*, February 27, 1970.
7. *Izvestiya*, April 21, 1970.
8. *Trud*, March 11, 1970.
9. *Izvestiya*, December 13, 1973; and *Pravda*, December 20, 1973.
10. *Pravda*, December 18, 1977.

11. Quoted in I. Ognev, "Yevropa-Sibir'," *Ekonomika i organizatsiya promyshlennogo proizvodstva*, No. 4 (1976), 170.

12. In the first half of the 1970s, it was the proponents of the so-called balanced energy approach who exerted the more visible efforts for the cause.

13. *Sovetskaya Rossiya*, December 8, 1978.

14. "Osnovnye problemy kompleksnogo razvitiya Zapadnoi Sibiri," (A conference report), *Voprosy ekonomiki*, No. 8 (1978), 37.

15. V. I. Dolgikh, "Povyshat' uroven' rukovodstva predpriyatiyami toplivno-energeticheskogo kompleksa," *Partiinaya zhizn'*, No. 1 (1980), 16-17.

16. *Ibid.*, p. 23.

17. When he died in June 1977, signatories to a statement of condolence included Brezhnev and other Soviet leaders. *Pravda*, June 17, 1977.

18. For example, see I. Ognev, "Yevropa-Sibir'," p. 170; *Sovetskaya Rossiya*, August 9, 1979; and *Literaturnaya gazeta*, January 1, 1981, p. 10 and July 15, 1981, p. 10.

19. W. C. Wilde, "Issues in the Development of Siberia and the Far East," in N. T. Dodge (ed.), *The Soviets in Asia* (Mechanicsville, Md., Cremona Foundation, 1972), pp. 30-31.

20. *Ibid.*, p. 31.

21. *Literaturnaya gazeta*, May 1, 1978, p. 10.

22. *Ibid.*, November 7, 1979, p. 11.

23. Thane Gustafson, *Reform in Soviet Politics: Lessons of Recent Policies on Land and Water* (Cambridge, Cambridge University Press, 1981), p. 90.

24. *Pravda*, April 1, 1978.

25. "Osnovnye problemy...," (A conference report), *Voprosy ekonomiki*, No. 8 (1978), 34.

26. "Pavlodar-Ekibastuz kompleks," *Ekonomicheskaya gazeta*, No. 22 (1978), p. 2.

27. Their career profiles are mainly derived from Soviet newspapers. But data on most local officials are unavailable. Other sources include *Bol'shaya Sovetskaya entsiklopediya* (Moskva, various years); *Yezhegodnik bol'shoi Sovetskoi entsiklopedii* (Moskva, various years); L. Crowley, A. I. Lebed, and H. E. Schulz (eds.), *Prominent Personalities in the USSR* (Methuen, N.J., The Scarecrow Press, 1968); Val Ogareff, *Leaders of the Soviet Republics, 1971-1980* (Canberra, The Australian National University Press, 1980); B. Lewytzkyj (ed.), *Who's Who in the Soviet Union* (Munich, K. G. Saur, 1984).

8

Conclusion

At the beginning of this study, two questions were raised: Is there a perceptible trend towards the expansion of participation by territorial interests in the Soviet policy process, and if so, what is the nature of their participation? In the subsequent chapters, the role of pro-West Siberian elements in Soviet energy policy-making was examined. From the evidence it was concluded that they successfully engaged in public campaigns for the rapid development of the oil and gas industry in the eastern part of the country. In this process, a policy coalition was formed.

As discussed earlier, Western scholars have put forward three explanations of policy grouping in Soviet politics: groupings as factions, tendencies, and policy complexes. As far as the West Siberian energy coalition is concerned, there is no evidence that it was a factional grouping. It had become a dominant or "winning" coalition owing to the involvement of Brezhnev. The Party leader himself announced two consecutive energy development programmes for the fast exploitation of West Siberian oil and gas resources. In other words, the pro-West Siberians owed their success to intervention by the top leader. Nevertheless, there is no indication that leading members of the coalition had personal links with the General Secretary. Their biographical data, though incomplete, strongly suggest that their appointments had been based largely on seniority and specialized competence rather than factional considerations. Most of them had retained their posts over a long period of time and a stable relationship seems to have been achieved between them. In the pro-West Siberians' case, functional specialization and stabilization of personnel were characteristic features of Soviet cadre policy during the Brezhnev period. Moreover, the West Siberians and their supporters displayed long-term commitment to the broad issues connected with West Siberian energy development--from oil and gas production to housing--regardless of the ups and downs of the country's energy strategy over the period. They were engaged in promotional discussions in the press before the leadership made a decision in their favor. All these characteristics clearly fail to meet the requirements of a faction as suggested by Uri Ra'anan and others.

Nor is the West Siberian coalition simply an aggregate of similar tendencies. At the initial stage of its formation, the coalition did look rather similar to what Franklyn Griffiths and others describe as tendencies, ad hoc lobbies, or loose coalitions. But it turned out to be highly stable in terms of its composition and of the demands made by its members. As stated above, the West Siberians experienced no major changes amongst their membership. Some of them were coopted to Moscow during the period to take charge of the oil and gas industry of the country at the center and they were succeeded in Siberia by those selected from among local cadres. None of them, even though transferred to Moscow, changed their position on the development of energy resources in West Siberia. As to the West Siberians' supporters, these also maintained both a relatively stable membership and consistency in their demands. The coalition proved not to be a short-term alliance dealing with only one temporally-bound issue, as suggested by John Lowenhardt. Instead, it involved a long-term alliance directed at broad issues that in turn subsumed many specific issues such as the siting of energy-consuming industries and the organizational set-up for comprehensive regional development. Finally, it combined individuals who explicitly and knowingly represented different groups and institutions. It was not composed of individuals whose representation of particular groups or institutions was merely tacit or unwitting, as suggested by Griffith and other scholars.

At the same time, however, it is not clear that the pro-West Siberian coalition formed a policy complex, or part of one, of various institutional actors working in the area of energy policy. There is no doubt that the coalition played a significant role in Soviet energy policy-making. But it failed to include apparently important elements of a policy complex such as officials of the central Party apparatus and relevant industrial ministries. Certainly, many such officials would have had sympathy with the West Siberians and their supporters. But as bureaucrats, it would appear that they preferred not to express sharp disagreements openly and preferred to withhold statements of position until the official Party line became clear. Like their counterparts in many Western countries, they may "attempt to influence policy primarily through the 'administrative' process, rather than through the more visible, and therefore risky, political process."[1] In any case, their absence makes the West Siberian coalition appear rather parochial in its composition.

However, if the assumption were made that the coalition represented a broader combination of relevant officials and institutions than can be ascertained from the Soviet press, such a model of policy complexes may appear a rather better fit. Although our analysis has been limited to the formation of the pro-West Siberian coalition, we know that there was a competing coalition, i.e. a coalition advocating a more or less balanced energy approach with relatively more emphasis on coal and atomic energy. We have seen that Brezhnev and Kosygin had been in disagreement over basic strategy in energy development. In Chapter 4, it was shown that those advocating the balanced approach included, amongst others, many central government officials and specialists working within the coal industry.

In conclusion, the nature of the pro-West Siberian energy coalition, all evidence considered, would seem to lie somewhere between that of "tendency" grouping and policy "complex." It brought together many organizational actors who explicitly and knowingly represented particular groups or institutions. It was a stable, long-term alliance directed at broad issues. Territorial elements constituted the major coalition partners. The alliance certainly allowed them more opportunity to represent their interests in energy policy-making. As concerns the motives of the West Siberians two broad possibilities suggest themselves. Initially they may have been spurred to make demands for their region by the heavy pressures upon them to fulfil targets set by the plan. Or, they may have been emboldened by earlier achievements in their province to press demands with a view to achieving favor and promotion. Whatever their initial motives, Tyumen' Party leaders--Shcherbina and then Bogomyakov--and other leading figures in the locality clearly earned personal and bureaucratic favors from Moscow in this process. Many of them received promotion during this period. Bogomyakov himself frequently won the honor of speaking at Party Congresses and other important meetings.

As for territorial interests, their influence in Soviet politics was not unknown in the early Soviet period. Stephen Cohen, for instance, argues that when Kirov and other provincial leaders swung almost unanimously behind Stalin in his struggle with Bukharin, "one significant factor was probably their understandable desire to obtain a share of Stalin's 'maximum investment' in heavy industry for their own regions."[2] Even at the height of Stalinism, territorial elements certainly continued lobbying for the development of their respective regions. Merle Fainsod warned that the totalitarian image of the Soviet system should not distort reality by ignoring "the fluid play of bureaucratic politics that underlies the monolithic totalitarian facade."[3] According to him, the battle among various sectoral and regional interests for a preferential position in the Soviet economy was waged "by negotiation, by personal influence, and by invoking the assistance of the powerful" within the framework of the ruling priorities of the leadership.[4] But what Fainsod called "bureaucratic politics" should be regarded more as an aspect of policy implementation than of policy formation. "The essence of bureaucratic politics in the Soviet system," he said, "consists in a search for a viable equilibrium between the pressures from above for maximal output (plan fulfillment) and the inescapable limitations which factors of scarcity and human frailty impose."[5] As argued above, many pro-West Siberian elements in the energy economy seem to have been guided by similar motives. These pro-West Siberian elements, however, proved to be active in influencing policy formation. More importantly, they were allowed to promote their cause more or less openly in the media. As witnessed by the pro-West Siberian case, the media debates among competing interests at least in the economic field during Brezhnev's era were clearly less inhibited than any previously. At the same time, the pro-West Siberian case indicates that the interests represented in the Soviet policy process during the Brezhnev period were based less on factional and more on institutional lines.

Last but not least, the phenomenon of growing representation by territorial and other elements outside the leadership prompts one to ask whether there has been an accompanying change in the structure of power in the Soviet political system. That is, has the leadership shared its authority in policy-making with those elements below it in the Soviet political structure? We have seen that Brezhnev's involvement in the energy area had long been preceded by promotional activities by the pro-West Siberian elements. But the West Siberian coalition could not achieve success without his direct involvement. Gyorgy Markus characterizes planning in Soviet-type economies as "a complicated process of semi-institutionalized *competition* and *bargaining* between the various horizontally and vertically articulated 'bureaucracies'."[6] But he is quick to add that "the last decision between the competing claims will be made by the political leadership itself: it is the ultimate broker, without appeal."[7] Our case seems to conform to his assertion. If such observations are right, what is the relation between the leadership and various elements below it in the Soviet condition? The major weakness of Soviet institutional and professional elements, vis-a-vis the leadership, is certainly that these do not possess independent sources of political influence. At the same time, however, the Soviet leadership may have become increasingly aware of the limited number of feasible possibilities for change available to them as the economy became more complex and resources grew scarcer. According to Valerie Bunce and John Echols, the recent tendency to incrementalism in Soviet policy-making signifies the presence of the "constraints on elites generated...particularly at the highest echelons."[8] In the energy area, there were apparently no practical alternatives for the Soviet leadership, or at least for Brezhnev, to the crash development of West Siberian hydrocarbons as a means of earning foreign currency and obtaining Western technology. The national problem thus became an important local opportunity for the West Siberians. Along with their supporters, they drew the attention of the leadership to the congruence of national and regional objectives. In turn, the leadership gave them the opportunity of expressing their opinions on the best means of realizing policy objectives. In connection with this, Richard Judy argues in his analysis of the role of Soviet economists that the leadership has actually encouraged them to put forward policy proposals in the area of economic development.[9] Similarly, we have seen that Brezhnev urged academics in Siberia to help resolve the country's fuel and power problems.[10] In this process, the West Siberian energy coalition has emerged. It is clearly connected with the attempt on the part of the pro-Siberian elements--including the Siberians themselves--to influence the leadership.

NOTES

1. Gordon B. Smith, "Bureaucratic Politics and Public Policy in the Soviet Union," in Gordon B. Smith (ed.), *Public Policy and Administration in the Soviet Union* (New York, Praeger, 1980), p. 8.

2. Stephen F. Cohen, "Stalin's Revolution Reconsidered," *Slavic Review*, Vol. 32 (June 1973), 267. See also Sheila Fitzpatrick, "Ordzhonikidze's Takeover of Vesenkha: A Case Study in Soviet Bureaucratic Politics," *Soviet Studies*, XXXVII (April 1985), 153-172.

3. Merle Fainsod, *How Russia Is Ruled*, Revised edition (Cambridge, Mass., Harvard University Press, 1963), p. 417.

4. *Ibid.*

5. *Ibid.*, p. 419. ( ) added. See also Andrew C. Janos, "Interest Groups and the Structure of Power: Critique and Comparisons," *Studies in Comparative Communism*, XII (Spring 1979), 9.

6. Gyorgy Markus, "Planning the Crisis: Remarks on the Economic System of Soviet-type Societies," *Praxis International*, Vol. 1 (October 1981), 247. Emphases in the original.

7. *Ibid.*, p. 249.

8. Valerie Bunce and John M. Echols III, "Power and Policy in Communist Systems: The Problem of 'Incrementalism'," *Journal of Politics*, Vol 40 (November 1978), 930-931.

9. Richard W. Judy, "The Economists," in H. Gordon Skilling and Franklyn Griffiths (eds.), *Interest Groups in Soviet Politics* (Princeton, Princeton University Press, 1971), pp. 249-250.

10. See Chapter 7, footnote 24.

Abbreviations

AN SSSR	USSR Academy of Sciences
Giprotyumenneftegaz	Tyumen' State Oil and Gas Research-Design Institute
GKNT	State Committee for Science and Technology
Glavtyumengeologiya	Chief Tyumen' Geology Administration
Glavtyumenneftegaz	Chief Tyumen' Oil and Gas Administration
Glavtyumenneftegazstroi	Chief Tyumen' Administration for Oil and Gas Industry Enterprises
Mingeo SSSR	USSR Ministry of Geology
Mingeo RSFSR	RSFSR Ministry of Geology
Minnefteprom SSSR	USSR Ministry of the Oil-Extracting Industry
Minneftegazstroi SSSR	USSR Ministry of Construction of Oil and Gas Industry Enterprises
SO AN SSSR	Siberian Department of the USSR Academy of Sciences
SOPS	Council for Study of Productive Forces, USSR Gosplan
Tyumengazprom	Tyumen' Gas-extracting Industry Association
ZapSibMVTK	Interdepartmental Territorial Commission on Problems of the West Siberian Oil and Gas Complex
ZapsibNIGNI	West Siberian Geological-Prospecting and Oil Research Institute

Bibliography

Newspapers and Journals

Ekonomicheskaya gazeta.
Izvestiya.
Literaturnaya gazeta.
Pravda.
Sotsialisticheskaya industriya.
Sovetskaya Rossiya.
Trud.

Ekonomika i organizatsiya promyshlennogo proizvodstva.
Planovoe khozyaistvo.
Voprosy ekonomiki.

Books and Articles

Aganbegyan, A. G. *Zapadnaya Sibiri na rubezhe vekov*, Sverdlovsk, Sredne-Ural'skoe izdatel'stvo, 1984.

Ageeva, S. D. and B. P. Orlov, "Nekotorye cherty investitsionnogo protsessa v Zapadno-Sibirskom neftegazovom komplekse," *Izvestiya Sibirskogo otdeleniya Akademii Nauk SSSR*, seriya obshchestvennykh nauk, No. 11, 1982, 85-89.

Alekseev, V. V., *Ocherki ekonomiki Sibiri*, Novosibirsk, Nauka, 1980.

Alekseev, A. M., Yu. T. Movsesyan, and L. I. Sevastyanov, "Dinamicheskaya model' razvitiya i razmeshcheniya neftedobyvayushchei promyshlennosti, stroitel'noi bazy i gorodov v raionakh Zapadno-Sibirskoi nizmennosti,"

Izvestiya Sibirskogo otdeleniya AN SSSR, seriya obshchestvennykh nauk, No. 11, 1969, 21-27.

Altunin, Ye. N., "Strategiyu vydirat' segodnya," *Ekonomika i organizatsiya promyshlennogo proizvodstva*, No. 2, 1979, 12-22.

Anderson, R. D., Jr., "Soviet Decision-Making and Poland," *Problems of Communism*, XXXI, March-April 1982, 22-36.

Arzhanov, F. G., "Vokrug burovoi," *Ekonomika i organizatsiya promyshlennogo proizvodstva*, No. 2, 1979, 23-31.

Bahry, Donna, "Measuring Communist Priorities: Budgets, Investments and the Problem of Equivalence," *Comparative Political Studies*, XIII, October 1980, 267-292.

Baibakov, N. K., "Zadacha narodnokhozyaistvennoi vazhnosti," *Ekonomicheskaya gazeta*, No. 11, 1974, 7-8.

Bandman, M. K., V. A. Kalmyk, B. P. Orlov, and Z. R. Tsim dina (eds.), *Sibir' v edinom narodnokhozyaistvennom komplekse*, Novosibirsk, Nauka, 1980.

Baranova, T. B., "Osnovnye pokazateli razvitiya promyshlennosti Sibiri v desyatoi pyatiletke," *Izvestiya Sibir skogo otdeleniya Akademii Nauk SSSR*, seriya obshche stvennykh nauk, No. 11, 1982, 72-74.

Beschinskii, A. and R. Vitebskii, "Energetika i razmeshchenie promyshlennogo proizvodstva," *Voprosy ekonomiki*, No. 5, 1977, 35-46.

Bialer, Seweryn, *Stalin's Successors: Leadership, Stability and Change in the Soviet Union*, Cambridge, Cambridge University Press, 1980.

_____ and Thane Gustafson (eds.), *The Soviet Union at the Crossroads: The 26th Congress of the CPSU*, London, George Allen & Unwin, 1982.

Biddulph, Howard L., "Local Interest Articulation at CPSU Congresses," *World Politics*, XXXVI, October 1983, 28-52.

Blackwell, Robert E., "Cadres Policy in the Brezhnev Era," *Problems of Communism*, XXVIII, March-April 1979, 29-42.

Bogomyakov, G. P. "Tyumenskii kompleks i ego budushchee," *Ekonomika i organizatsiya promyshlennogo proizvodstva*, No. 5, 1976, 9-11.

Bokserman, Yu., "Puti povysheniya effektivnosti transporta topliva," *Planovoe khozyaistvo*, No. 2, 1975, 20-29.

Bol'shaya Sovetskaya entsiklopediya, Moskva, various years.

Brenner, M., "Effektivnost' ispol'zovaniya toplivno-energeticheskikh resursov," *Voprosy ekonomiki*, No. 6, 1977, 37-48.

Brenner, M., "Chtoby uvelichit' moshch' neftyanogo potoka strany," Ekonomika i organizatsiya promyshlennogo proizvodstva, No. 1, 1978, 129-144.

Breslauer, George W., *Khrushchev and Brezhnev as Leaders: Building Authority in Soviet Politics*, London, George Allen & Unwin, 1982.

_____, "Is There A Generation Gap in the Soviet Political Establishment?: Demand Articulation by RSFSR Provincial Party First Secretaries," *Soviet Studies*, XXXVI, January 1984, 1-25.

Brezhnev, L. I., "Otchetnyi doklad TsK KPSS XXIII s'ezdu KPSS" (March 29, 1966), in L. I. Brezhnev, *Leninskim kursom: rechi i stat'i*, Vol. 1, Moskva, Politizdat, 1970.

_____, "Otchetnyi doklad TsK KPSS XXIV s'ezdu KPSS," *Pravda*, March 31, 1971.

_____, "O pyatidesyatiletii SSSR," (December 21, 1972), in L. I. Brezhnev, *Ob osnovnykh voprosakh ekonomicheskoi politiki KPSS na sovremennom etape, rechi i doklady*, Vol. 2 (Moskva, Politizdat, 1979), pp. 120-142.

_____, "Otchet TsK KPSS i ocherednye zadachi partii v oblasti vnutrennei i vneshnei politiki," (February 24, 1976), in *Materialy XXV s'ezda KPSS*, Moskva, Politizdat, 1976, p. 3-89.

_____, "Iz vystupleniya na plenume TsK KPSS," (December 13, 1977), in L. I. Brezhnev, *Ob osnovnykh voprosakh ekonomicheskoi politiki KPSS na sovremennom etape, rechi i doklady*, Vol. 2, Moskva, Politizdat, 1979, pp. 445-457.

_____, "Otchet Tsentral'nogo Komiteta KPSS XXVI s'ezda KPSS i ocherednye zadachi partii v oblasti vnutrennei i vneshnei politiki," (February 23, 1981), *Pravda*, February 24, 1981.

Bunce, Valerie, and John M. Echols III, "Power and Policy in Communist Systems: The Problem of 'Incrementalism'," *Journal of Politics*, Vol 40, November 1978, 911-932.

Campbell, Robert W., *The Economics of Soviet Oil and Gas*, Baltimore, Md., Johns Hopkins University Press, 1968.

_____, *Trends in the Soviet Oil and Gas Industry*, Baltimore, Md., Johns Hopkins University Press, 1976.

_____, *Soviet Energy Technologies: Planning, Policy, Research and Development*, Bloomington, Indiana University Press, 1980.

_____, "Energy," in A. Bergson and H. S. Levine (eds.), *The Soviet Economy: Toward the Year 2000*, London, George Allen & Unwin, 1983, p. 191-217.

Central Intelligence Agency, *Prospects for Soviet Oil Production*, ER-77-10270, April 1977.

_____, Directorate of Intelligence, *Prospects for Soviet Oil Production: A Supplemental Analysis*, ER 77-10425, July 1977.

_____, National Foreign Assessment Center, *Energy Decision Making in the Soviet Union: A Reference Aid*, An organizational chart, CR 80-10623, August 1980.

Churikov, L. I., N. A. Sesin, and V. A. Dyukanov, "Geologorazvedka i neft'," *Ekonomika i organizatsiya promyshlennogo proizvodstva*, No. 6, 1977, 43-46.

Cocks, Paul, "Administrative Rationality, Political Change, and the Role of the Party," in Karl W. Ryavec (ed.), *Soviet Society and the Communist Party*, Amherst, The University of Massachusetts Press, 1978, pp. 41-59.

Colton, Timothy J., *Commissars, Commanders, and Civilian Authority: The Structure of Soviet Military Politics*, Cambridge, Mass., Harvard University Press, 1979.

Crowley, L., A. I. Lebed, and H. E. Schulz (eds.), *Prominent Personalities in the USSR*, Methuen, N.J., The Scarecrow Press, 1968.

Dienes, Leslie, and Theodore Shabad, *The Soviet Energy System: Resource Use and Policies*, New York, Wiley, 1979.

Dolgikh, V. I., "Povyshat' uroven' rukovodstva predpriyatiyami toplivno-energeticheskogo kompleksa," *Partiinaya zhizn'*, No. 1, 1980, 15-23.

Dzirkals, Lilita, Thane Gustafson, and A. Ross Johnson, *The Media and Intra-Elite Communication in the USSR*, Santa Monica, Ca., Rand Corporation, 1982.

Feitel'man, N., "Mineral'no-syr'evaya baza SSSR i perspektivy ee razvitiya," *Voprosy ekonomiki*, No. 12, 1982, 59-70.

Filanovskii, V., "Zapadno-Sibirskii neftegazovyi kompleks: rezul'taty i perspektivy," *Planovoe khozyaistvo*, No. 3 1980, 19-26.

Friedgut, Theodore H., "Interests and Groups in Soviet Policy-Making: The MTS Reforms," *Soviet Studies*, XXVIII, October 1976, 524-547.

Goldman, "The Changing Role of Raw Material Exports and Soviet Foreign Trade," in U.S. Congress, Joint Economic Committee, *Soviet Economy in a Time of Change*, Vol. 1, Washington, D.C., 1979, p. 177-195.

_____, *The Enigma of Soviet Petroleum: Half-empty or Half-full?*, London, George Allen & Unwin, 1980.

Golubnichii, A. M., V. P. Gur'ev, V. T. Permyakov, and N. A. Sesin, "Voprosy sovershenstvovaniya planirovaniya na novom etape razvitiya neftyanoi promyshlennosti Zapadnoi Sibiri," in S. N. Starovoitov (ed.), *Problemy razvitiya Zapadno-Sibirskogo neftegazovogo kompleksa*, Novosibirsk, Nauka, 1983, p. 91-114.

"The Government of the USSR," *Radio Liberty Research*, RL 338/82, August 20, 1982.

Griffiths, Franklyn, "A Tendency Analysis of Soviet Policy-Making," in H. Gordon Skilling and Franklyn Griffiths (eds.), *Interest Groups in Soviet Politics*, Princeton, Princeton University Press, 1971, pp. 335-377.

Gustafson, Thane, *Reform in Soviet Politics: Lessons of Recent Policies on Land and Water*, Cambridge, Cambridge University Press, 1981.

_____, "Soviet Energy Policy: From Big Coal to Big Gas," in Seweryn Bialer and Thane Gustafson (eds.), *The Soviet Union at the Crossroads: The 26th Congress of the CPSU*, London, George Allen & Unwin, 1982, pp. 121-139.

_____, *The Soviet Gas Campaign: Politics and Policy in Soviet Decision-making*, Santa Monica, Ca., Rand Corporation, 1983.

Guzhnovskii, L. P., "Sibirskii vklad v neftyanoe mogushchestvo strany," *Ekonomika i organizatsiya promyshlennogo proizvodstva*, No. 6, 1977, 35-43.

_____, "Neftyanaya i gazovaya promyshlennost'," in V. E. Popov (ed.), *Toplivno-energeticheskii kompleks Sibiri*, Novosibirsk, Nauka, 1978, p. 26-76.

Hewett, Edward A., *Energy, Economics, and Policy in the Soviet Union*, Washington, D.C., Brookings Institution, 1984.

Hoffmann, Erik P., and Robbin F. Laird, *The Politics of Economic Modernization in the Soviet Union*, Ithaca, N.Y., Cornell University Press, 1982.

Holubnychy, Vsevolod, "Spatial Efficiency in the Soviet Economy," in V. N. Bandera and Z. L. Melnyk (eds.), *The Soviet Economy in Regional Perspective* (New York, Praeger, 1973), pp. 1-44.

Hough, Jerry F., *The Soviet Prefects: The Local Party Organs in Industrial Decisionmaking*, Cambridge, Mass., Harvard University Press, 1969.

_____ and Merle Fainsod, *How the Soviet Union Is Governed*, Cambridge, Mass., Harvard University Press, 1979.

Jermol, M. M., and L. A. Magnusson, *Soviet Preparations for Major Boost of Oil Exports*, Malmo, Sweden, Petro Studies Rept. GOP-782, 1978.

Jones, Ellen, "Committee Decision Making in the Soviet Union," *World Politics*, XXXVI, January 1984, 165-188.

Judy, Richard W., "The Economists," in H. Gordon Skilling and Franklyn Griffiths (eds.), *Interest Groups in Soviet Politics*, Princeton, Princeton University Press, 1971, pp. 209-251.

Katz, Abraham, *The Politics of Economic Reform in the Soviet Union*, New York, Praeger, 1972.

Kelley, Donald R., "Interest Groups in the USSR: The Impact of Political Sensitivity on Group Influence," *The Journal of Politics*, Vol. 34, August 1972, 860-888.

_____, "Environmental Policy-Making in the USSR: The Role of Industrial and Environmental Interest Groups," *Soviet Studies*, XXVIII, October 1976, 570-589.

Khrushchev, Nikita S., "O kontrol'nykh tsifrakh razvitiya narodnogo khozyaistva SSSR na 1959-1965 gody," *Vneocherednoi XXI s'ezd KPSS*, stenograficheskii otchet, I (Moskva, Gospolitizdat, 1959), pp. 12-120.

_____, *Khrushchev Remembers*, Trans. by S. Talbott, London, Andre Deutsch, 1971.

_____, *Khrushchev Remembers: The Last Testament*, Trans. by Talbott, Boston, Little, Brown & Co., 1974.

Kirillin, V., "Energetika--problemy i perspektivy," *Kommunist*, No. 1, 1975, 43-51.

"Kompleksnoe razvitie proizvoditel'nykh sil Zapadnoi Sibiri--v tsentre vnimaniya uchenykh i prakticheskikh rabotnikov," *Planovoe khozyaistvo*, No. 9, 1978, 97-114.

Kononov, Yu. D., "Toplivno-energeticheskii kompleks v sisteme narodnokhozyaistvennykh svyazei," *Ekonomika i organizatsiya promyshlennogo proizvodstva*, No. 4, 1983, 17-32.

Kosygin, A. N., "Direktivy XXIV s'ezda KPSS po pyatiletnemu planu razvitiya narodnogo khozyaistva SSSR na 1971-1975 gody," *Pravda*, April 7, 1971.

_____, "Osnovnye napravleniya razvitiya narodnogo khozyaistva SSSR na 1976-1980 gody," (March 1, 1976), *Materialy XXV s'ezda KPSS*, Moskva, Politizdat, 1976, pp. 109-155.

_____, "Kurs na effektivnost'--vazhneishee zveno ekonomicheskoi politiki partii," *Planovoe khozyaistvo*, No. 7, 1979, 3-17.

_____, *K velikoi tseli: izbrannye rechi i stat'i*, Vol. 2, Moskva, Politizdat, 1979.

Kozlov, I. D., *Energeticheskoe khozyaistvo stran SEV*, Moskva, Nauka, 1980.

KPSS v rezolyutsiyakh i resheniyakh s'ezdov, konferentsii i plenumov TsK, Vol. 10, 1969-1971, Moskva, Politizdat, 1972.

Kuramin, V. P., S. S. Pesotskii, V. T. Permyakov, N. A. Sesin, and S. N. Starovoitov, "Problemy planirovaniya i upravleniya razvitiem Zapadno-Sibirskogo neftegazo vogo kompleksa," in S. N. Starovoitov (ed.), *Problemy razvitiya Zapadno-Sibirskogo neftegazovogo kompleksa*, Novosibirsk, Nauka, 1983, p. 33-46.

Kuzovatkin, R. I., "Front i tyl Samotlora," *Ekonomika i organizatsiya promyshlennogo proizvodstva*, No. 6, 1976, 79-87.

Lalayants, A., "Dva obshchestva--dve linii v razvitii toplivno-energeticheskogo kompleksa," *Planovoe khozyaistvo*, No. 4, 1975, 20-31.

Lee, J. Richard, and James R. Lecky, "Soviet Oil Developments," in U.S. Congress, Joint Economic Committee, *Soviet Economy in A Time of Change*, Vol. 1, Washington, D.C., 1979, pp. 581-599.

Lewytzkyj, Borys (ed.), *Who's Who in the Soviet Union*, Munich, K. G. Saur, 1984.

Linden, Carl A., *Khrushchev and the Soviet Leadership, 1957-1964*, Baltimore, The Johns Hopkins University Press, 1966.

Lipanovich, V. I., "Osobennosti dinamiki i struktury kapital'nykh vlozhenii v shirotnykh mezoregionakh Zapadnoi Sibiri," in A. G. Granberg (ed.), *Ekonomika Sibiri v razreze shirotnykh zon*, Novosibirsk, Nauka, 1985, pp. 63-85.

Lowenhardt, John, *Decisionmaking in Soviet Politics*, London, Macmillan, 1981.

Lukes, Stephen, *Power: A Radical View*, London, Macmillan, 1974.

Maksimov, K., "Sistema pokazatelei effektivnosti kapital'nykh vlozhenii v toplivnykh otraslyakh," *Planovoe khozyaistvo*, No. 6, 1984, 25-34.

Maksimov, Yu. I., "Dobycha toplivno-energeticheskikh resursov v Sibiri," *Izvestiya Sibirskogo otdeleniya Akademii Nauk SSSR*, seriya obshchestvennykh nauk, No. 6, 1982, 34-38.

Margulov, R. D., *Razvitie gazovoi promyshlennosti i analiz tekhniko-ekonomicheskikh pokazatelei*, Moskva, VNII Gazprom, 1976.

Markus, Gyorgy, "Planning the Crisis: Remarks on the Economic System of Soviet-type Societies," *Praxis*

International, Vol. 1, October 1981, 240-257.

"Materialy k vsesoyuznoi konferentsii po razvitiyu proizvoditel'nykh sil Sibiri," *Izvestiya Sibirskogo otdeleniya Akademii Nauk SSSR*, seriya obshchestvennykh nauk, No. 6, 1980, 10.

Mazover, Ya. A. (ed.), *Problemy razvitiya i razmeshcheniya toplivnykh baz SSSR*, Moskva, Nauka, 1982.

Medvedev, Roy A., and Zhores A. Medvedev, *Khrushchev: The Years in Power*, London, Oxford University Press, 1977.

Melent'ev, L. A., and A. Makarov, "Perspektivnoe razvitie toplivno-energeticheskogo kompleksa," *Planovoe khozyaistvo*, No. 4, 1980, 87-94.

_____ (eds.), *Energeticheskii kompleks SSSR*, Moskva, Ekonomika, 1983.

Mel'nikov, N., and V. Shelest, "Toplivno-energeticheskii kompleks SSSR," *Planovoe khozyaistvo*, No. 2, 1975, 8-19.

Meyerhoff, Arthur A., "Soviet Petroleum: History, Technology, Geology, Reserves, Potential and Policy," in Robert G. Jensen, Theodore Shabad and A. W. Wright (eds.), *Soviet Natural Resources in the World Economy*, Chicago, University of Chicago Press, 1983, pp. 306-362.

Miller, John, "Nomenklatura: Check on Localism?," in T. H. Rigby and Bohdan Harasymiw (eds.), *Leadership Selection and Patron-Client Relations in the USSR and Yugoslavia*, London, George Allen & Unwin, 1983, pp. 62-97.

Moses, Joel C., "Regionalism in Soviet Politics: Continuity as A Source of Change, 1953-1982," *Soviet Studies*, XXXVII, April 1985, 184-211.

Muravlenko, V. I., and V. I. Kremnev (eds.), *Sibirskaya neft'*, Moskva, Nedra, 1977.

Narodnoe khozyaistvo SSSR, Moskva, Statistika, various years.

Narodnoe khozyaistvo RSFSR, Moskva, Statistika, various years.

Narodnoe khozyaistvo Tyumenskoi oblasti za gody vos'moi pyatiletki (1966-1970 gody), Omsk, Statistika, 1971.

Nekrasov, A. M., and A. A. Troitskii (eds.), *Energetika SSSR v 1981-1985 godakh*, Moskva, Energoizdat, 1981.

Nelson, Daniel, "Conclusion: Participatory and Policy-making Dilemmas in Local Communist Politics," in Daniel Nelson (ed.), *Local Politics in Communist Countries*, Lexington, Ky., The University Press of Kentucky, 1980, pp. 211-224.

Nelson, Daniel, "Vertical Integration and Political Control in Eastern Europe: The Polish and Romanian Cases," *Slavic Review*, Vol. 40, Summer 1981, 23-54.

Nesterov, I., "Neftegazovyi potentsial Zapadnoi Sibiri," *Ekonomicheskaya gazeta*, No. 11, 1980, p. 15.

North, Robert N., "Soviet Northern Development: The Case of NW Siberia," *Soviet Studies*, XXIV, October 1972, 171-199.

_____, *Transport in Western Siberia: Tsarist and Soviet Development*, Vancouver, University of British Columbia Press and the Center for Transportation Studies, 1979.

"Ob investitsionnykh programmakh perspektivnogo razvitiya raionov Sibiri i Srednei Azii," *Ekonomika i organizatsiya promyshlennogo proizvodstva*, No. 6, 1971, 3-51.

Odom, William E., "A Dissenting View on the Group Approach to Soviet Politics," *World Politics*, XXVIII, 1976, 542-567.

Ogareff, Val, *Leaders of the Soviet Republics, 1971-1980*, Canberra, The Australian National University Press, 1980.

Ognev, I., "Yevropa-Sibir'," *Ekonomika i organizatsiya promyshlennogo proizvodstva*, No. 4, 1976, 154-180.

Orlov, B. P., "Razvitie ekonomiki Sibiri na otdel'nykh etapakh sotsialisticheskogo stroitel'stva," *Izvestiya Sibirskogo otdeleniya AN SSSR*, seriya obshchestvennykh nauk, No. 11, 1982, 60-70.

_____ and R. I. Shniper, "Obzor opyta programmnogo resheniya narodnokhozyaistvennykh problem v Sibiri," *Izvestiya Sibirskogo otdeleniya Akademii Nauk SSSR*, seriya obshchestvennykh nauk, No. 6, 1980, 11-19.

"Osnovnye problemy kompleksnogo razvitiya Zapadnoi Sibiri," *Voprosy ekonomiki*, No. 8, 1978, 15-37.

Park, D., *Oil and Gas in Comecon Countries*, London, Kogan Page, 1978.

Ploss, Sidney, *Conflict and Decision-Making in Soviet Russia: A Case Study of Agricultural Policy, 1953-1963*, Princeton, Princeton University Press, 1965.

Pravdin, A., and M. Matthews, "Inside the CPSU Central Committee: Interview by M. Matthews," *Survey*, Vol. 20, Autumn 1974, 94-104.

Probst, A., *Voprosy razmeshcheniya sotsialisticheskoi promyshlennosti*, Moskva, Nauka, 1971.

_____, *"Puti razvitiya toplivnogo khozyaistva SSSR,"* *Voprosy ekonomiki*, No. 6, 1971, 51-63.

_____, "O dolgosrochnoi perspektive razmeshcheniya proizvodstva," *Voprosy ekonomiki*, No. 5, 1973, 17-30.

Ra'anan, Uri, "Soviet Decision-Making and International Relations," *Problems of Communism*, XXIX, November-December 1980, 41-47.

"Razvedochnoe burenie na neft' v SSSR," *Ekonomika i organizatsiya promyshlennogo proizvodstva*, No. 6, 1977, 37.

Razvitie narodnogo khozyaistva Sibiri, Novosibirsk, Nauka, 1978.

Resheniya partii i pravitel'stva po khozyaistvennym voprosam, Vol. 5, 1962-1965, Moskva, Politizdat, 1968.

Rumer, Boris, "Soviet Investment Policy: Unresolved Problems," *Problems of Communism*, XXXI, September-October 1982, 53-68.

Shashin, V. D., "Puti povysheniya effektivnosti neftyanoi promyshlennosti," *Planovoe khozyaistvo*, No. 4, 1973, 15-22.

_____, "Gorizonty neftyanoi industrii," *Ekonomicheskaya gazeta*, No. 22, 1976, p. 4.

Shcherbina, B. Ye., "Novye rubezhi tyumenskikh neftyanikov," *Ekonomicheskaya gazeta*, No. 6, 1970, p. 5.

_____, "Industrial'nye metody sooruzheniya ob'ektov toplivnoi energetiki," *Planovoe khozyaistvo*, No. 3, 1980, 3-11.

Shell Oil, *Enhanced Oil Recovery*, Shell Briefing Service, March 1979.

Sidorenko, A., "Yevropeiskaya chast' strany raskryvaet nedra," *Kommunist*, No. 18, 1970, 60-70.

Smirnov, V. A., Yu. I. Maksimov, V. I. Konstantinov, I. F. Maksimova, "Spetsializirovannye modeli perspektivnogo planirovaniya gazovoi promyshlennosti," in Yu. I. Maksimov and Z. R. Tsimtsina (eds.), *Optimizatsiya razvitiya i razmeshcheniya neftegazovoi promyshlen nosti*, Novosibirsk, Nauka, 1977, pp. 52-80.

Smith, Gordon B., "Bureaucratic Politics and Public Policy in the Soviet Union," in Gordon B. Smith (ed.), *Public Policy and Administration in the Soviet Union*, New York, Praeger, 1980, pp. 1-17.

Solomon, Peter H., Jr., *Soviet Criminologists and Criminal Policy: Specialists in Policy-Making*, London, Mac millan, 1978.

Starovoitov, S. N., "Voprosy nadezhnosti v perspektivnom planirovanii razvitiya neftyanoi promyshlennosti," in Yu. I. Maksimov and Z. R. Tsimtsina (eds.), *Optimizatsiya razvitiya i razmeshcheniya neftegazovoi promyshlennosti*, Novosibirsk, Nauka, 1977, pp. 81-93.

Stern, Jonathan P., *Soviet Natural Gas Development to 1990*, Lexington, Mass., Lexington Books, 1980.

Stewart, Philip D., "Soviet Interest Groups and the Policy Process: The Repeal of Production Education," *World Politics*, XXII, October 1969, 29-50.

Tatu, Michel, *Power in the Kremlin, From Khrushchev to Kosygin*, New York, Viking, 1968.

Tikhonov, N. A., "Segodnya FRG--eto odin iz nashikh krupnykh partnerov v delovom vzaimovygodnom sotrudnichestve s zapadom," (1976) in N. A. Tikhonov, *Izbrannye rechi i stat'i*, Moskva, Politizdat, 1980, pp. 226-228.

_____, "Osnovnye napravleniya ekonomicheskogo i sotsial'nogo razvitiya SSSR na 1981-1985 gody i na period do 1990 goda," *Pravda*, February 28, 1981.

Trofimov, B., "Formirovanie Tyumenskogo neftegazovogo kompleksa," *Planovoe khozyaistvo*, No. 9, 1981, 84-88.

Trofimuk, A. A. "Nauka v Sibiri--dlya Sibiri," *Ekonomika i organizatsiya promyshlennogo proizvodstva*, No. 3, 1977, 35-36.

Umanskii, L. M., and M. M. Umanskii, *Ekonomika neftyanoi i gazovoi promyshlennosti*, Moskva, Nedra, 1965.

"Uskorennoe razvitie proizvoditel'nykh sil Sibiri--vazhneishaya narodnokhozyaistvennaya zadacha," *Planovoe khozyaistvo*, No. 3, 1980, 120-125.

Vainshtein, B., A. Khaitun, and N. Sokolov, "Effektivnost' neftegazovogo kompleksa Zapadnoi Sibiri," *Voprosy ekonomiki*, No. 10, 1978, 19-27.

Varlamov, V., and I. Panfilov, "Osnovnye napravleniya formirovaniya territorial'no-proizvodstvennogo kom pleksa Zapadno-Sibirskoi ravniny," *Planovoe khozyaistvo*, No. 10, 1974, 53-62.

Welsh, William A., *Understanding Stability in East European Political Systems*, A monograph, Cologne, Bundesinsti tut fur Ostwissenschaftliche und Internationale Studien, 1980.

Wilde, W. C., "Issues in the Development of Siberia and the Far East," in N. T. Dodge (ed.), *The Soviets in Asia*, Mechanicsville, Md., Cremona Foundation, 1972, pp. 29-35.

Wiles, Peter, "A Note on the Cost of Soviet Oil," in NATO, Economic and Information Directorates (eds.), *CMEA: Energy, 1980-1990*, Newtonville, Mass., Oriental Research Partners, 1981, pp. 129-141.

Wilson, David, *Soviet Oil and Gas to 1990*, London, The Economist Intelligence Unit, 1980.

Yakovets, Yu., "Ekonomicheskie rychagi i povyshenie effektivnosti mineral'no-syr'evogo kompleksa," *Planovoe khozyaistvo*, No. 1, 1978, 69-77.

Yatrov, S., "Toplivno-energeticheskii kompleks," *Ekonomicheskaya gazeta*, No. 10, 1980, p. 10.

Yefremov, Ye. P., M. K. Mikhalev, L. I. Churikov and G. L. Chudnovskii, "Sostoyanie i napravleniya dal'neishei realizatsii programmy kompleksnogo razvitiya neftedobyvayushchei promyshlennosti Zapadnoi Sibiri," in S. N. Starovoitov (ed.), *Problemy razvitiya Zapadno-Sibirskogo neftegazovogo kompleksa*, Novosibirsk, Nauka, 1983, pp. 57-90.

Yezhegodnik bol'shoi Sovetskoi entsiklopedii, Moskva, various years.

Index

Academy of Sciences, USSR, 17
Aganbegyan, A. G., 74, 76, 91, 94, 95, 105, 111-113, 138, 147, 151, 154, 162
Aleksandrov, A. P., 75, 111, 155
Altunin, Ye. N., 65, 77, 95, 109, 147, 153, 160
Arzhanov, F. G., 32, 109, 153, 161
Baibakov, N. K., 36-37, 88, 118
Batalin, Yu. P., 88, 98, 147, 152, 162
Belorusov, D., 87, 148
Beschinskii, A. A., 102
Bialer, S., 2
Biddulph, H., 2
Bidzhakov, V., 109
Bikkenin, N. B., 152
Bogomyakov, G. P., 64, 70, 88, 89, 94, 97-98, 104, 115, 117, 139-140, 147, 149-150, 153, 160
Bokserman, Yu. I., 90
Breslauer, G., 2, 117
Brezhnev, L. I. 40-44, 114-115, 129-140, 158
Bulgakov, R., 153, 161
Bureaucratic organizations, USSR, 1
Churikov, L. I., 103, 151
Colton, T., 9
Dolgikh, V. I., 96, 139, 152, 155
Dymshits, V. E., 96, 115
Dzirkals, L., 5, 6
Ekonomicheskaya gazeta, 105, 159
CIA, 137
Chief Tyumen' Administration for the Construction of Oil and Gas Industry Enterprises, 18
Chief Tyumen' Geology Administration, 18
Chief Tyumen' Oil and Gas Administration, 18
Coalition
Definition, 6
Coalition-formation, 4
As a faction, 7-8
As a tendency of articulation, 8
As a policy "complex," 9-10
See West Siberian Coalition
Conference
Tyumen', 90-91
Novosibirsk, 92
Controversy
See West Siberian controversy
Council of Ministers, USSR, 18
West Siberian Commission, 18-19
Council for Study of Productive Forces, 17, 90, 148, 158
Demands
See West Siberian demands
Development drilling, 51, 53-54
Development drilling in West Siberia, 33

Democratic centralism, 1
Development priority
 West Siberia, 116
Development programme
 West Siberia, 86-88, 110-113
EKO, 108-109
Energy development policy, USSR, 34-44
 1969 decree, 34-35, 92
 European oil, 35-38
 Coal policy, 38-39
 1977 oil policy, 40-41
 1981 gas policy, 41-44
Erv'e, Yu. G., 65, 85-86, 95, 100, 147, 150, 161
Filanovskii, V. Yu., 67-68, 88-89, 93, 109-110, 112, 147, 154, 161
Five-year plans
 Ninth, 35
 Tenth, 38-39, 43
Fuel production, USSR, 26
Galonskii, P. P., 90
Goldman, M., 137-138
Gosplan, USSR
West Siberian Commission, 17, 20
Griffiths, F., 8, 170
Groupings, USSR
 See Coalition
Gustafson, T., 4
Guzhnovskii, L. P., 102, 151, 163
Holubnychy, V., 148
Horizontal integration, 3
Hough, J., 2, 9-10
Influence, 2, 4-5
Interest
 Articulation, 2
 Bureaucratic, 2
 Functional, 2
 Groupings, 6
 Representation, 9
 Vertical, 2
Investment, Soviet energy
 Between fuel industries, 45-49
 Between fuel-producing regions, 49-54
Karyagin, I., 85, 147
Khrushchev, N. S., 7, 25
Kirillin, V., 75
Kiselev, E., 93
Kistanov, V., 87, 91, 148
Koptyug, V., 112
Kosolapov, R. I., 152-153
Kosygin, A. N., 38-39, 129-137
Kozlov, V., 104
Kremnev, V., 71, 92, 147, 164
Krylov, A. P., 66
Kuramin, V., 115, 153, 162
Kuzovatkin, R. I., 98, 101, 105, 151, 161
Lalayants, A., 75, 96
Lavrent'ev, M., 85, 147
Ligachev, Ye., 87, 90, 104, 139, 150, 160
Literaturnaya gazeta, 87
Lowenhardt, J., 8, 170
Lukbyanenok, N. V., 93, 146
Makarov, A., 110
Maksimov, V. P., 89, 93-95, 146, 160
Mal'tsev, N. A., 66, 72, 111, 155, 164
Marchuk, G. I., 111, 154, 157-158, 162
Mazover, Ya. A., 73, 165
Melent'ev, L. A., 75, 110, 154
Miller, J., 2
Ministry, energy, 16-17
Moses, J., 1
Muravlenko, V. I., 71, 92, 96, 99-101, 147, 150, 161
Murzin, A., 67, 93, 98, 100-101, 104, 151, 165
Musin, M., 89
Nekrasov, N. N., 64, 69, 91, 94, 99, 104, 107-109, 148,

Nekrasov (cont'd), 151, 154, 165
Nelson, D., 3
Nesterov, I. I., 65, 68-70, 95, 97, 109, 147, 151, 163
Ognev, I., 99, 151, 155, 163
Oil industry, USSR, 3
 Achievements, 25-28
 Controversy, 4
 Enhanced recovery, 35-38
 Problems, 33
 Production, 26-27, 29, 33, 39
 Production by location, 29
 Production and transportation indices, 31
 Recovery rate, 28
 Reserves, 30, 37, 41
 Wells drilled, 31
 West Siberia, 3, 27-28, 29
Opinion groupings, 8
Organization, Soviet energy, 15-20
 West Siberia, 18-19, 112-15
Orudzhev, S.A., 96, 152, 164
Ostryi, G., 85, 89
Panfilov, I., 98
Participation, USSR, 1, 3
Patron-client relationship, 7
Pervukhin, M., 73, 88, 107
Pipeline construction, USSR, 45
Piskotin, M. I., 105
Policy coalition, 8
Policy-making, USSR, 2-3, 172-173
Popov, V. E., 94, 147, 163
Pravda, 83-84, 114
Privedennye zatraty, 32-33, 71-72
Probst, A., 71, 151, 165
Protozanov, A., 64, 84-86, 88-89, 91-92, 146, 160
Prudenskii, G., 85, 147
Public discussions, 5, 117-118
Ra'anan, Uri, 7, 170
Referentura, 18
Rovnin, L. I., 87, 147, 161
Rumer, B., 50
Salmanov, F. K., 66, 69, 70, 97, 151, 153, 161
Secretariat, CPSU, 18
Sevastyanov, V., 113
Shaevskii, Yu., 85
Shashin, V. D., 66, 88, 95, 96, 98, 147, 151, 164
Shatokhin, E., 104, 165
Shcherbina, B., 45, 63, 64, 71, 72, 86, 90-92, 94-96, 116, 145, 149, 152, 159
Shidlovskii, I., 89, 147
Shmal', G., 100, 150, 160
Shmarev, A. T., 69
Shupta, S., 85
Siberians, 4
Siberian Department, the USSR Academy of Sciences, 18-19, 110-111, 156-157
Sidorenko, A. V., 65-66, 90
Simzen, M., 65, 147
Solomon, P., 2
Soviet leadership on West Siberian oil, 129-140
Soviet press, 6
Sovetskaya Rossiya, 95
State Committee for Science and Technology, 17
Strizhov, N., 67, 153
Sulimenkov, G., 110
Party Congress,
 23rd, 35
 24th, 35
 25th, 38
 26th, 41-42
Territorial interests, 1-2
 West Siberia, 10
Tikhonov, N. A., 139
Timonin, V., 85
Titov, I., 93
Tokarev, S., 91, 148, 165
Tomsk, 86, 89-90
Trofimov, B., 115, 153, 160

Trofimuk, A. A., 64, 65, 72-73, 89-92, 94-95, 97, 104, 112-113, 147, 151, 154, 162
Tyumen' Gas Industry Association, 18
Udovenko, V., 65, 147
Utrobin, Ye., 86, 146, 160
Vainshtein, B., 76, 105
Varlamov, V., 98
Veselkov, G. G., 146
Vitebskii, R. Ya., 102
Vtorushin, S., 100, 101, 104, 113, 155, 165
West Siberian coalition,
  Formation, 156-159
  Nature, 169-172
  Party apparatus, Siberia, 145-146, 149-150, 153
  Party apparatus, Moscow, 147, 151-152, 155
  Government agencies, Siberia, 146
West Siberian coalition (cont'd)
  Government agencies, Moscow, 147, 151, 154
  Industrial enterprises, Siberia, 146-147, 150-151, 153
  Research institutions, Siberia, 147, 150-151, 154
  Research institutions, Moscow, 148, 151, 154
  Media organs, Moscow, 148
West Siberian fuel controversy, 63-77
  Reserves, 64-70
  Costs, 71-77
West Siberian demands, 83, 115-116
  Coordination, 105
West Siberians
  Recruitment pattern, 165-166
Yamnov, A. A., 92, 147, 163
Yeronin, N., 71, 92, 147, 163